IMAGES
of America

PITTSBURGH'S EAST LIBERTY VALLEY

On the cover: **PENN AVENUE.** This view of Penn Avenue, previously Forbes Road from Ligonier to Fort Pitt, looks west towards the tavern at Black Horse Hill some four miles from downtown Pittsburgh. The spire is that of the third East Liberty Presbyterian Church built in 1864 on the same site of South Highland and Penn Avenues with gas lighting and horse stalls. (Courtesy of the East End/East Liberty Historical Society.)

IMAGES
of America

PITTSBURGH'S EAST LIBERTY VALLEY

East End/East Liberty Historical Society

ARCADIA
PUBLISHING

ISBN 978-0-7385-5489-1

Published by Arcadia Publishing
Charleston, South Carolina

Printed in the United States of America

Library of Congress Catalog Card Number: 2007926962

For all general information contact Arcadia Publishing at:
Telephone 843-853-2070
Fax 843-853-0044
E-mail sales@arcadiapublishing.com
For customer service and orders:
Toll-Free 1-888-313-2665

Visit us on the Internet at www.arcadiapublishing.com

Contents

ACKNOWLEDGMENTS

This book of representative selections draws upon the support and private collections of many persons. The East End/East Liberty Historical Society appreciates a variety of contributions from Annette Balsamico, Peter Bolanis, Paul Brecht, Elizabeth Buchanan, Christian Breitkreutz, Andy and Kitty Cheatham, George Clark, Arlene Dyer, James Edwards, Michael Eversmeyer, Marilyn Evert, Anne Franks, Jane Fulton, William Gibson, Cheryl Hall, John Henne, Celia Hindes, Charles Honeywell, Cyrus Hosmer III, the Honorable Justin Johnson, Leonard Lachina, Edward Lesoon, Rudolph Maceyko, Al Mann, the Reverend Elwood Martin, Patricia Miller, Wendi Miller, Eugene Myers, Pasquale Navarro, Christopher Reiling, Robert Sampson, Raymond Schinhofen, Leigh Seabright, Philip Simpson, Peggy Spangler, Rob Stephany, Robert Tortorete, Al Vento, Carl Vitti, Walter Werner, Franklin West (deceased), James West, and Dr. Sara West.

Photograph and postcard credits are due to Calvary Episcopal Church, Carnegie Museum of Art, City of Pittsburgh Department of Engineering and Construction, East Liberty Branch of the Carnegie Library, East Liberty Development, Frick Art and Historical Center, George Westinghouse Museum Foundation, McCune family archives, Pennsylvania Department of the Main Carnegie Library, *Pittsburgh Post-Gazette*, Senator John Heinz Regional History Center, University of Pittsburgh, and Variety The Children's Charity.

Very special appreciation is due to the late John Fulton Stuart Collins, Jr. of North Euclid Avenue, a 1915 graduate of Peabody High School and the author of Stringtown on the Pike, published by the East Liberty Chamber of Commerce in 1966.

Should there be errors, corrections, or additions, the Society would much appreciate your contacting us at 5907 Penn Avenue, Ste. 305, Pittsburgh, PA, 15206; 412-661-9660; or www.eastlibertychamber.org.

INTRODUCTION

At the beginning of the 18th century, the western Pennsylvania region was a great wilderness occupied by wandering bands of Iroquois hunters. English traders had begun lucrative activity in the area before Capt. Celeron de Bienville traveled down the Allegheny River in 1749, past the site of the present Highland Park, claiming the territory for France.

Virginia and Pennsylvania vied for possession of the Forks of the Ohio, both claiming ownership of the land on which legally set boundaries had not yet been established. The Forks of the Ohio, where the Allegheny and Monongahela Rivers join to form the Ohio, became the center of a contest between the British and the French to control the inland rivers. In 1753, Gov. Robert Dinwiddie of Virginia sent the young George Washington to warn the French to leave. It was in a report to Governor Dinwiddie that Washington makes reference to the "Northern Liberties," an English "liberty" being the grazing land around the city. Pittsburgh also had a West and an East Liberty.

After Gen. Edward Braddock's disastrous attempt to take the Forks of the Ohio in 1755, the English sent Gen. John Forbes and his army to capture Fort Duquesne. In 1758, Forbes ordered the then Colonel Washington to widen the old Indian trail from Fort Ligonier through East Liberty to support the army's supply wagons on their way to capture the French fort. This was the first road-building in the valley. First called the Forbes Road, it was also known as the Old Glade Road, the Philadelphia/Greensburg Pike, and now Penn Avenue.

The strategic positioning of this road as it crossed what is now Fifth Avenue in East Liberty was a major factor in the area's growth. Conestoga wagons, the railroad, horse car, trolley, and finally, the automobile used these road systems as the valley grew.

After the Revolutionary War, many soldiers remained or returned, realizing the advantages of the beautiful and fertile surroundings of the East Liberty Valley. They bought huge parcels of land and settled on farms that, as most were Virginians, they called plantations. It was not until 1784 that a southern Pennsylvania boundary was established with completion of the Mason-Dixon Line. Early maps of the plantations in the East Liberty Valley include what are now the neighborhoods of Shadyside, Wilkinsburg, Homewood, Lincoln, Larimer, Bloomfield, and Lawrenceville. Caspar Taub, Alexander Negley, Henry Heth, Peter Parchment, James Ross, Thomas Ross, Conrad Winebiddle, and Thomas Mellon were among the first land owners in the valley.

Jacob Negley, a son of Alexander Negley, was a surveyor and engineer who greatly expanded his father's holdings. In 1817, he laid out a town in the valley with its center at Penn and Frankstown Avenues and named it East Liberty. It was also at one time called Negleystown. In

1837, the county surveyor at the time, Robert Hilands, subdivided the Negley landholdings. He laid out Negley and Hiland Avenues, the latter of which was changed by the city to Highland in 1890. The village's tremendous growth, particularly in the 1860s, made it an appealing object for consolidation, and in 1868, it was annexed to the city of Pittsburgh. Today the Highland Park neighborhood, once Negley-owned land, is listed in the National Register of Historic Places as a historic district in recognition of its significance as a model streetcar suburb of the late 19th and early 20th centuries.

The images and stories that follow are designed to show our birth, growth, and the great years, as well as today's efforts to bring a new birth and hope to the East Liberty Valley.

One

The Setting

In the 1700s, what was to become known as East Liberty Valley was a land of dense forests, streams, meadows, and wild game. Archeological evidence reveals Native American habitation in the Pittsburgh region thousands of years ago. Although dominated by the Iroquois, several Native American groups inhabited the rich hunting grounds. Among them were the Lenne Lenape, Shawnee, and Delaware, who had migrated from eastern and southern regions that were being settled by Europeans.

There were several white traders in the valley in the mid-1700s. George Croghan, a prominent American colonist, was an early advocate of western expansion and an experienced Native American agent and fur trader. By 1760, he was trading with as many as 1,000 Native Americans in western Pennsylvania and was the owner of large tracts of land in the area.

Control of the Forks of the Ohio (1747–1763) began the struggle between Native Americans and the French and British. Col. George Washington, by orders from Gen. John Forbes, began the work of widening an existing Native American trail (now Penn Avenue) for Forbes' advance toward the Forks (the Point) and the capture of Fort Duquesne in 1758. Washington had visited the area earlier when he met Guyasuta, the Seneca who became a principal chief and negotiator between the Iroquois and the English. Guyasuta had accompanied Washington to talks with the French in 1753.

In 1762, Col. Henry Bouquet, needing provisions of food for his soldiers at Fort Pitt, looked to Caspar (Caspard) Taub, a German immigrant who had a successful farm near the Forbes Road in the valley. The first recorded land grant of 303 acres was issued to Taub in exchange for one third of his crops. The influence of Taub and his descendants was to play a formidable role in the growth of the East Liberty Valley.

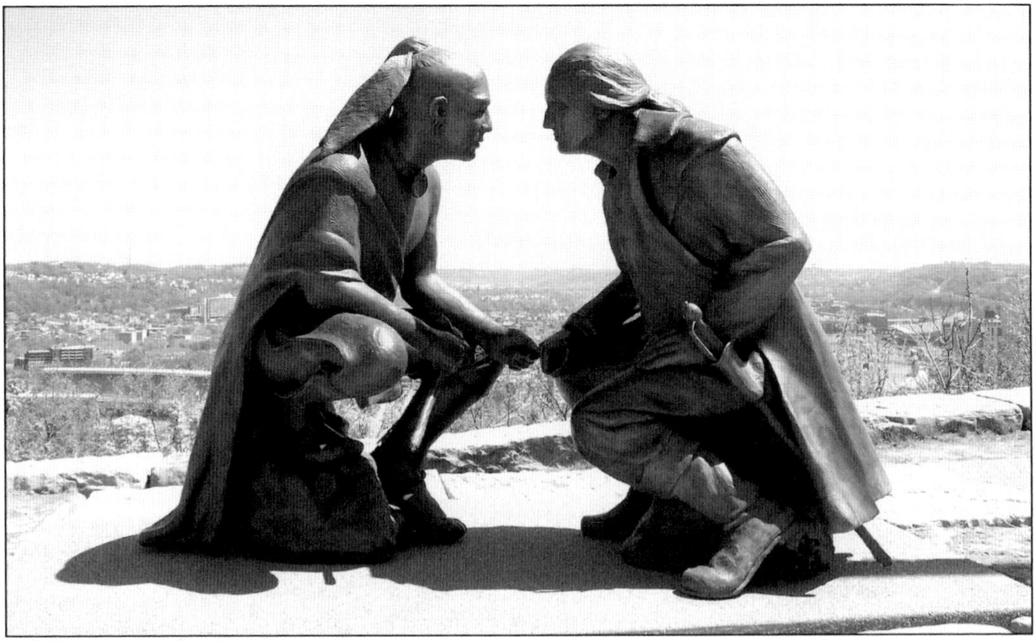

POINT OF VIEW, 2006. This dramatic bronze sculpture by Pittsburgh artist James West was recently erected on Pittsburgh's Mount Washington. The Seneca leader Guyasuta (*c.* 1725–1794) and George Washington shared a nine-day council in 1770 at which white settlement in the area was at issue. Guyasuta had years earlier been a guide to Washington but later sided with the British. In spite of their differences, Washington asserted that they parted from the council as friends. The aging Guyasuta later endeavored to establish peaceful relations with the United States.

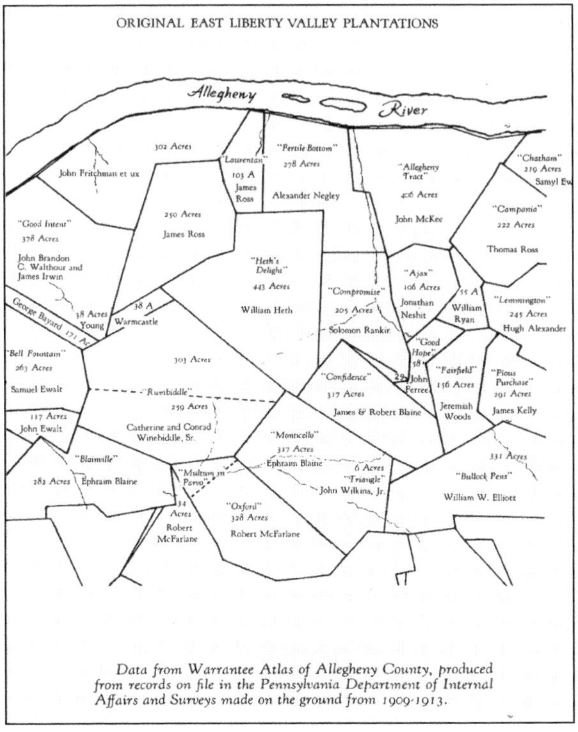

EARLY PLANTATIONS. The term plantation rather than farm was customary in Virginia, which claimed jurisdiction over Pittsburgh and southwestern Pennsylvania under her royal charter until Revolutionary War times. It was not until 1784 that a definitive southern Pennsylvania boundary was established with completion of the Mason-Dixon Line. Alexander Negley (1734–1809) purchased his 278-acre plantation in 1778.

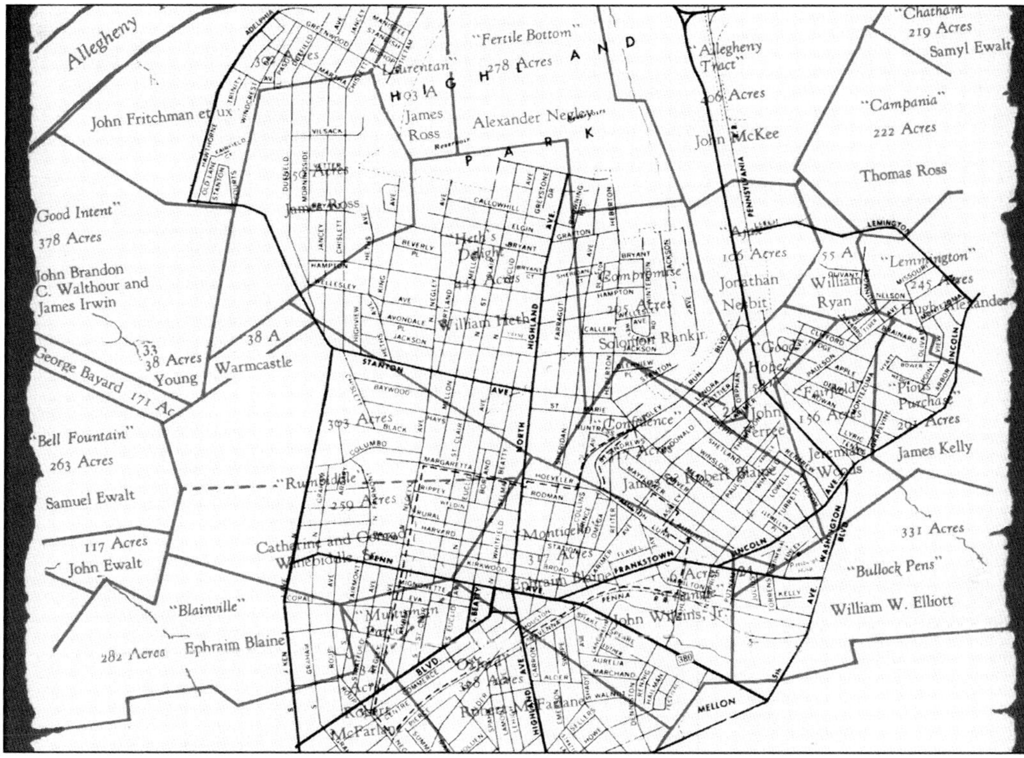

PLANTATIONS WITH MODERN STREET GRID. This picture shows the early plantation map superimposed on the present-day East Liberty street grid. The city park known as Highland Park occupies a major portion of Alexander Negley's plantation. The Ross log house is located on the Thomas Ross plantation known as Campania.

Copy of Original Grant of land in East Liberty by Colonel Bouquet to Caspard Taub

Fort Pitt 12th November 1762

This is to certify that I have permitted Caspard Taub to clear a plantation at the Four Mile Spring on the old road going to Ligonier, in order to raise provisions for the use of this garrison and corn for the King's horses, and the conditions of the said grant are that the said Caspard Taub shall pay every year, to the commanding officer at this post for the King's use, one-third of all the Produce, of the said Plantation, horses and cattle excepted, under penalty of forfeiting his improvement to the Crown.

Given under my hand as above.
H. Bouquet, Col.

TAUB LAND GRANT, 1762. Col. Henry Bouquet granted 303 acres to German immigrant Caspard Taub in exchange for one-third of his crops to feed Bouquet's soldiers at Fort Pitt. Taub named his property Rumbiddle. He was the first to have legal possession of land in the East Liberty Valley. Through marriage, the land later became part of Jacob Negley's vast holdings.

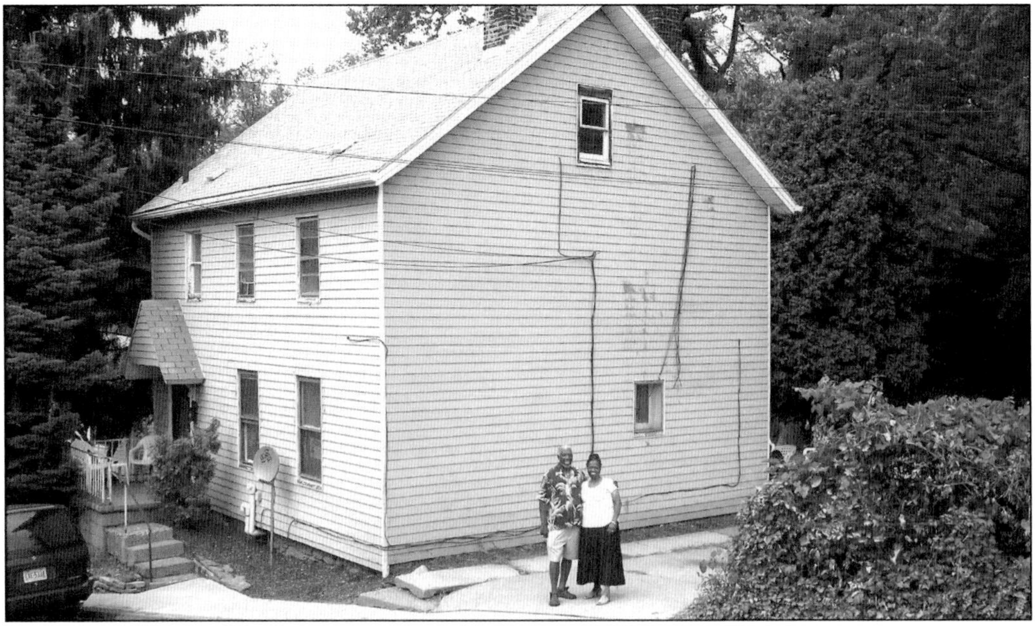

Ross Log House, 1794. Thomas Ross, a Revolutionary War soldier, built a two-story log house on his 222 acres of land deeded in 1788 called Campania. It still stands on Ross Garden Road in the Lincoln district. Now under a shell of vinyl siding, it was bought in 1976 by Ralph and Celeste Carter. There is considerable interest in restoring this historic landmark.

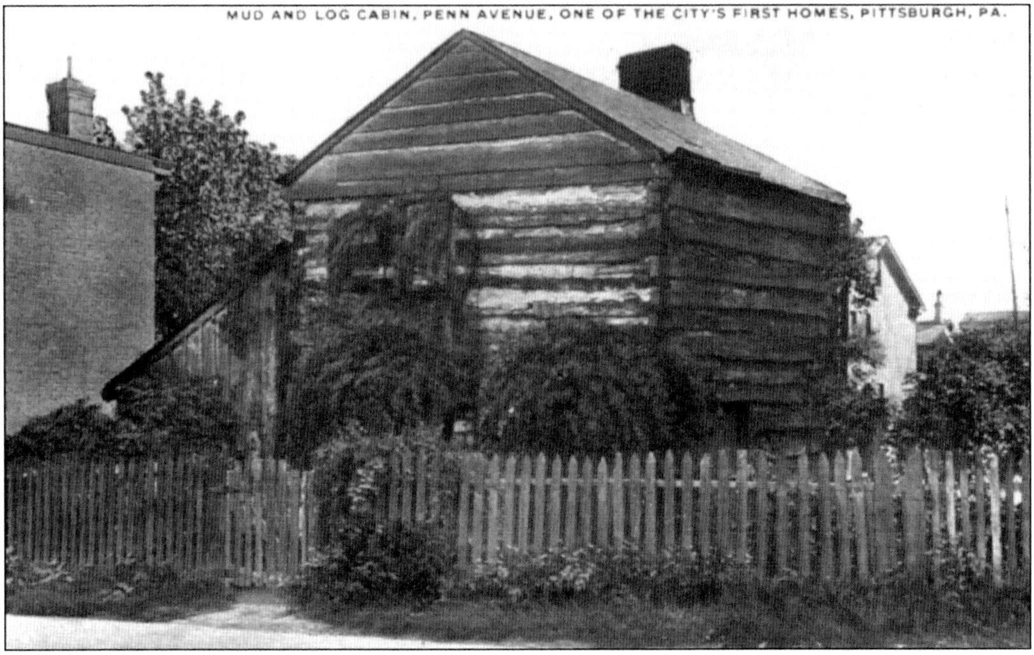

Forsythe Log House, Late 1700s. Using logs believed to be from British barracks at Braddock's Field, this house was built by Capt. Peter Parchment for his daughter Mary and her husband, Hugh Forsythe. It was moved from Wilkinsburg to Penn Avenue near St. Clair Street about 1840. In 1917, Thomas Mellon II moved the house to Penn and Negley Avenues and maintained it as a museum. It was removed about 1948.

PETER PARCHMENT PLAQUE, 1921. This plaque was placed by the Daughters of the American Revolution on the Forsythe Log House to honor Peter Parchment (1749–1844), who served in the 13th Virginia Regiment from 1777 to 1780 and was made captain of the Fifth Company of the Allegheny County Brigade of Militia. Descendant George Clark lives in Highland Park.

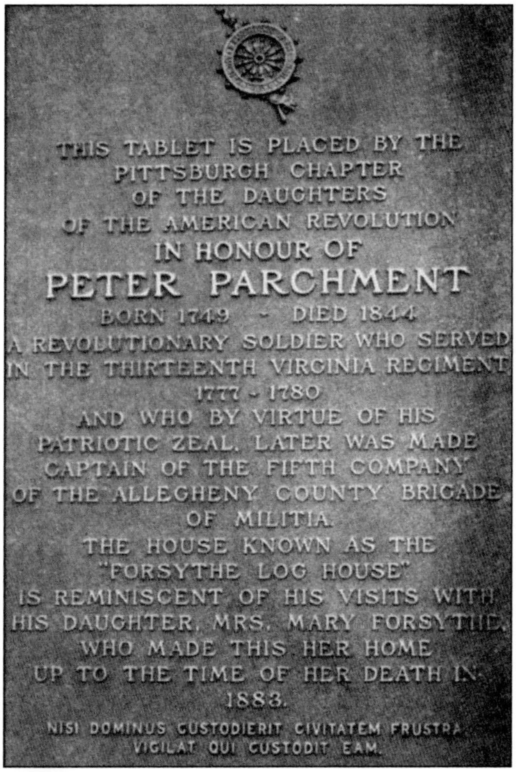

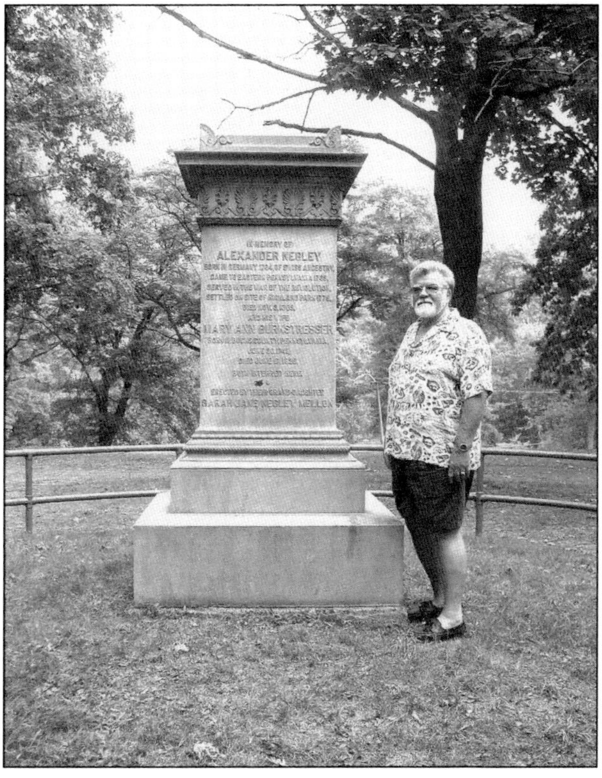

NEGLEY MARKER, 1912. This monument, located in Highland Park, was erected at the bequest of Sarah Jane Negley Mellon (1817–1909), the widow of Thomas Mellon (1813–1908), in memory of her grandparents, Alexander Negley and Mary Ann Burkstresser, who are buried here. Also here are the remains of some 50 early settlers in the East Liberty Valley. Descendant William Gibson is pictured here.

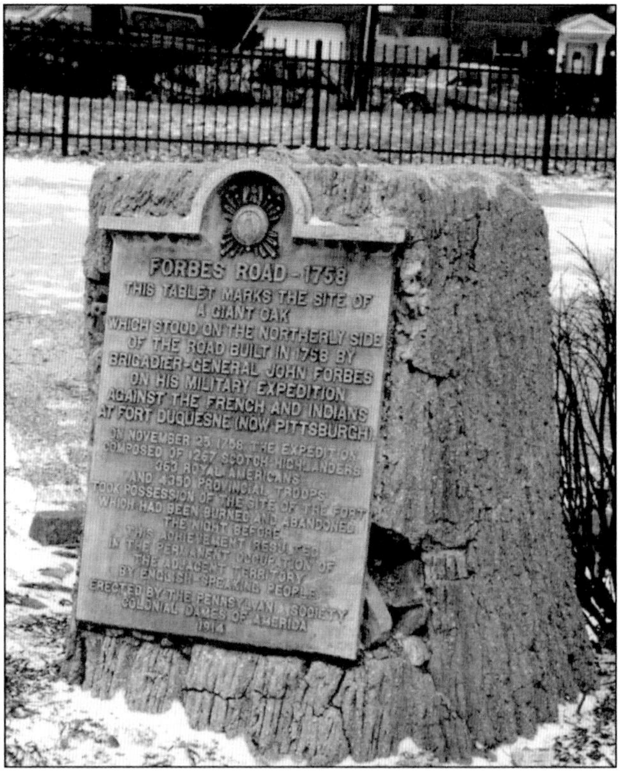

FORBES ROAD STUMP, 1914. The first road, carved through East Liberty Valley from Native American trails, was built by Col. George Washington in 1758 at the direction of British Gen. John Forbes and was named Forbes Road. A bronze plaque at 6805 Penn Avenue shows where the Forbes Oak stood. It is said that the sword of an English officer was found in the tree when it was cut down in 1909.

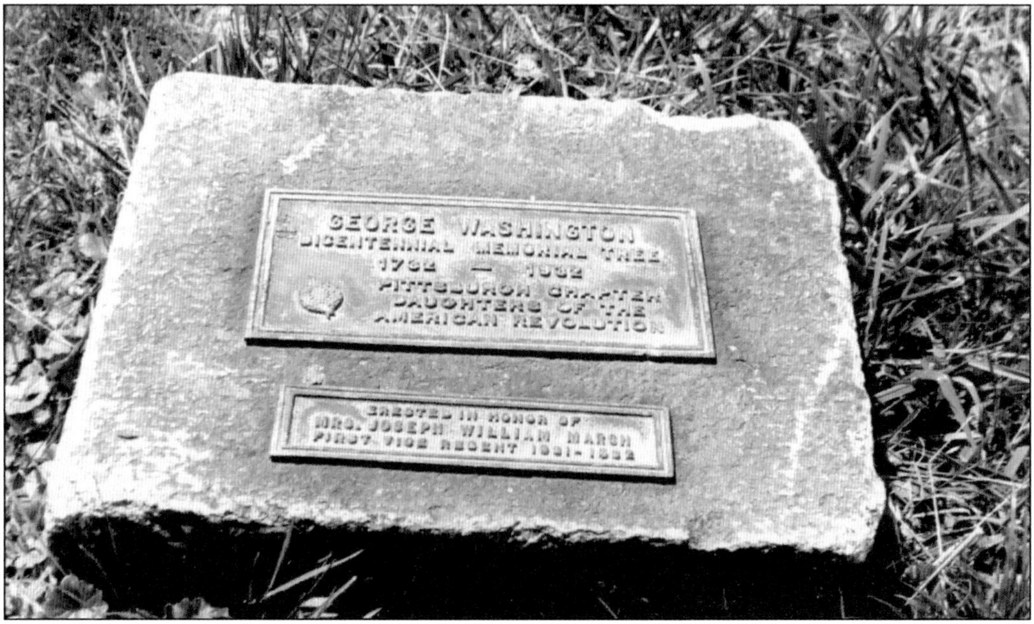

WASHINGTON MARKER, 1952. This marker was placed in Highland Park by the Pittsburgh Chapter of the Daughters of the American Revolution. Washington made seven journeys into this western frontier. His first was as a 21-year-old colonial major to inform the French that they were trespassing on English soil. One of his guides was the Seneca Native American Guyasuta. The present location of this marker is unknown.

Two

The Village of East Liberty

Early memoirs and histories such as those of William Graham Johnston affirm the rural charm of the village of East Liberty in the early and mid-19th century. His description of the valley is of a "scene of tranquil beauty . . . spread at our feet,——one which I doubt has its equal this side of heaven."

In the 1830s, the village was mainly log houses, woodland, and farms. About a half-dozen taverns, more than would be expected in such a small village, were a respite for travelers along the Forbes Road (later called the Greensburg Pike). Beitler's Tavern, the Black Horse Tavern, and McCall's Tavern were among them. Negley's General Store was also a welcomed stop.

Alexander Negley had extensive farm land and orchards on the hilltop above the Allegheny River in what is now Highland Park. The family farmed and ran a steam gristmill. In 1809, Alexander's son Jacob built a school near what is now Penn and Highland Avenues. Thomas Mellon, a young lawyer who lived nearby, married Jacob's daughter, Sarah Jane, in 1843, considerably increasing his holdings in the valley.

Three churches appeared in East Liberty before 1855, and there were 154 "heads of families" in 1856, among whom were 20 farmers, 24 merchants, 13 carpenters, 6 inn keepers, and 6 physicians, as well as tailors, tanners, saddlers, and 7 "gentlemen." The latter is likely a reference to evidence that country houses had begun to appear in the neighborhood. As early as 1832, William Wilkins (1779–1865), an early prominent judge and ambassador to Russia, purchased 650 acres in the valley on which he built, in 1835, his great Greek revival country home, Homewood.

In 1852, the first train stopped in East Liberty. With this and its strategic crossroads, East Liberty and the valley became well positioned for future growth.

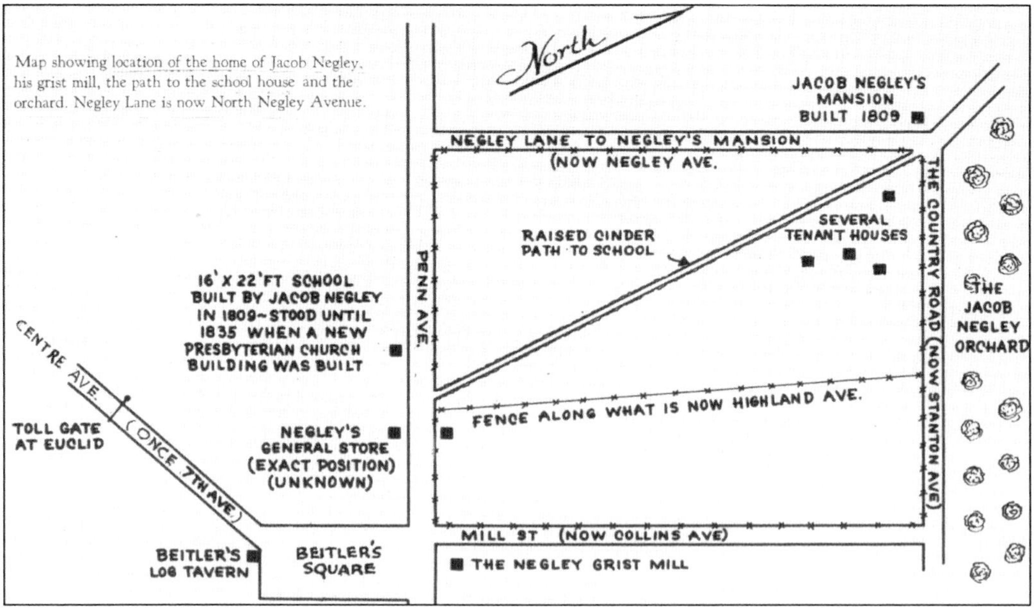

VILLAGE OF 1819. This map shows the Negley farm and gristmill, and Beitler's Tavern. Jacob Negley had the foresight to lay out the Greensburg and Pittsburgh Turnpike (Penn Avenue) to be 100 feet wide. This width has been maintained to this day through the East Liberty business district. At the time of the survey, some property owners objected to having to move their existing fences.

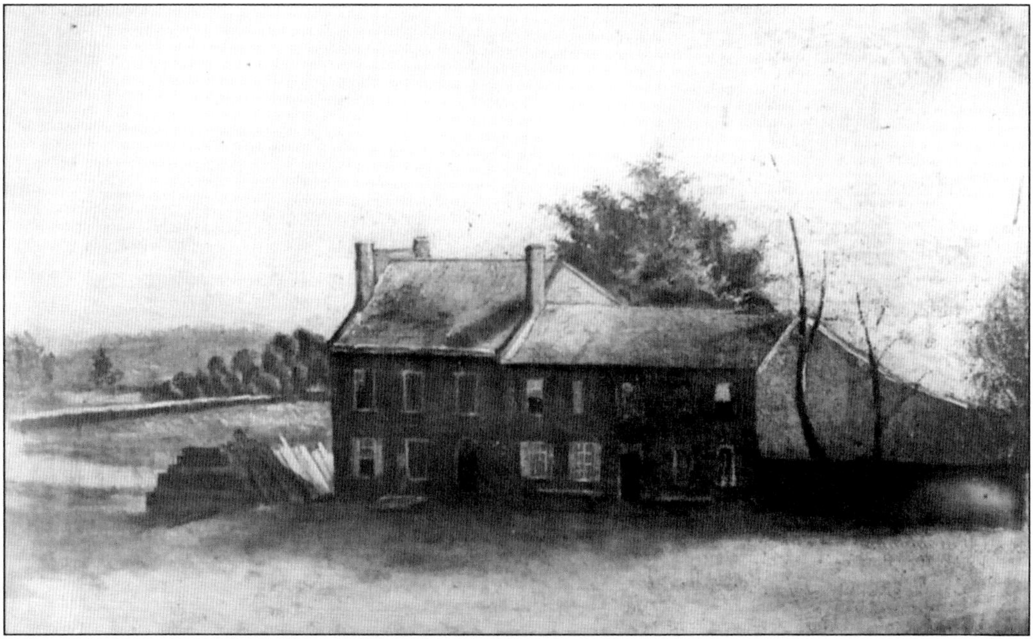

BEITLER'S TAVERN, 1819. John "Pap" Beitler owned a downtown tavern before moving to East Liberty in 1815, "a little way beyond the [Negley] church," on Penn Avenue at Collins Avenue. Here Conestoga wagons and stagecoaches stopped where passengers and horses were refreshed. It was famous for its suppers of spring chickens and waffles. The building, facing the cobblestoned Beitler's Square centered with a well, was also rented for a village school.

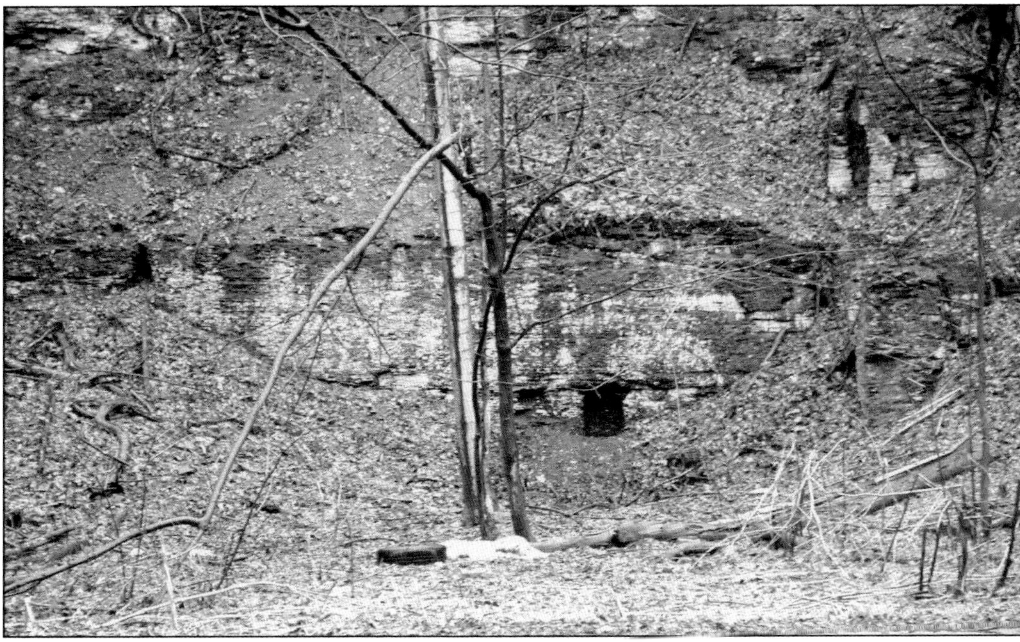

NEGLEY GRIST MILL, EARLY 1800S. This photograph shows a possible location for Jacob Negley's water-powered gristmill at the foot of Negley Run near what is now Washington Boulevard. The square-cut hole might have accommodated the axle bearing of the waterwheel. Archeological investigation is needed to verify this assumption.

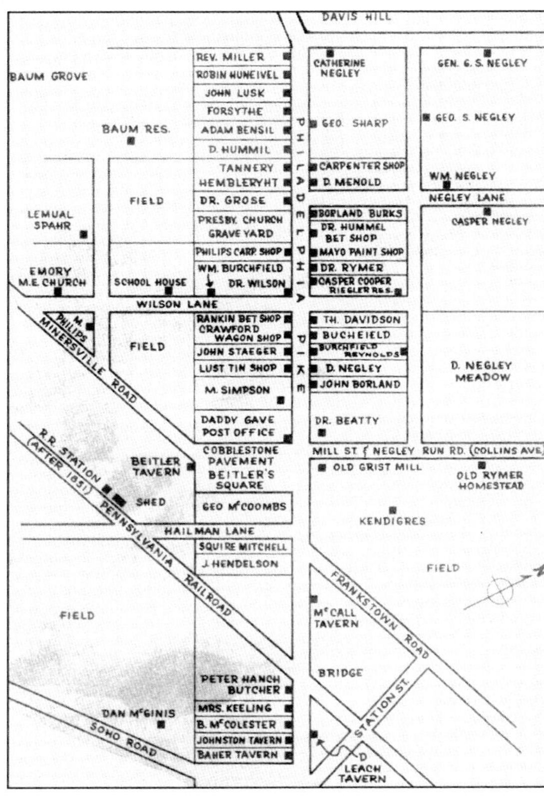

VILLAGE OF 1839. This map shows the locations of major East Liberty homes and businesses in 1839. The road shown as Philadelphia Pike is Penn Avenue, and Negley Lane is the current North Negley Avenue. At the eastern edge of the business district was Mill Street, which later became Collins Avenue. Since the 1960s redevelopment, Collins Avenue terminates at Penn Circle, thus eliminating its intersection with Penn Avenue.

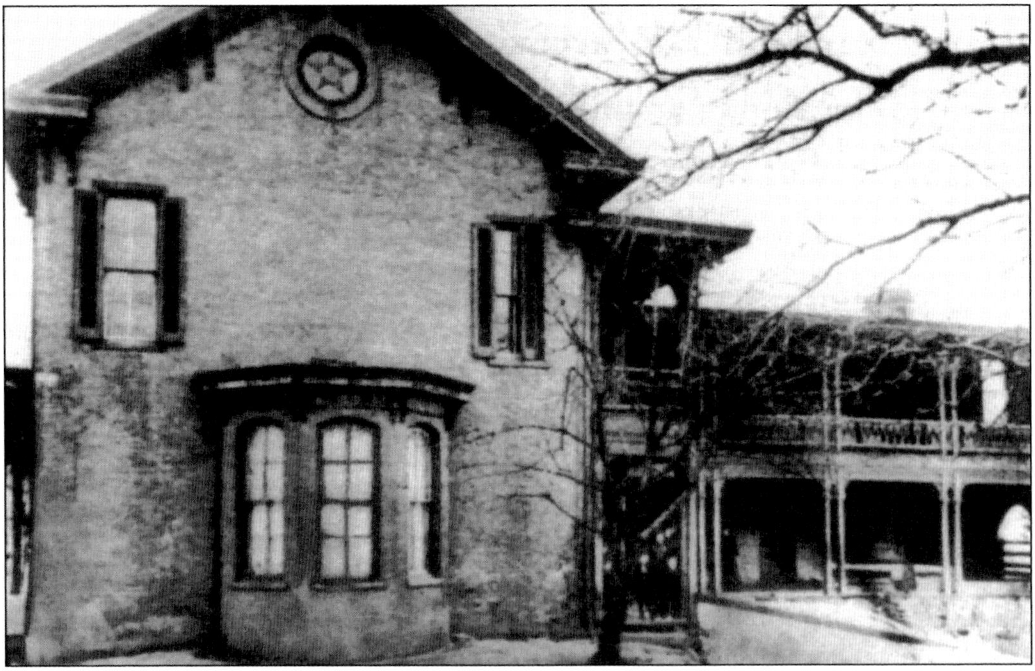

JACOB NEGLEY MANSION, 1809. Jacob Negley (1766–1827), son of Alexander Negley (1734–1809) and Mary Ann Burkstresser (1741–1829), built this home at Stanton and Negley Avenues. It was L-shaped and constructed of yellow brick made on site. The estate included a large apple orchard and a spring used by passing horses. The home was demolished in 1903.

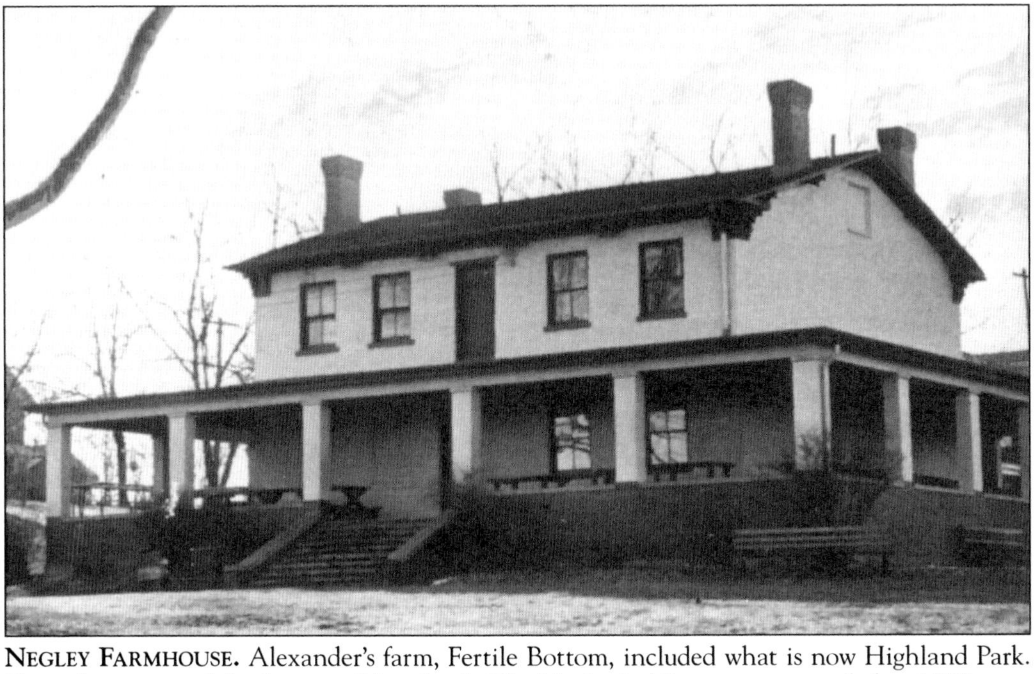

NEGLEY FARMHOUSE. Alexander's farm, Fertile Bottom, included what is now Highland Park. His widow operated the farm until her death. The Negley holdings were expanded to 1,500 acres by their son Jacob. The date of construction of this farmhouse is not known. It has had many uses, including a dairy and a private golf club. The building is now used for park activities.

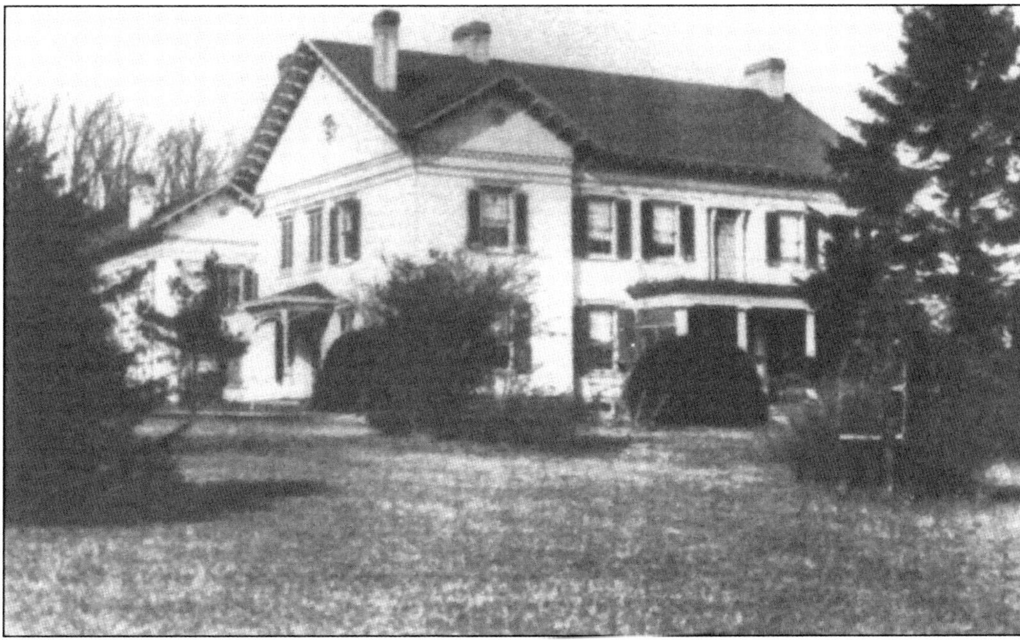

JUDGE THOMAS MELLON HOME, 1851. Thomas Mellon emigrated from Ireland in 1818. While a young attorney, he married Sarah Jane Negley. They built a 22-room, gray brick country home at 401 North Negley Avenue, less than a half-mile from the home of her father, Jacob Negley. They lived here for 57 years. The home was razed in 1955, and the property was subdivided.

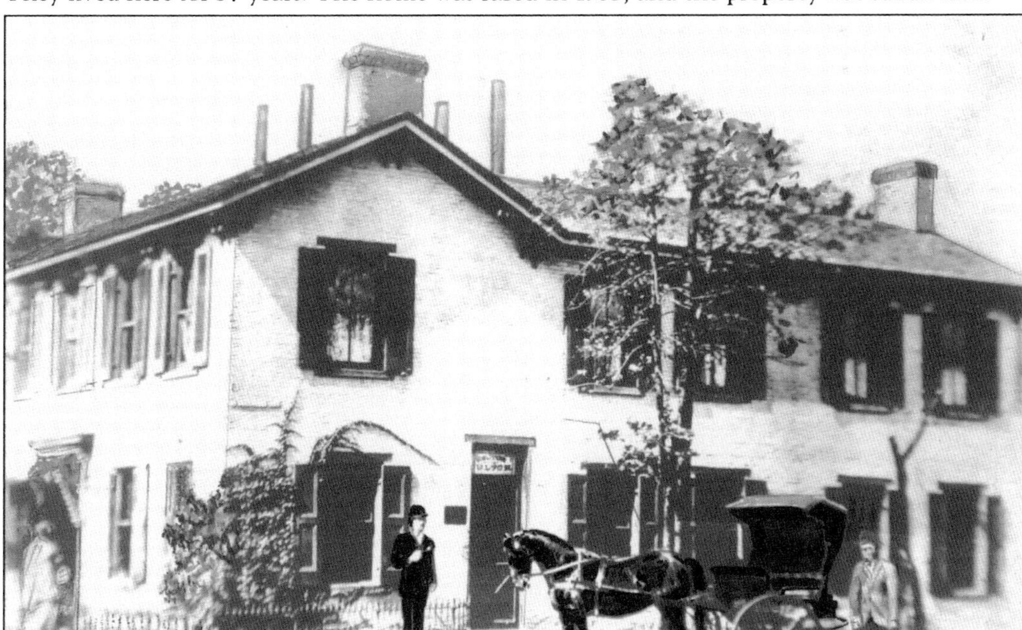

DR. FULTON'S RESIDENCE. This brick, tree-shaded house was the home of Dr. Henry W. Fulton (1838–1907), a prominent East Liberty physician. It was located at the northwest corner of Penn and Highland Avenues, where subsequently stood Rowe's department store, then Sander's market followed by the May-Stern furniture store. Dr. Fulton served in the Civil War. Members of the Fulton family still live in the area.

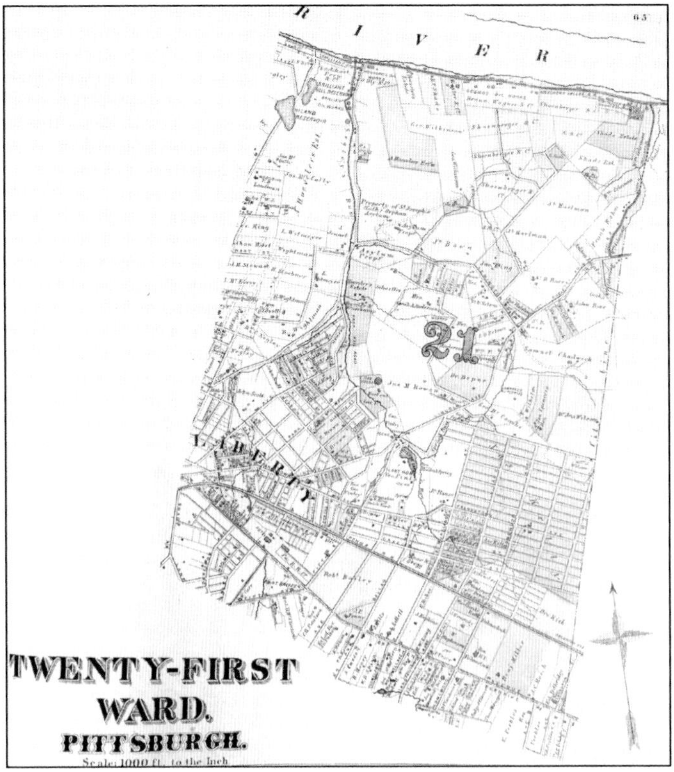

PITTSBURGH PLAT MAP, 1872. This map shows Silver Lake on Fifth Avenue extension, now Washington Boulevard. Near the Allegheny River is the Brilliant Oil Works, owned by Lockhart, Frew, and Company.

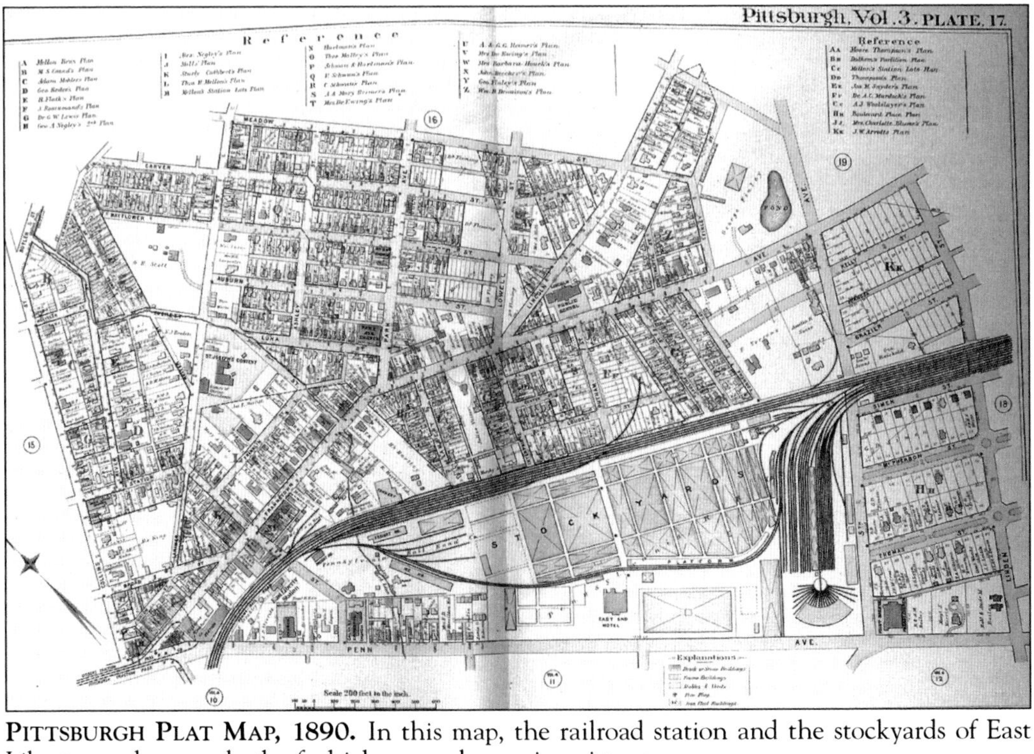

PITTSBURGH PLAT MAP, 1890. In this map, the railroad station and the stockyards of East Liberty can be seen, both of which are no longer in existence.

Three

The Growing Years

The opening of the Pennsylvania Railroad in 1852 through the center of the East Liberty Valley brought an influx of people and new businesses. It also brought the stockyards at Penn Avenue next to the station just below the crossroads. The railroad profoundly influenced all manner of enterprises and was a stimulus for growth.

In 1861, East Liberty became the home of a new industry when Charles Lockhart started the Brilliant Oil Works on the southern banks of the Allegheny River in what is now Highland Park. It was the first commercial oil refinery in the United States and represented the birth of the modern oil industry.

Thomas Mellon made his fortune in real estate, investments, and numerous transportation ventures connected with his land. In 1859, he was strongly behind the two horse car lines that connected East Liberty through Oakland, Lawrenceville, and downtown Pittsburgh. Other entrepreneurs brought new manufacturing enterprises and commercial activity to the area.

Kuhn Grocery, Henne Jewelry, Mansmann's Department Store, and other markets and stores of all kinds lined Penn Avenue. The Mellon-built Liberty Market (now AAA headquarters) opened on Centre Avenue. There was an active golf club that held tournaments and a merry-go-round that attracted crowds at Baum Boulevard and South Highland Avenue. Residents enjoyed skating, running meets, bicycle clubs, and dancing academies.

The opening of the railroad was also a factor in the construction of residences of the wealthy in the East Liberty Valley. Downtown offices could now easily be reached, and many businessmen, industrialists, and magnates of the steel industry located their homes here. Henry Clay Frick, Alexander Peacock, Andrew Carnegie, Thomas Carnegie, George Westinghouse, H. J. Heinz, and other millionaires built large houses of every architectural description away from the city and in the green pastures and clean air of the East Liberty Valley.

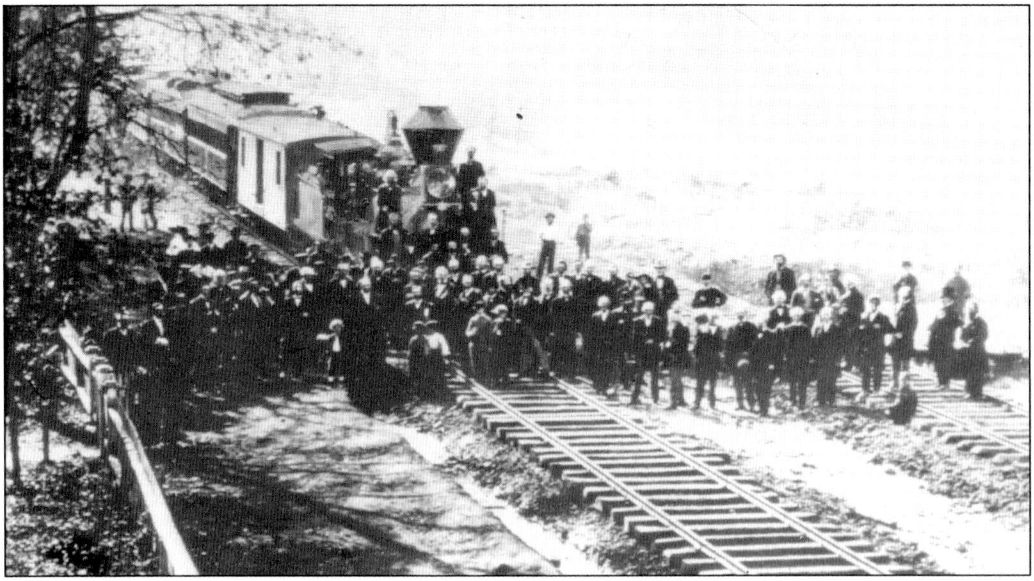

PENNSYLVANIA RAILROAD, 1852. This celebration marks the arrival of the first train from Philadelphia. It consisted of a wood-burning steam locomotive with three passenger cars. Two years later, the Pennsylvania Railroad completed its main line to Chicago, thus providing passenger and freight service from the East to the Midwest. Stagecoaches and Conestoga wagons no longer stopped at Beitler's Tavern. The East Liberty station was built on this site in 1905.

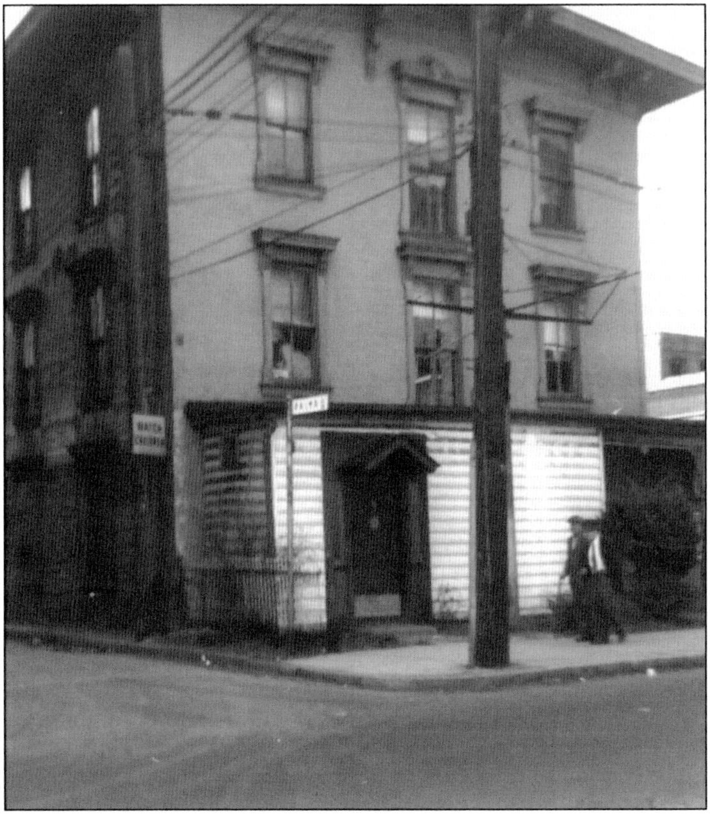

KUHN'S GRIST MILL, 1851. In the early 1800s, Jacob Negley built a gristmill on Negley Run, but it was unable to operate in times of low water. In 1816, he built a steam-powered mill at the northeast corner of Penn Avenue and Mill Street, capable of year-round operation. In 1851, David Kuhn erected a mill at 219 Collins Avenue, near where Negley's steam-powered mill had stood.

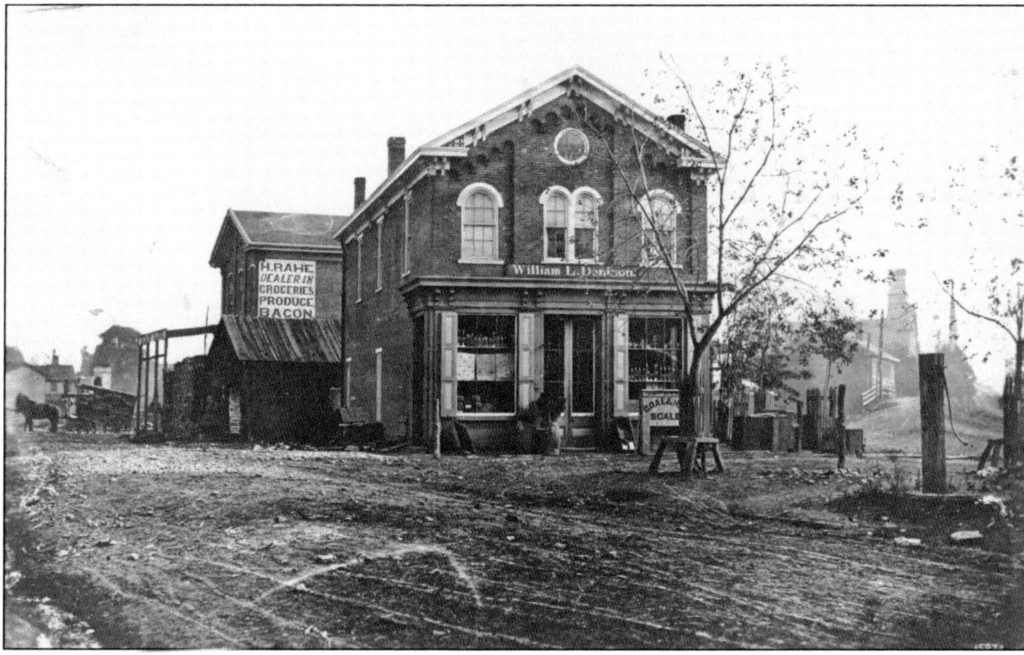

DENISON'S GENERAL STORE, 1865. This store, located at Penn and Frankstown Avenues, sold coal, coke, brooms, oil lamps, and chimneys. Note the water pump at the right of the picture. The building was destroyed by fire on July 4, 1870.

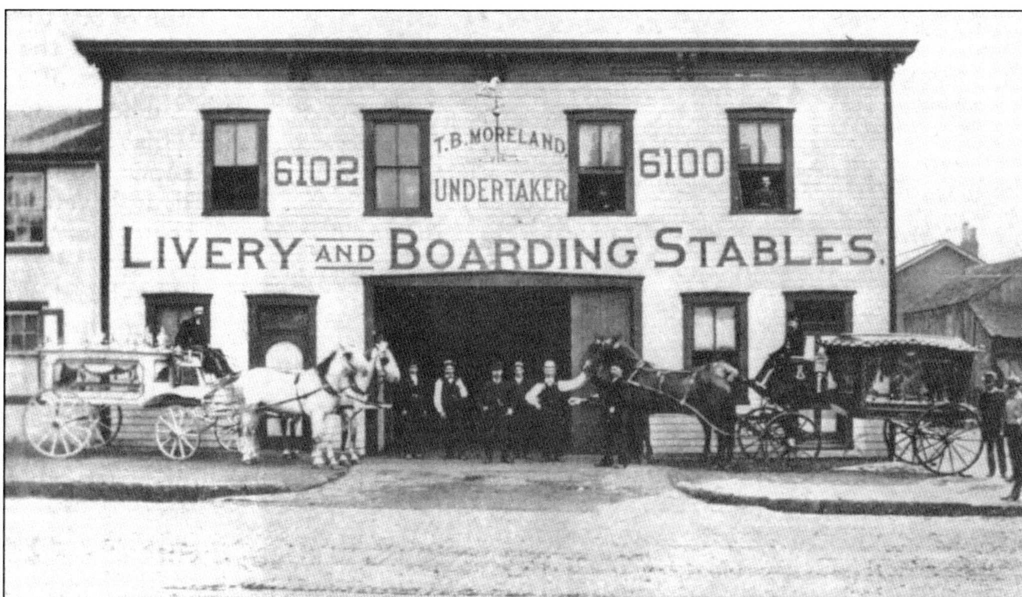

MORELAND LIVERY, 1870. T. B. Moreland operated a livery and boarding stables at 6100 Penn Avenue at Sheridan Avenue. He was also an undertaker catering to the social elite. He used a black hearse with black horses for the funerals of adults and a small white hearse drawn by white horses for children. He later moved his business to a converted mansion on North Highland Avenue, now occupied by Vintage.

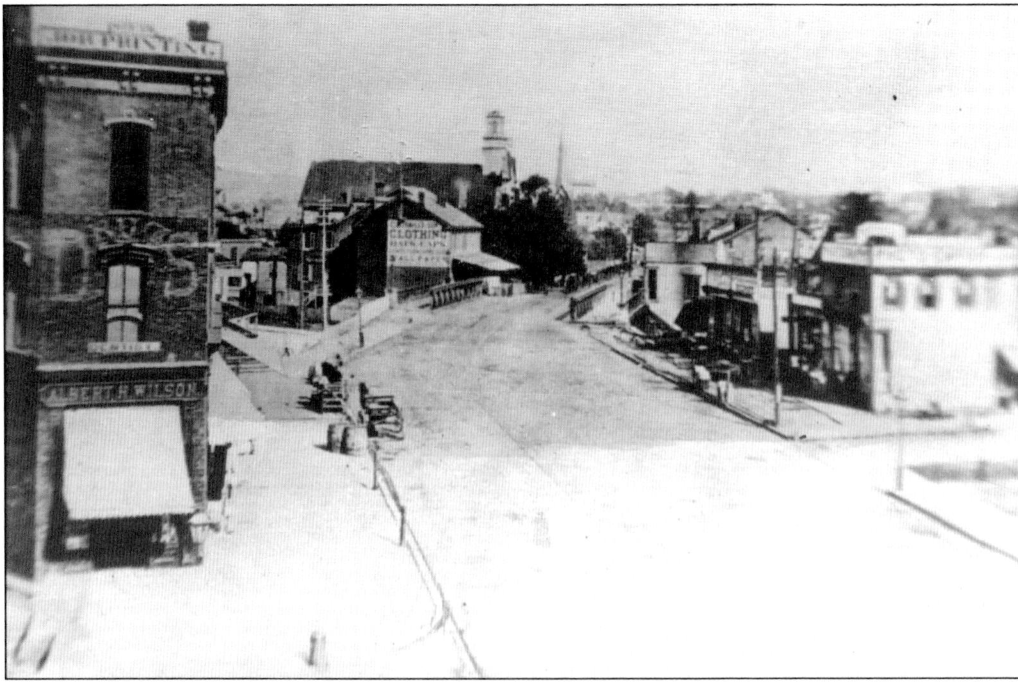

PENN AND FRANKSTOWN AVENUES, 1875. This photograph shows commercial growth at the same corner. The street has been paved, Denison's store has been replaced with a brick building, and a horse car is shown traveling east over the new bridge to Wilkinsburg. The store was bought by W. J. Spahr in 1880.

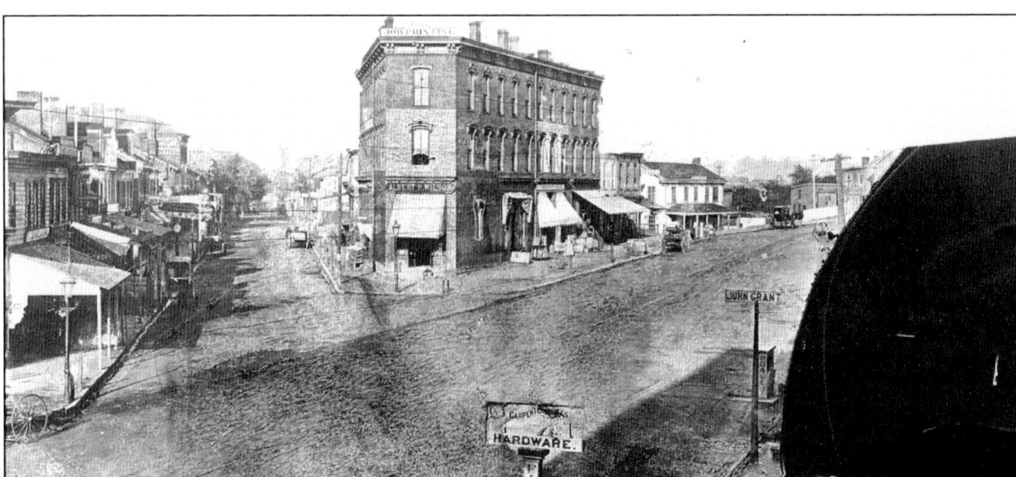

PENN AND FRANKSTOWN AVENUES, LATE 1800S. Here further business growth at the same intersection is seen.

KUHN AND BROTHER GROCERY, 1880. This market at 6113–6115 Penn Avenue, established by James C. and Harry P. Kuhn, served East Liberty for many years. Their first store, built in 1875, was at Collins Avenue and Station Street. The same family operated the gristmill, ran a catering establishment at 6262 Penn Avenue, and built the Rittenhouse Hotel at North Highland Avenue and Kirkwood Street.

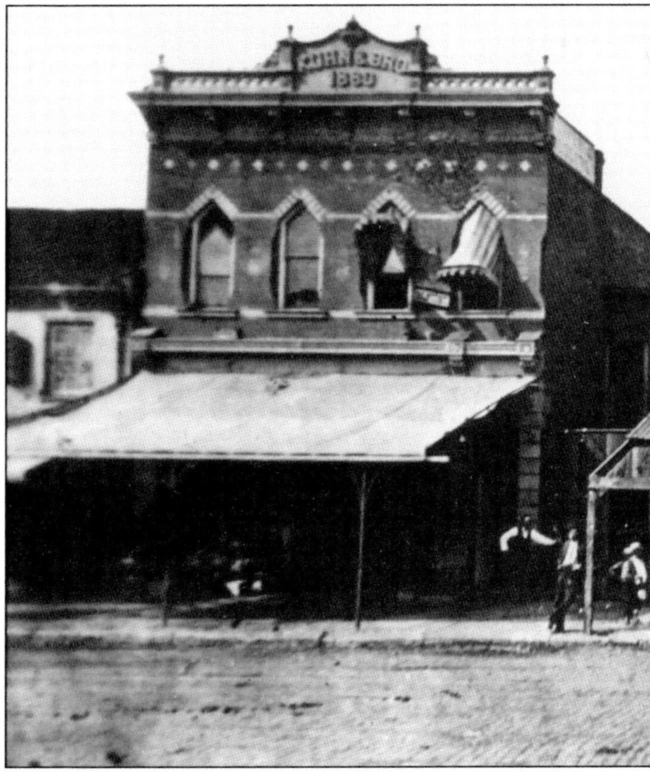

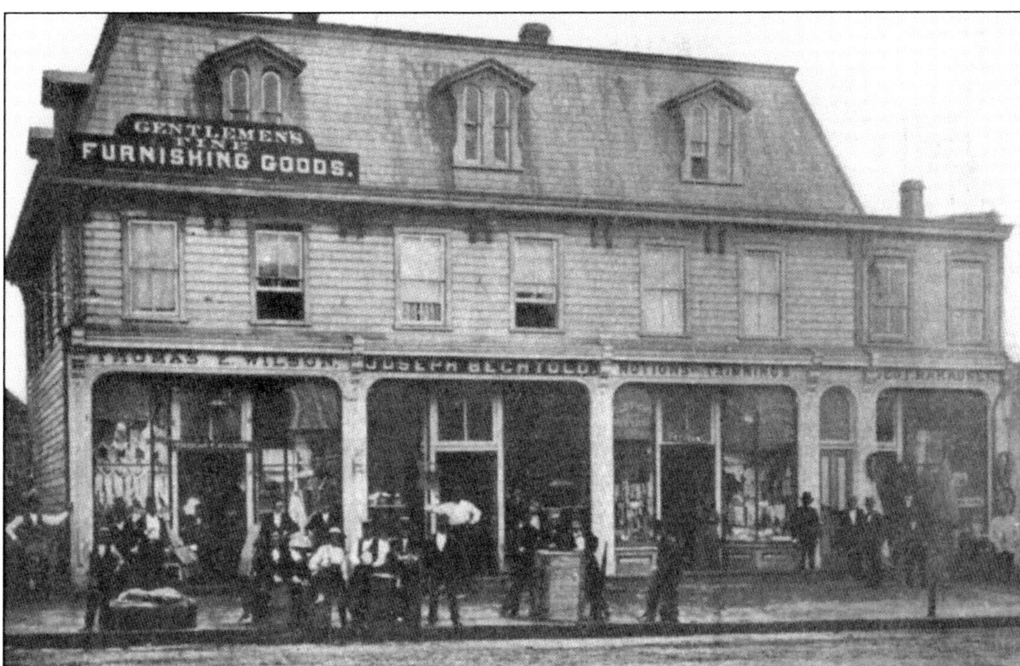

PENN AND CENTRE AVENUES. This photograph taken before 1880 shows several businesses, including Thomas Wilson's store offering "Gentlemen's Fine Furnishing Goods," as well as a store operated by Joseph Bechtold, and one featuring "Notions & Trimmings."

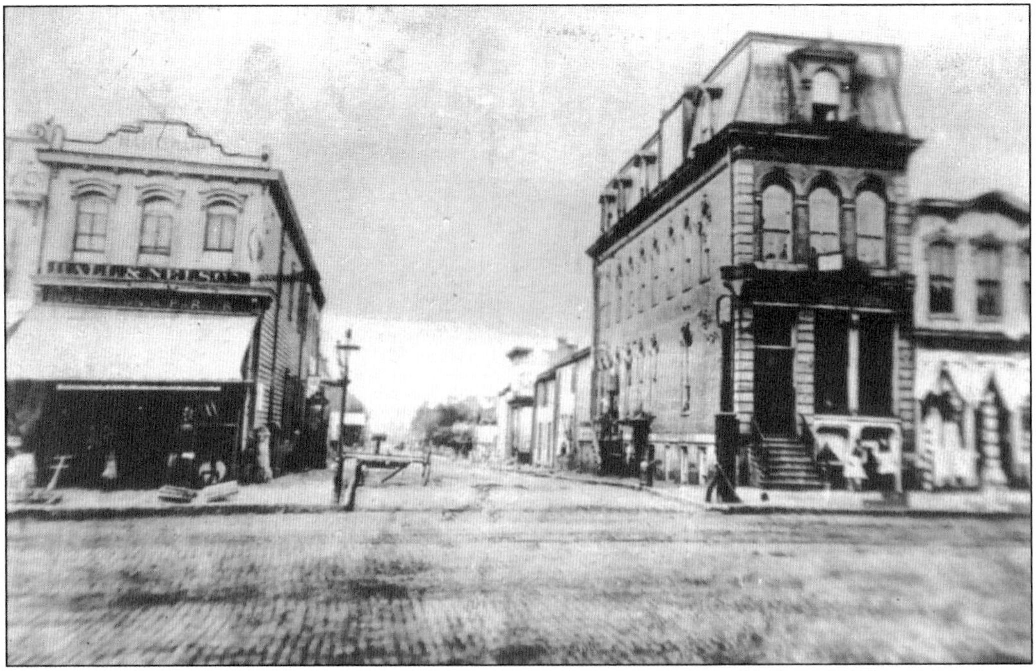

PENN AND COLLINS AVENUES, C. 1875. On the northwest corner is Hall and Nelson's hardware and general merchandise store. There was an apartment on the second floor, and the plow on the roof advertises the nature of the business. On the sidewalk are a lawn mower and bushel baskets. A hay rake sits on the Collins Avenue side.

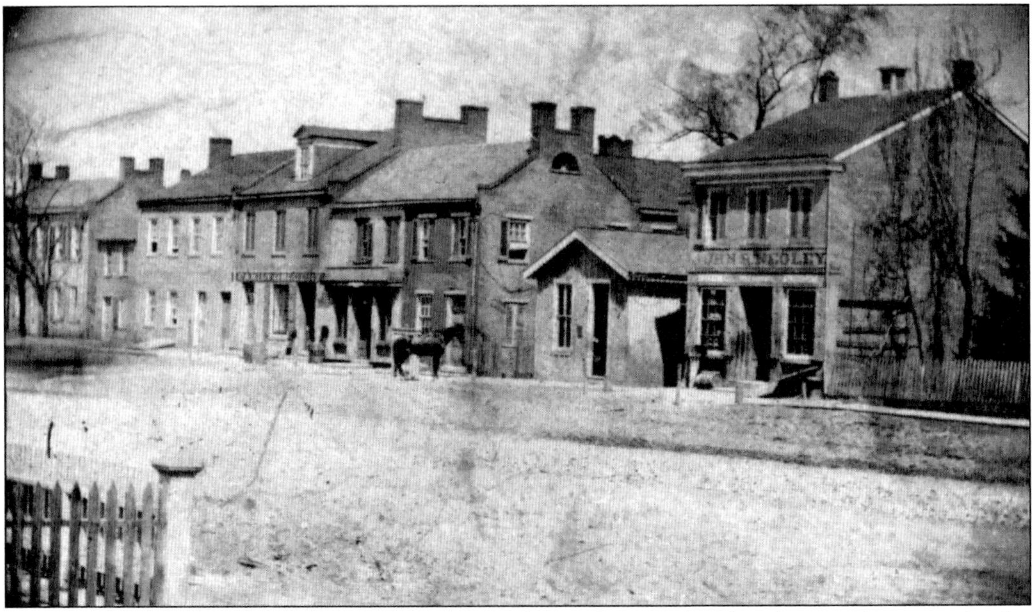

PENN AVENUE, 1868. This rare photograph shows the north side of Penn Avenue. At the corner of Negley Street (now Sheridan Avenue) stood the residence of Thomas Davison, justice of the peace, seen on the right. To the left is Andrew Davis, physician; William Reynolds, lumber merchant; Negley's grocery store; and Dr. John and Dr. Peter Perchment, brothers, physicians, and grandsons of early settler Peter Parchment (the earlier spelling was changed).

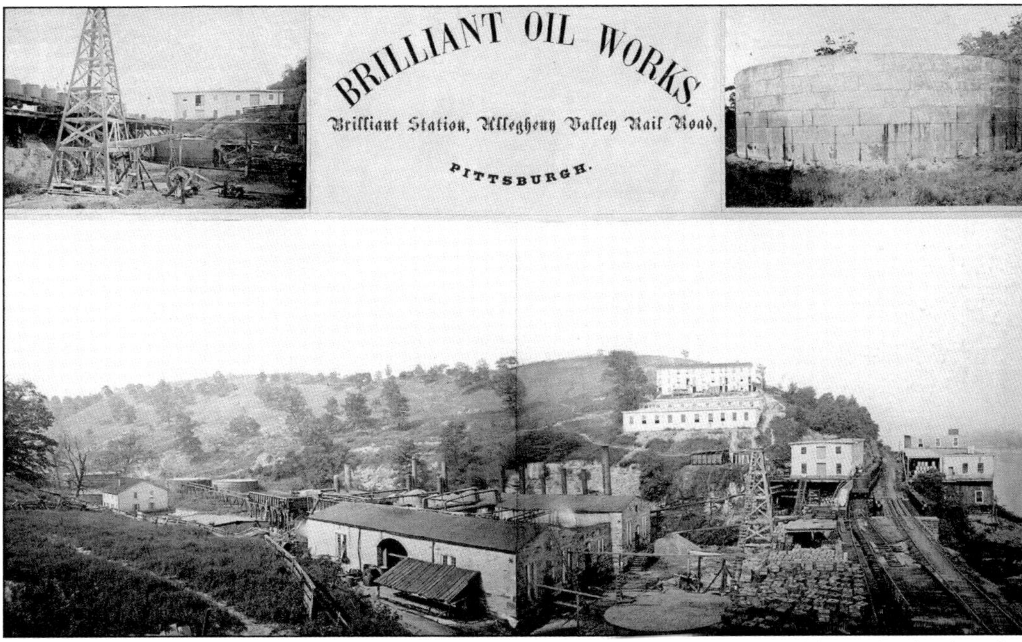

BRILLIANT OIL WORKS, 1861. Pittsburgh entrepreneur Charles Lockhart built the first commercial oil refinery in the United States at Brilliant, along the Allegheny River at Washington Boulevard, in what is now Highland Park. This plant processed crude petroleum barged from Oil City, Pennsylvania. In 1868, Lockhart and John D. Rockefeller met in East Liberty to form the Standard Oil Company.

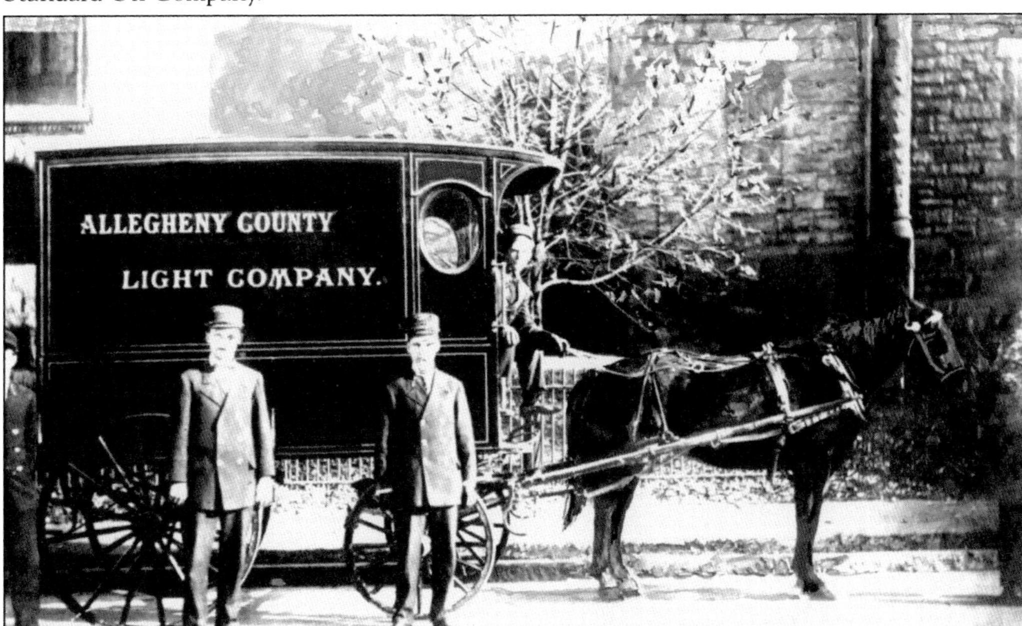

SERVICE WAGON, 1880. This horse-drawn wagon belonged to the Allegheny County Light Company, which was founded in 1880. Its competitor, the Electric Light and Power Company, was chartered in 1882 and included Dr. Henry W. Fulton as one of the incorporators. Allegheny County Light Company was absorbed by Duquesne Light Company in 1913.

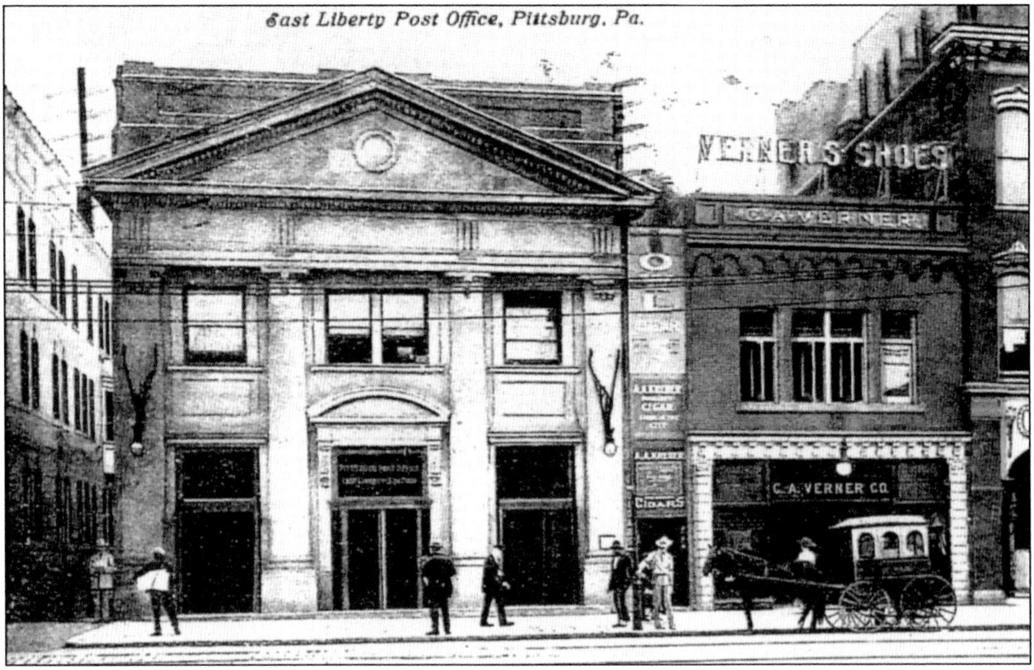

POST OFFICE, 1860S. This post office replaced one initially operated in John R. Negley's grocery store on Penn Avenue, where mail was sorted into pigeonholes, and there was no home delivery. The post office later relocated several times and, in 1929, was on Penn Avenue near Station Street. The 1929 location now houses a Trader Joe's store.

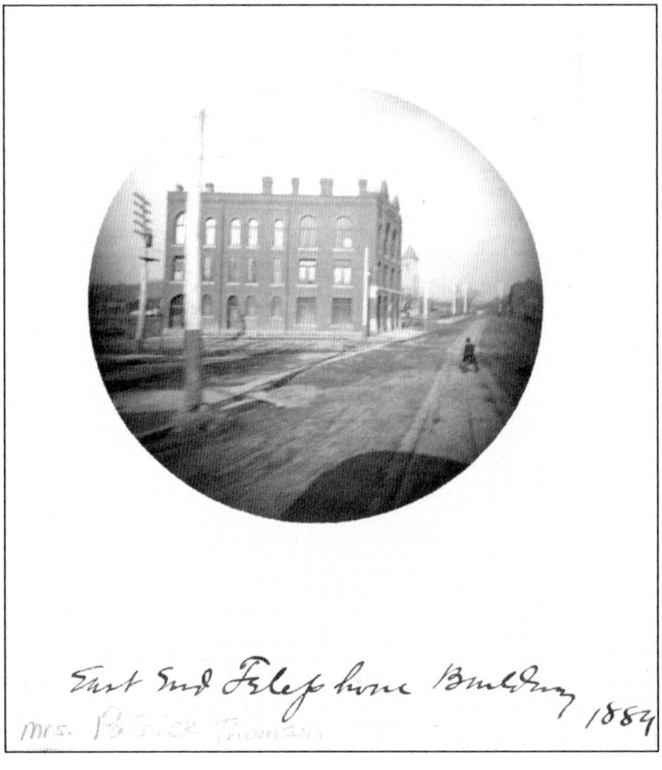

TELEPHONE BUILDING, 1889. In 1877, the first telephone in Allegheny County was installed at 232 Shady Avenue in the home of Thomas David, president of a local telegraph company, who had been approached by Gardiner Hubbard, the father-in-law of Alexander Graham Bell. The company built their first offices here at South Highland and Centre Avenues. The building now houses offices and a five-star restaurant.

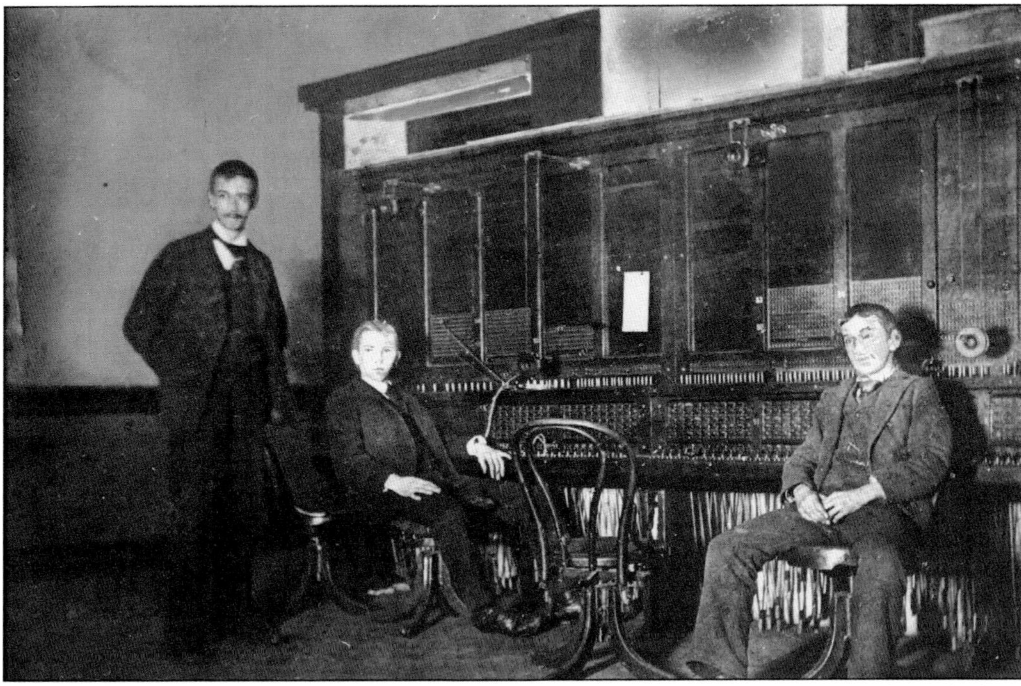

TELEPHONE SWITCHBOARD, 1889. Young men served as night operators in the telephone company building at South Highland and Centre Avenues.

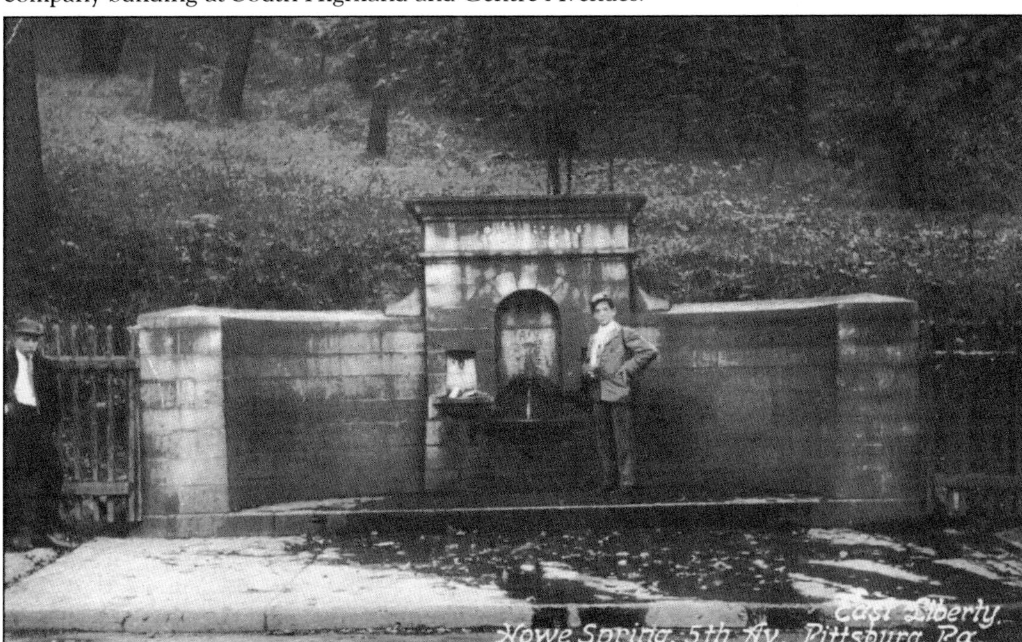

HOWE SPRINGS. This classical structure, located on Fifth Avenue below the campus of Chatham University, housed a natural spring. It was part of the estate of Thomas M. Howe (1808–1877), president of the Exchange National Bank of Pittsburgh. His mansion, Greystone, built around 1860, was located above the spring. In 1911, famous wildcatter Michael Benedum built an equally magnificent home at the same location, retaining the same name.

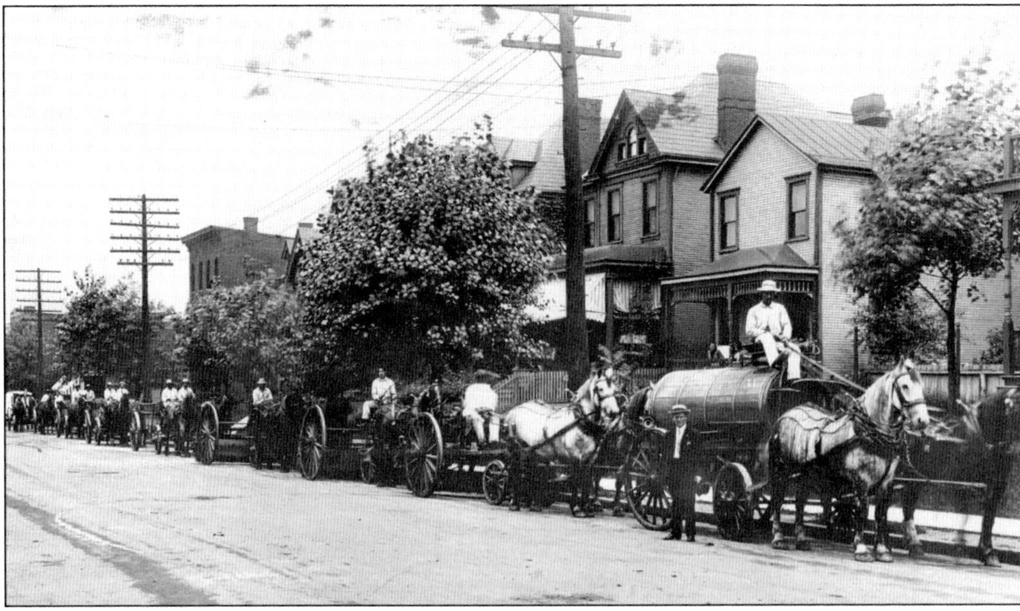

STREET CLEANING, C. 1895. This impressive lineup is the third division of the City of Pittsburgh's street-cleaning department before motorization in 1900.

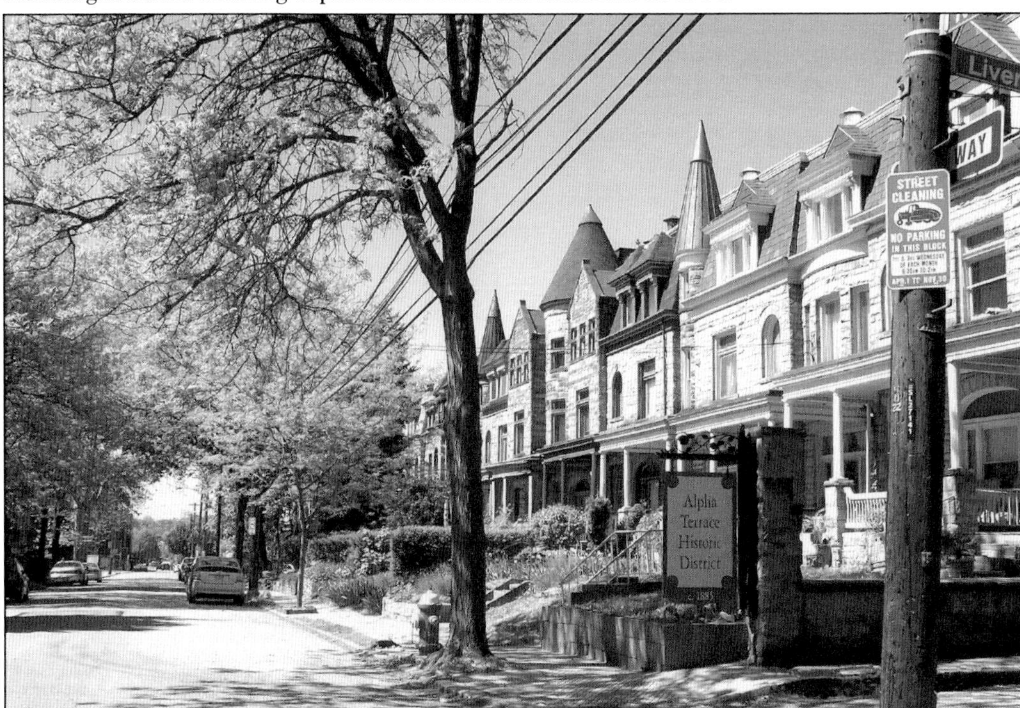

ALPHA TERRACE. These two dozen sturdy townhouses, located off North Beatty Street, were built as rental properties by Isabel Sargent. Those on the east side were built in 1885 in the Queen Anne style, and those on the west side in 1894 in the Richardsonian Romanesque style. They were sold in the 1950s. They are considered "one of the distinctive experiments in multifamily housing in late-Victorian America."

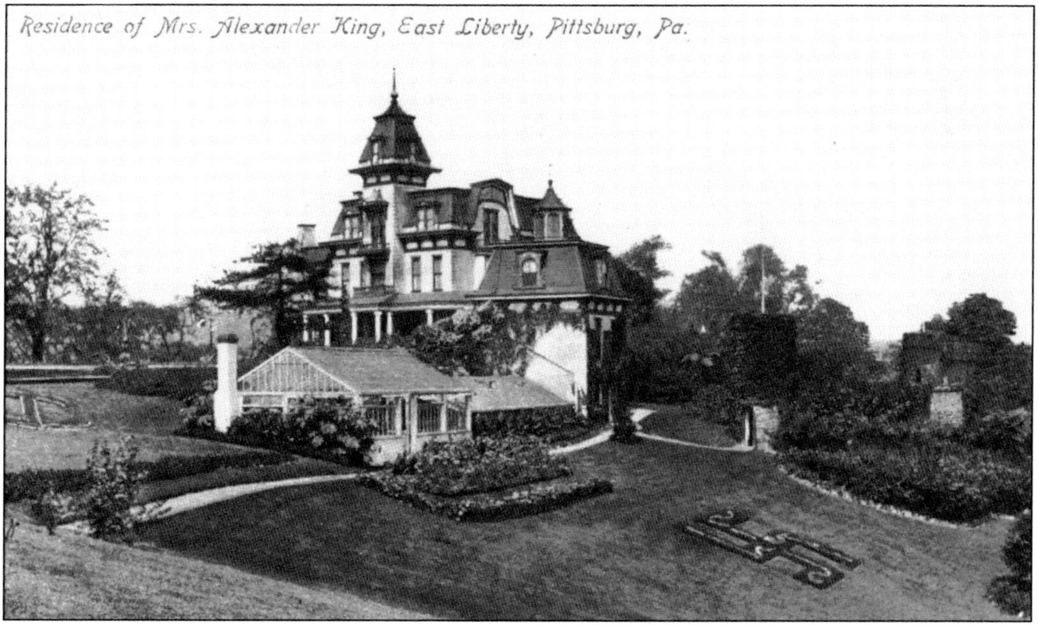

KING MANSION, 1880. The original mansion was built in 1869 for James Scott Negley on almost 100 acres off Elgin Street and North Negley Avenue. It burned in 1879, was purchased by glass magnate Alexander King, and rebuilt in 1880 as Baywood. King's widow lived here until her death in 1911. Her son occupied the home until his death in 1954. It is now a beautifully restored private residence.

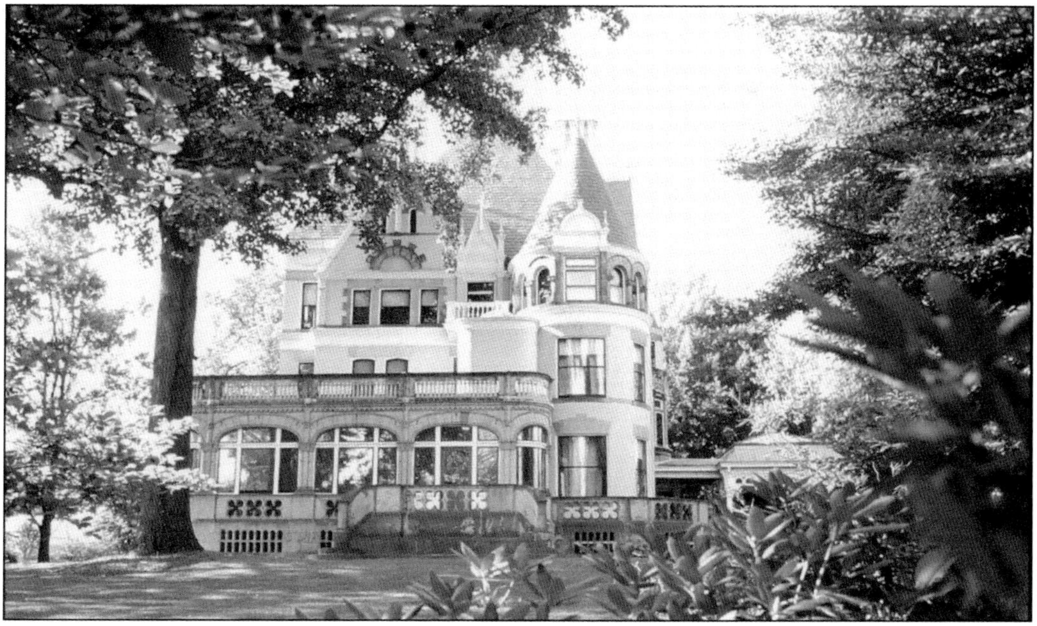

FRICK MANSION, 1882. Coke and steel magnate Henry Clay Frick (1849–1919) bought this 5.5-acre property at Penn and Homewood Avenues and remodeled an existing 1866 structure into a 23-room chateau-style mansion, named Clayton, where he lived until he moved to New York City in 1905. Beautifully maintained, the mansion and associated buildings, including an art gallery, an antique automobile museum, and a greenhouse, are open to the public.

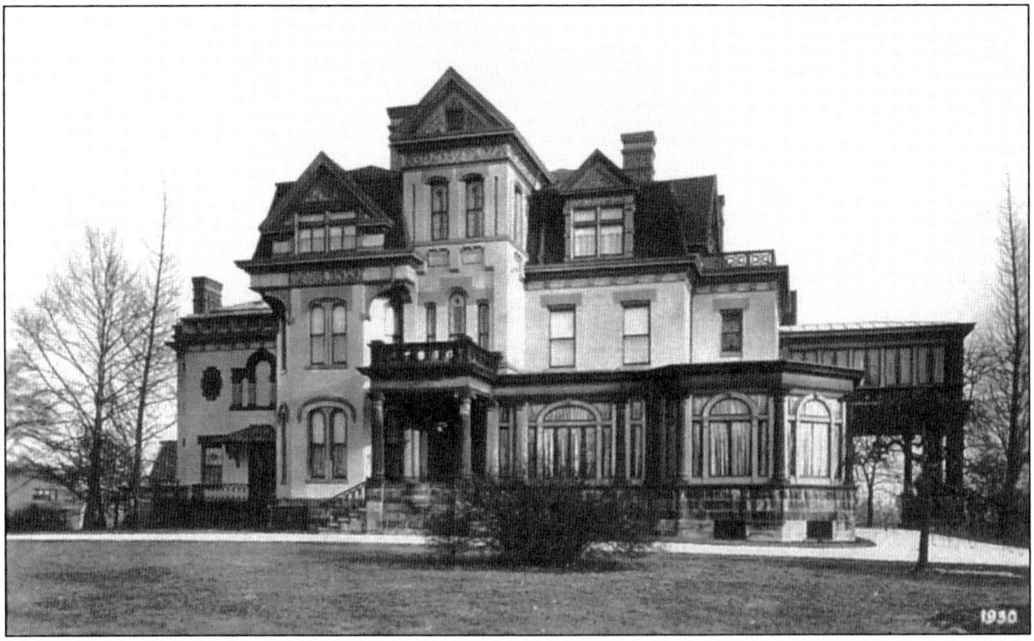

LOCKHART MANSION, MID-1800S. Charles Lockhart, who emigrated from Scotland in 1836, achieved major success in the oil business beginning with the Brilliant Oil Refinery on Washington Boulevard. His mansion at 608 North Highland Avenue, built on 10 acres, was demolished in 1952. The property was donated by his heirs to the Pittsburgh Theological Seminary when it relocated from Pittsburgh's North Side.

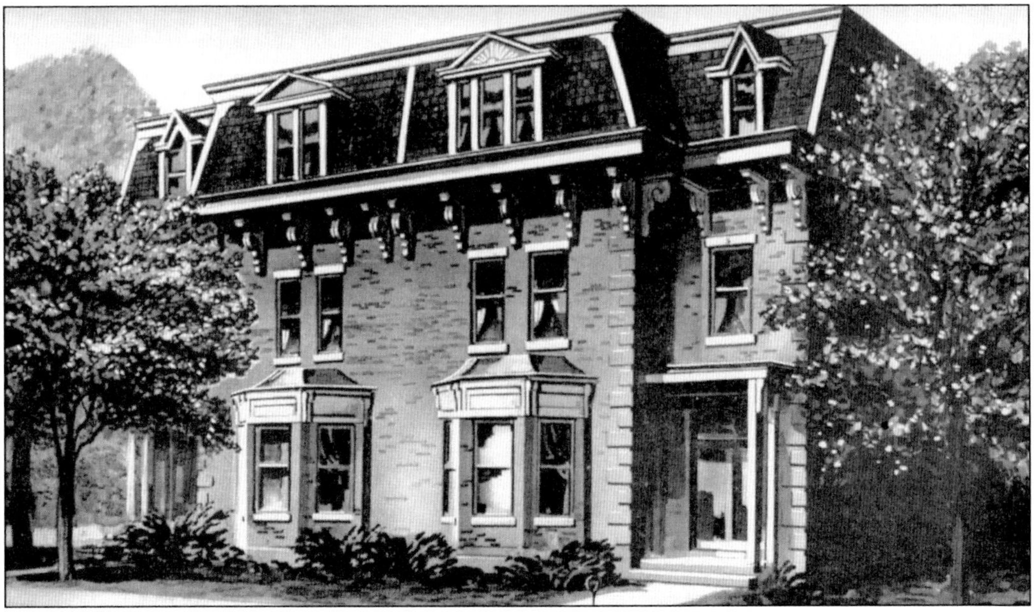

HUNT RESIDENCE, 1888. Alfred E. Hunt (1855–1899) was a metallurgical graduate from Massachusetts Institute of Technology who lived at 272 Shady Avenue when he founded the Pittsburgh Reduction Company for manufacturing aluminum using the Hall-Héroult process. This enterprise ultimately became the multinational corporation ALCOA, of which Hunt was the first president. This building currently houses the offices of Franklin West.

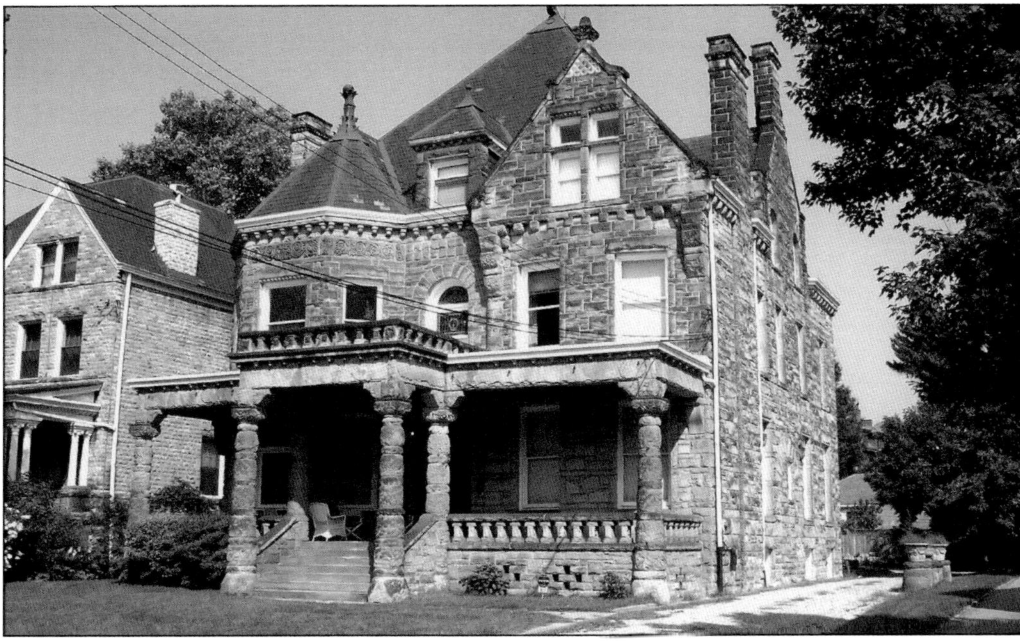

WERNER HOME, 1891. This house at 830 North Highland Avenue was built by Oswald Werner, great-grandfather of Highland Park resident Walter Werner. Oswald Werner and Sons Dyeing and Cleaning Works was the first dry-cleaning establishment in downtown Pittsburgh, established in 1864. They moved to East Liberty in the 1880s. The company pioneered in the development and use of Stoddard solvent, an odorless and non-flammable cleaning fluid.

HEINZ MANSION, 1892. H. J. Heinz (1844–1919), founder of the company that bears his name, resided in this French chateau-style home, Greenlawn, on Penn Avenue between North Lang Avenue and North Murtland Street. On the grounds were a conservatory, museum, and greenhouses. After Heinz's death, the home was demolished. Still visible is the low stone wall topped by an intricate wrought-iron fence.

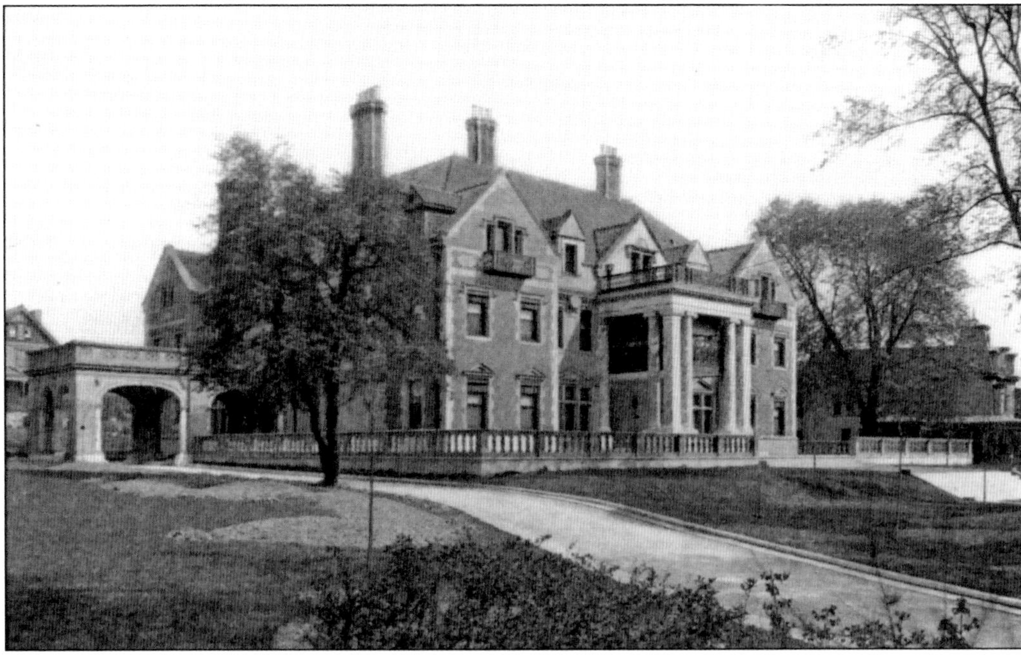

Peacock Mansion, 1901. Alexander Peacock (1863–1928) was a partner in Carnegie Steel. He became the prototypical "Pittsburgh millionaire" created when Carnegie sold out to J. P. Morgan. Peacock built Rowanlea, designed by Alden and Harlow, on North Highland Avenue. The estate covered the area from Highland Avenue to Farragut Street between Jackson Street and Wellesley Avenue. The home was razed in 1924 after Peacock's move to New York City.

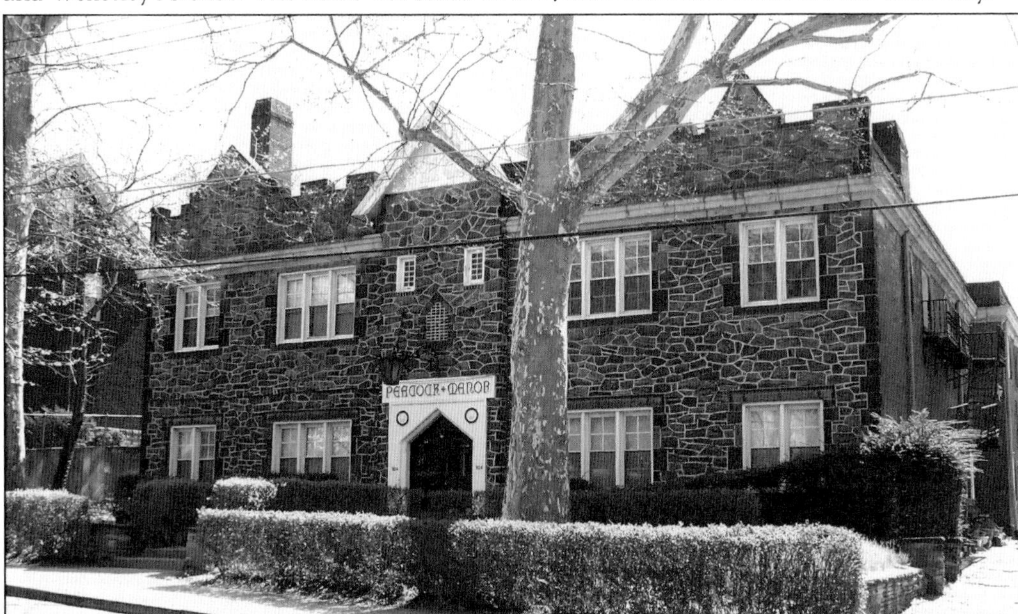

Peacock Manor, 1901. Now converted to contain apartments, this structure at 924 Farragut Street was originally the stables of the Peacock mansion. The estate also had large gardens and a greenhouse to accommodate plants and safeguard palm trees in winter for summer display along the mansion's drive.

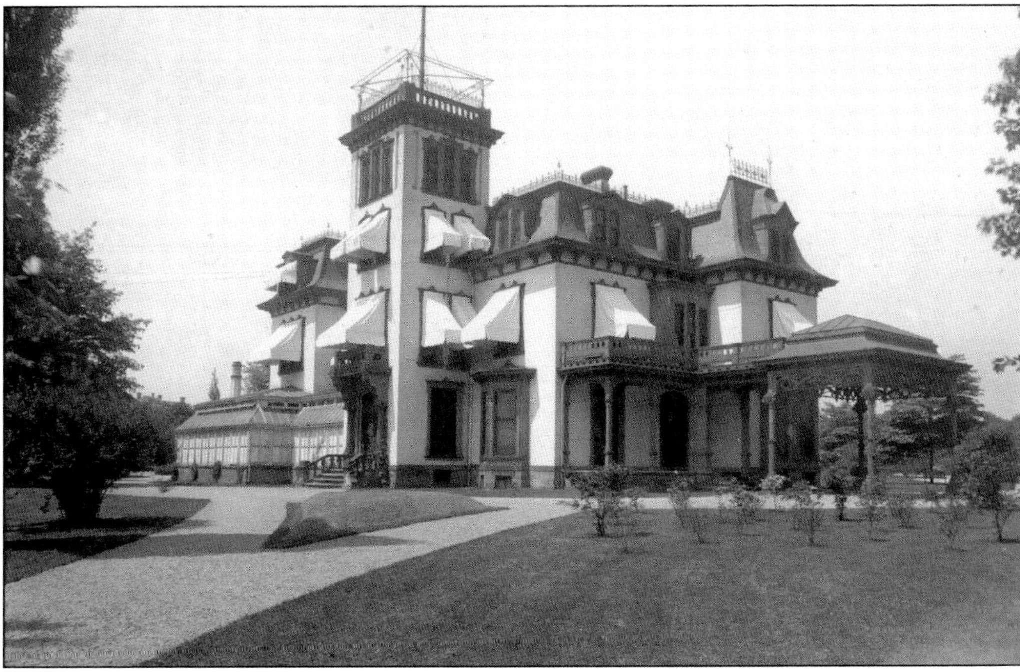

Westinghouse Mansion, 1867. George Westinghouse (1846–1914), noted inventor and industrialist, moved here with his bride and purchased five acres on Thomas Boulevard between North Lang Avenue and North Murtland Street, on which their home Solitude was built. A lighted tunnel provided access to his ceramic-tile lined laboratory. The mansion was torn down in 1919, and the property made into a city park.

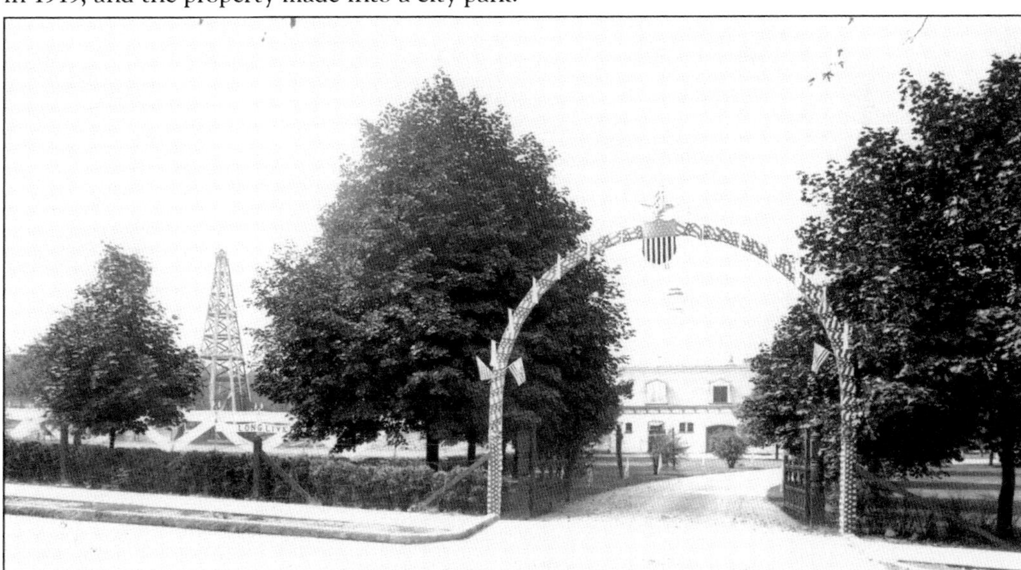

Gas Well, 1884. On his property, Westinghouse drilled the city's first gas well, leading to the formation of the Equitable Gas Company. The derrick is seen at the left. Westinghouse was enthusiastic about the potential for natural gas as an energy source for residential, commercial, and industrial purposes. The laboratory and boiler house are shown in the middle of the photograph.

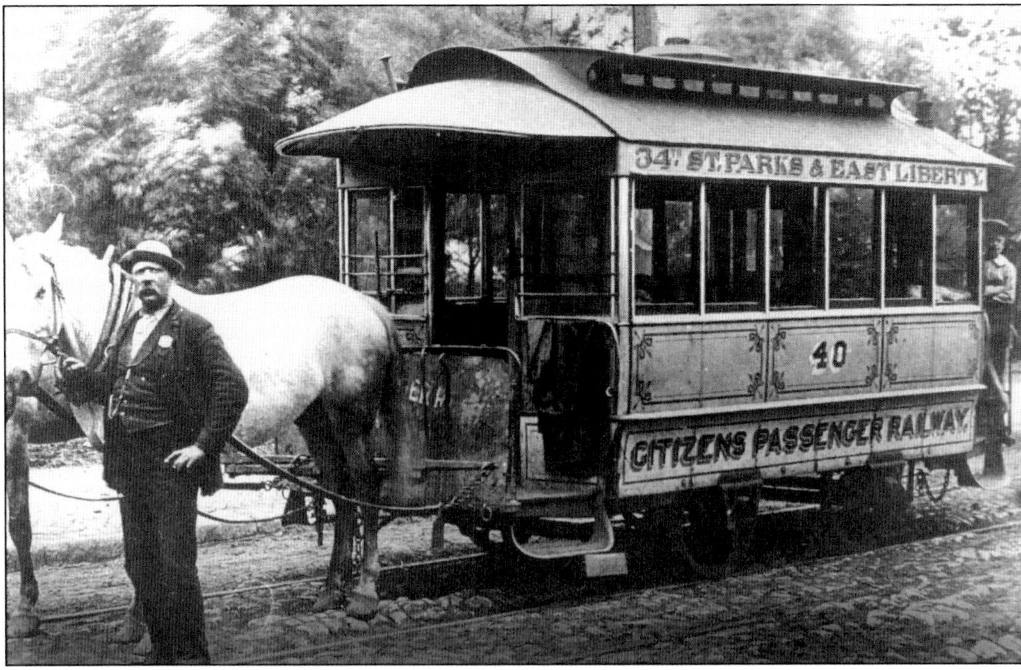

HORSE-DRAWN CAR, LATE 1880S. The Citizens Passenger Railway was the first horse car line in Pittsburgh. It operated along Penn Avenue to Thirty-fourth Street and later was extended to the growing East Liberty. These cars were used in Pittsburgh until 1924.

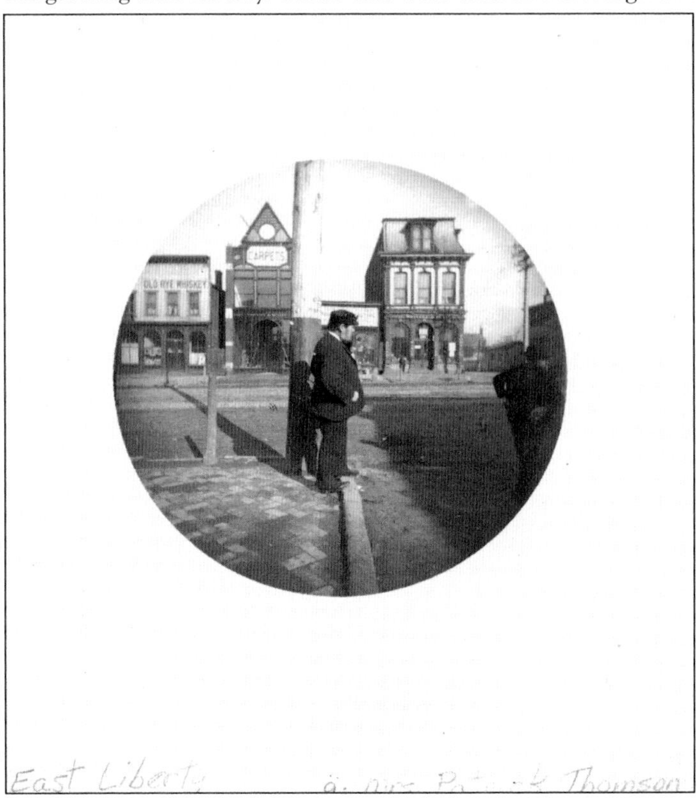

AN ENGLISHMAN CHATS WITH A PASSERBY, C. 1889. The building to the left reads Old Rye Whiskey, next to it Carpets, and to the far right H. Swisshelm, Books, Tobacco. The exact location of this encounter in East Liberty is unknown.

Four

THE YEARS OF GLORY

East Liberty reached its peak in the early decades of the 20th century. Industry was booming, schools were being built, and entertainment options were at an all-time high. It was served by 104 trains a day, and electric streetcar service made the community a convenient and popular shopping area. By the 1920s, electric lighting and telephone service was available for homes. The area had its own newspaper, the *East Liberty Tribune*. Population increased from 46,623 in 1910 to 59,570 by 1930.

The great theater era began around 1913, and soon there were many theaters within a few blocks of each other. In the late 1940s, Silver Lake, a popular swimming area, was drained to make way for the Silver Lake Drive-in, the first outdoor theater in Pittsburgh. Motor Square Garden featured boxing events and bicycle races in the 1920s and 1930s; in 1938, it became a Cadillac sales and service department.

The automobile made its appearance and by 1906, there were 12 car dealers in the East End. Of the 3,000 cars in Pittsburgh at that time, 2,000 were in the East Liberty area. Thomas Mellon's grandson William Larimer Mellon, president of Gulf Oil Company, started one of the first drive-in gas stations in 1913 at the corner of Baum Boulevard and St. Clair Street. The Ford Motor Company had a subsidiary assembly plant on the southeast corner of Baum Boulevard and Morewood Avenue, and repair shops, automobile accessory stores and garages filled the boulevard.

The Kenmawr, Rittenhouse, and Kirkwood hotels served the new needs of increasing population and associated commercial activity. In 1910, Henry Clay Frick built the 13-story Highland Building at South Highland Avenue, and the Frederick Scheibler–designed Highland Towers were erected a few blocks away in 1913. The Nabisco plant opened on Penn Avenue in 1919 and growth necessitated enlargement in 1948.

The terrain of the East Liberty Valley, with its watercourse run-offs, determined development patterns of the neighborhoods. In the early 1900s to the late 1930s, several bridges were built across these runs, as they were called, to increase access and consequent growth to the region.

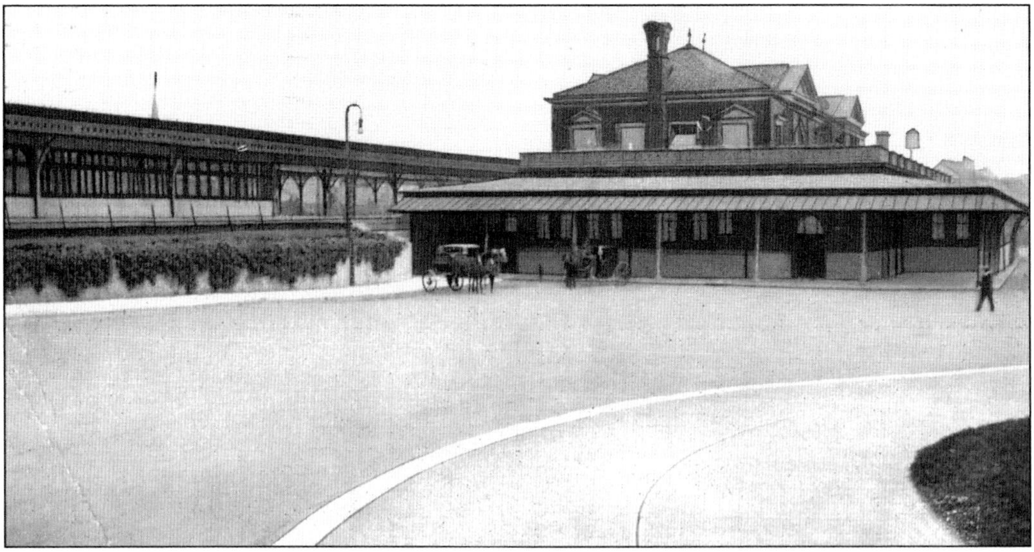

PENNSYLVANIA RAILROAD STATION, 1905. The coming of the railroad in 1852 greatly helped accelerate the growth of East Liberty. A two-platform, four-track station was constructed on seven acres. The station was designed by famed Philadelphia architect Frank Furness. Local commuter traffic ceased in 1953. The station was demolished in 1963 and the site is now a commercial shopping center called the Village of Eastside.

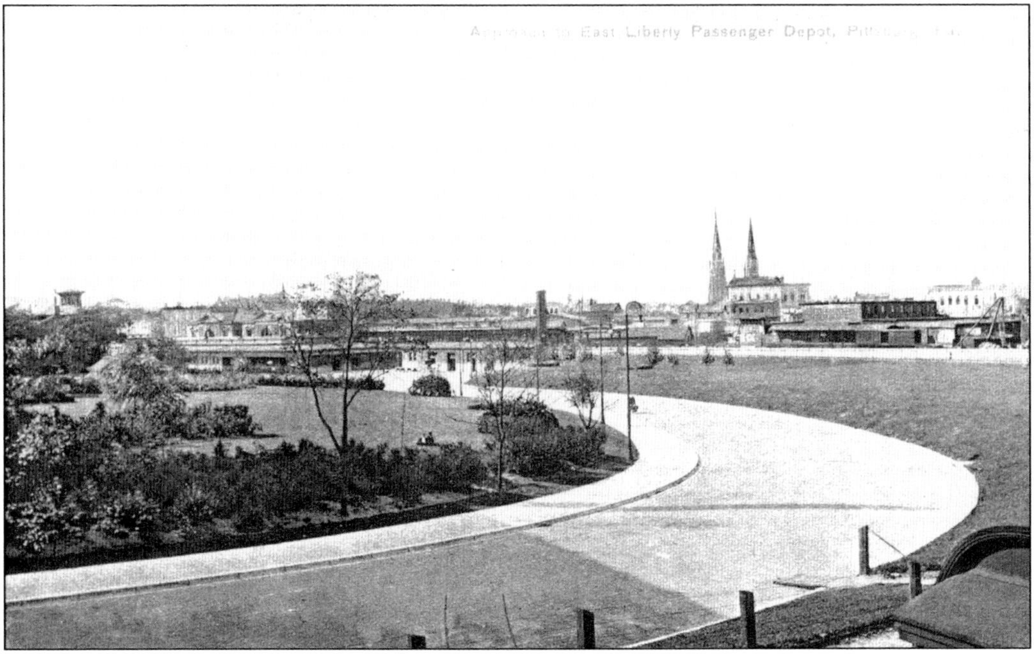

APPROACH TO RAILROAD PASSENGER STATION, EARLY 1900S. This photograph shows the road leading to the East Liberty station of the Pennsylvania Railroad. In the background are the twin towers of Ss. Peter and Paul Roman Catholic Church.

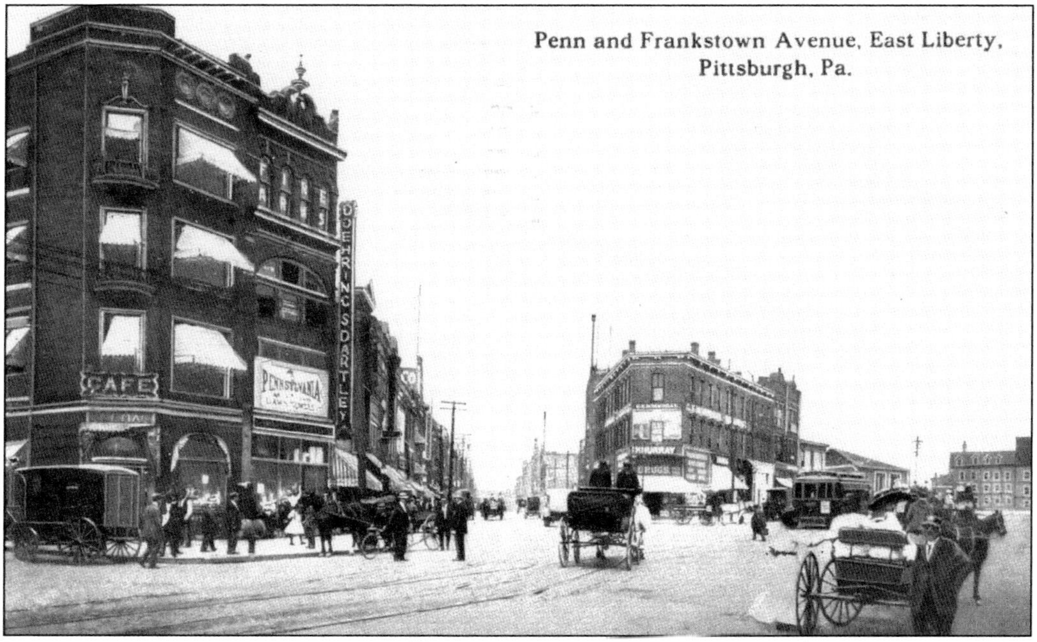

PENN AND FRANKSTOWN AVENUES, EARLY 1900S. As the 20th century began, activity at this familiar intersection increased, but there was still a preponderance of horse-drawn carts and carriages, with an occasional streetcar.

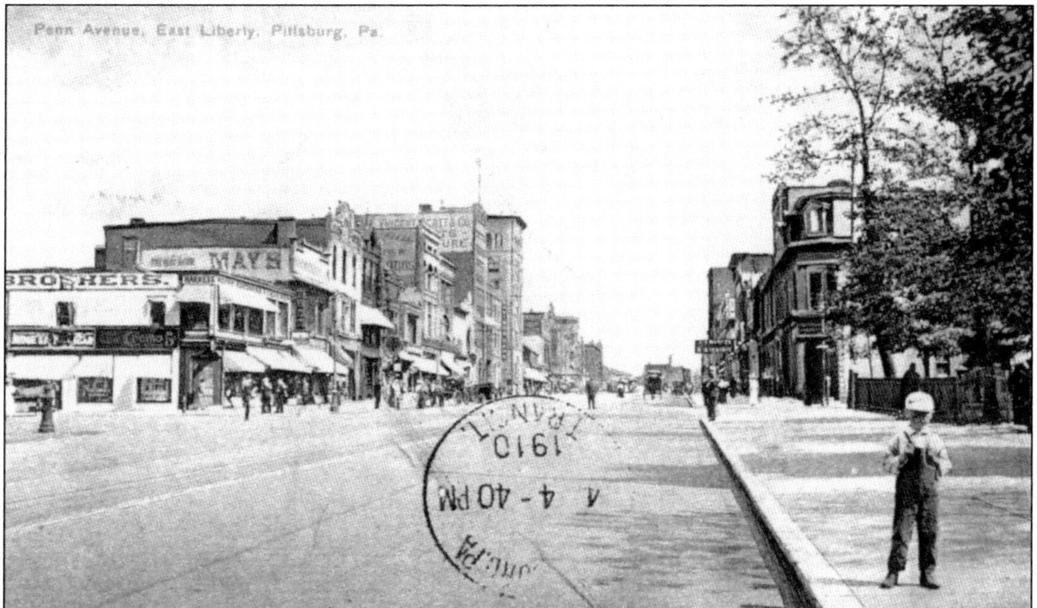

PENN AVENUE, 1910. This photograph, highlighting a young boy, dramatically shows the 100-foot width of Penn Avenue as originally laid out by Jacob Negley in the early 1800s.

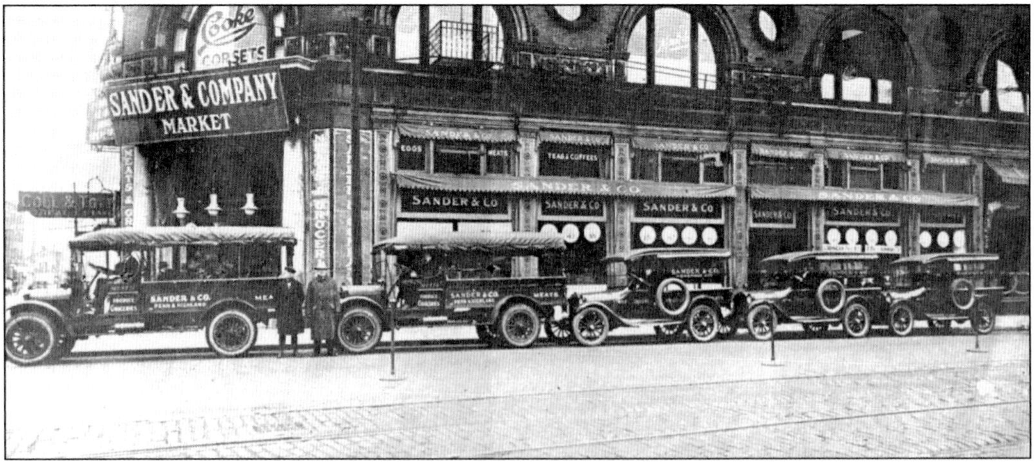

SANDER'S MARKET. Beginning in 1898, the four-story building at the northwest corner of Penn and Highland Avenues housed the C. H. Rowe department store, which was a household name for dry goods with wagon delivery. It was occupied by Sander's grocery in the 1920s and by May-Stern Furniture from 1930 to 1965. With its exterior restored to the original design in 1989, it now houses shops and offices.

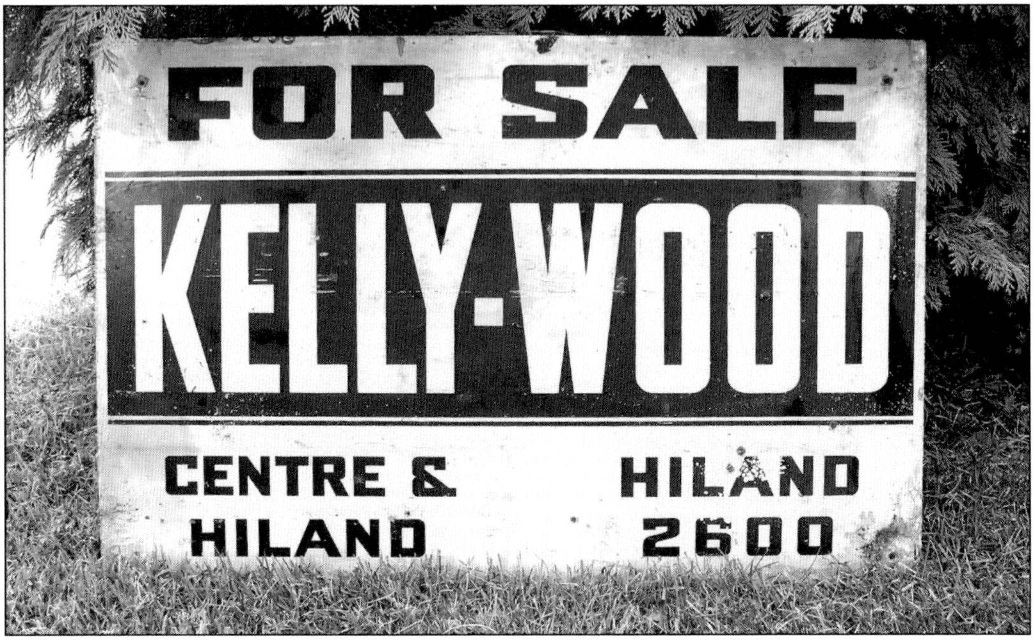

REALTY SIGN, EARLY 1900S. Kelly-Wood was a prominent East End realty company founded in 1893 at a time of residential and commercial growth in the East End. The spelling here derives from county surveyor, Robert Hilands, who laid out Negley and Hiland Avenues through the Negley lands in 1837. City council changed the name to Highland in 1890. It appears that the earlier version continued for some time.

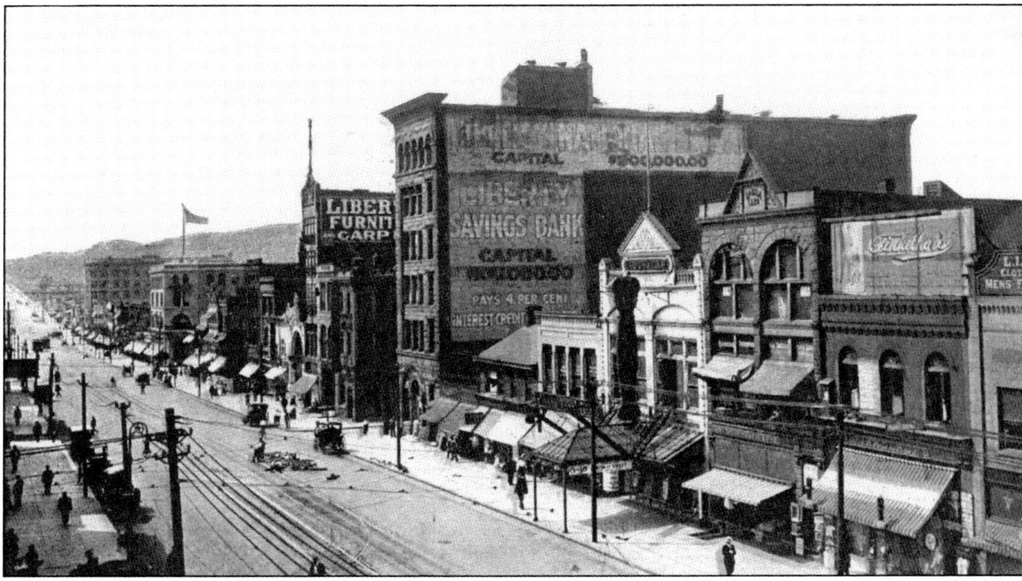

PENN AVENUE, 1918. Business on the north side of Penn Avenue had grown substantially by the beginning of the 20th century. Prominent is the six-story Liberty Building, which was designed by the noted architect Frederick Osterling and built in 1890. This venerable building still stands, currently housing East Liberty Development and other offices.

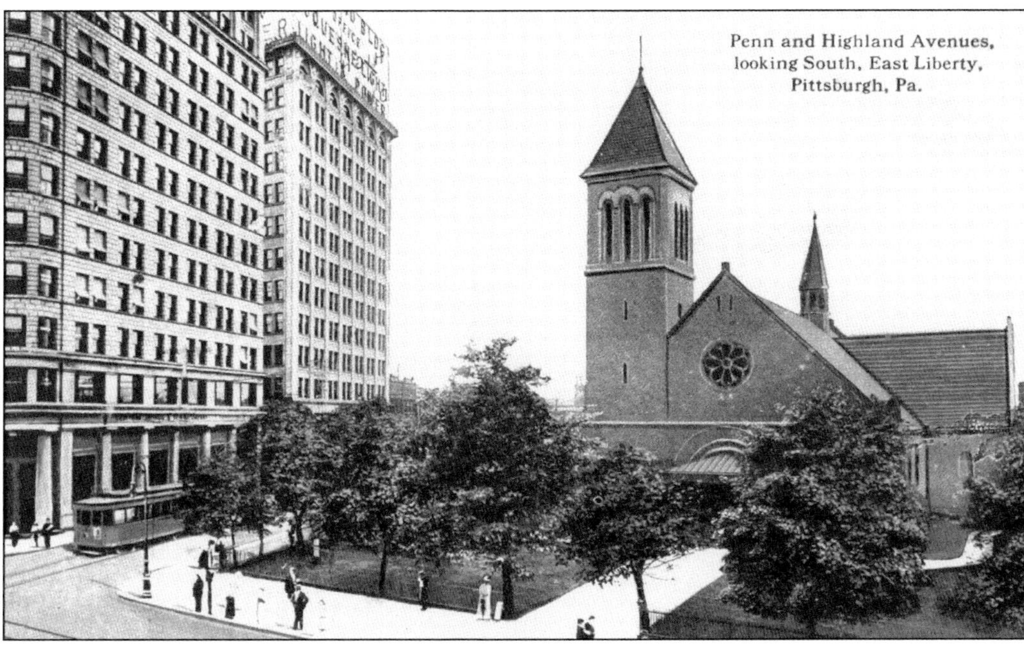

PENN AND HIGHLAND AVENUES, C. 1920. On the right is the 1888 home of East Liberty Presbyterian Church. At the far left is the 13-story East End Savings Building, built in 1910 and demolished in 1969. Next to it is the 13-story Highland Building, designed by Daniel Burnham of Chicago and built by Henry Clay Frick in 1910. It is currently not occupied.

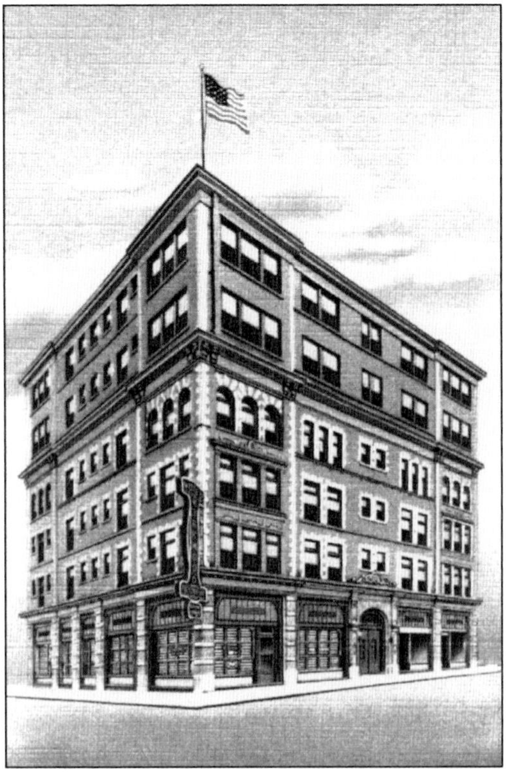

Kirkwood Hotel. This 100-room hotel was located at the northeast corner of Kirkwood and North Whitfield Streets. More recently, it was called the Metropolitan Hotel and housed the Embers Club. The building still stands and is currently slated for redevelopment.

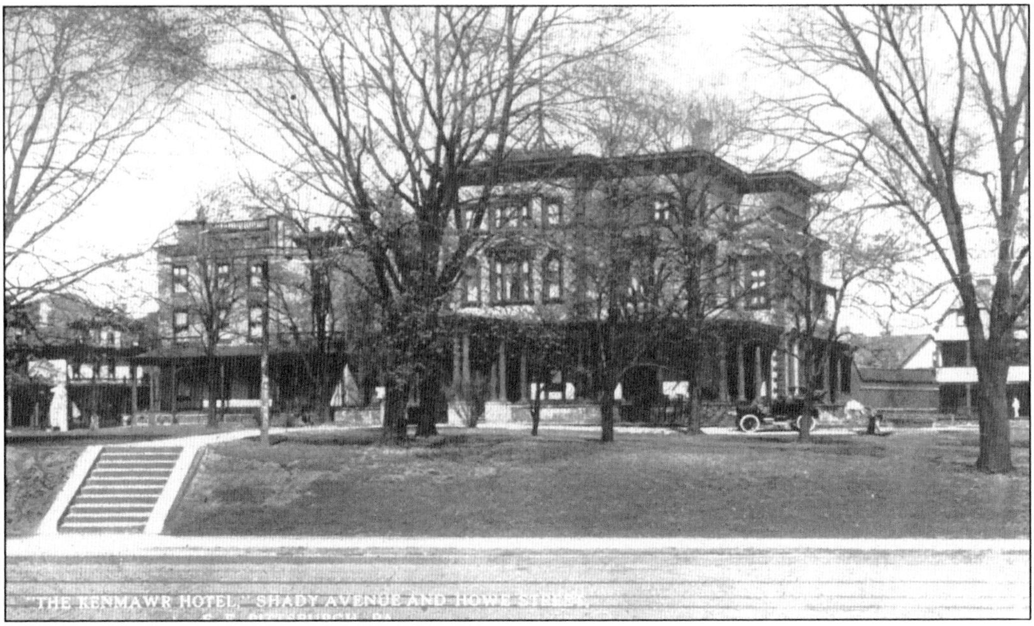

Kenmawr Hotel, 1890. W. R. Kuhn bought the Hailman estate at Shady Avenue and Walnut Street, converting the home into a hotel and the lawn into a park. In 1890, three stories and cottages were added. It was torn down in 1954 and replaced by the 13-story Kenmawr Apartments. This became the new home of the popular Joyce McClements Restaurant after a 1957 fire destroyed their Penn Avenue location.

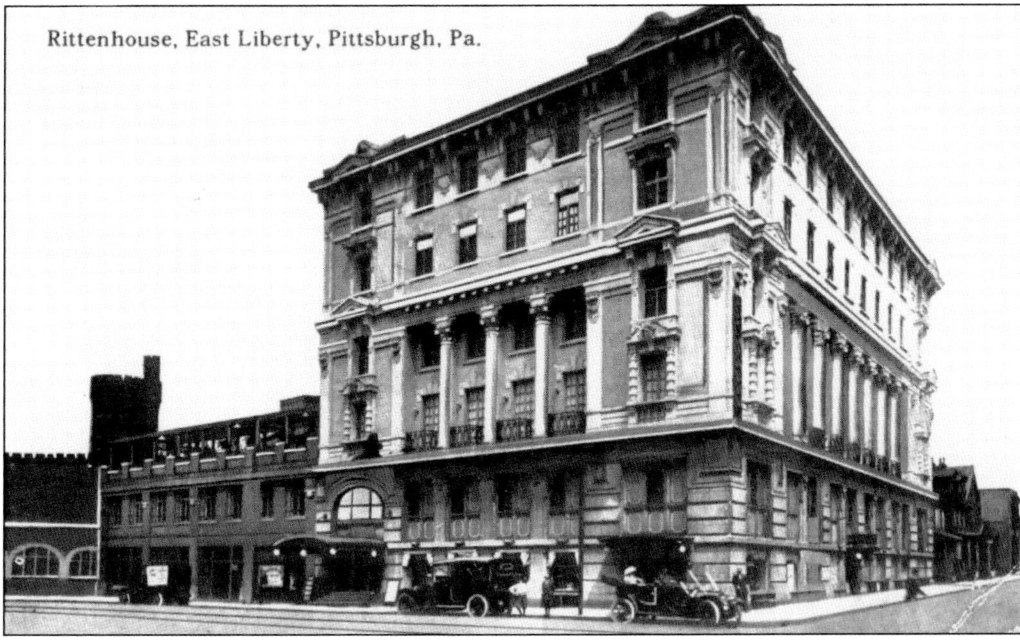

RITTENHOUSE HOTEL, 1908. Located on North Highland Avenue at Kirkwood Street, this hotel was built by William Rittenhouse Kuhn. It featured a beautiful ballroom and a restaurant. Many social events took place at the Rittenhouse Hotel. One of the first buildings razed in the redevelopment of the 1960s, it was so well constructed that its demolition was more challenging than expected.

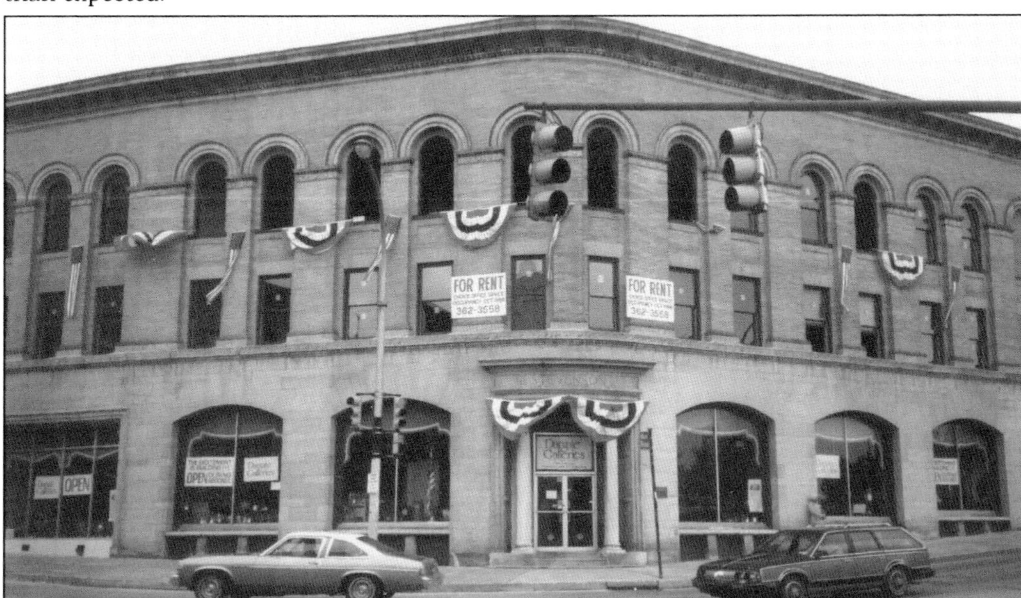

STEVENSON BUILDING, 1896. The George K. Stevenson grocery originated downtown at First and Market Streets. George Stevenson's sons expanded and moved in 1826 to fashionable Sixth Avenue. They built a new store in 1896 on the southeast corner of South Highland and Centre Avenues, offering home delivery to their carriage-trade clientele. The company closed in 1977, and the building is now occupied by businesses and a social service agency.

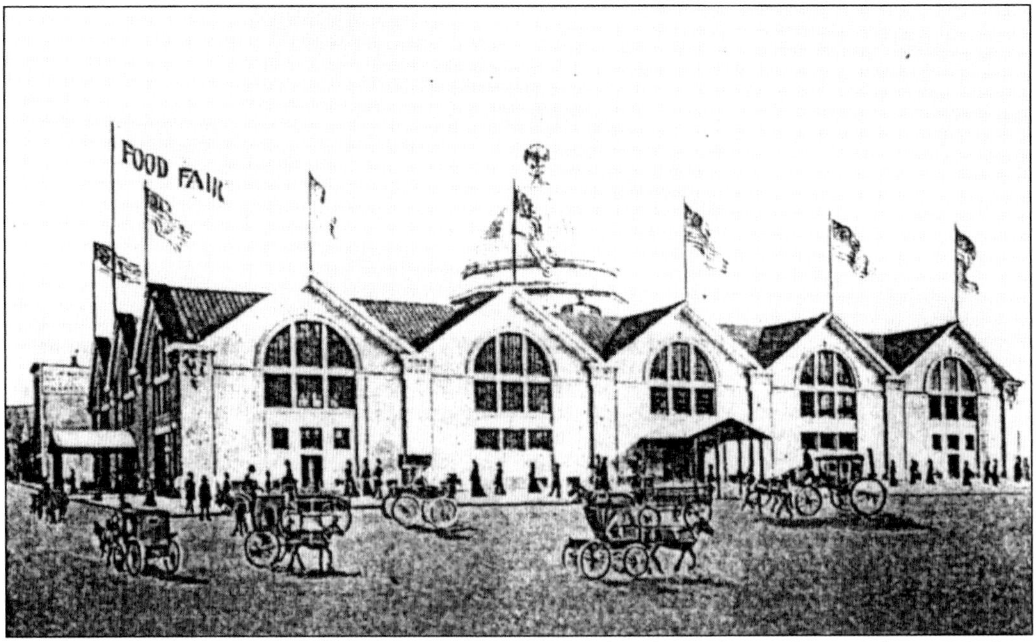

LIBERTY MARKET AND MOTOR SQUARE GARDEN. The above figure shows Liberty Market, a structure on Centre Avenue at South Beatty Street that was built in 1900 by the Mellons, designed by Peabody and Stearns. It was one of four major public markets in Pittsburgh. The market failed and closed in 1915, after which the building was remodeled into Motor Square Garden, shown in the picture below. The unique architecture of Motor Square Garden includes exposed steel trusses topped by a great windowed dome. Over the years, this landmark building has had several uses including a sports arena featuring boxing matches and bicycle races. It later became a car dealership and exhibition hall. In 1986, it was renovated for retail shops on three levels, and has been occupied by AAA since 1992.

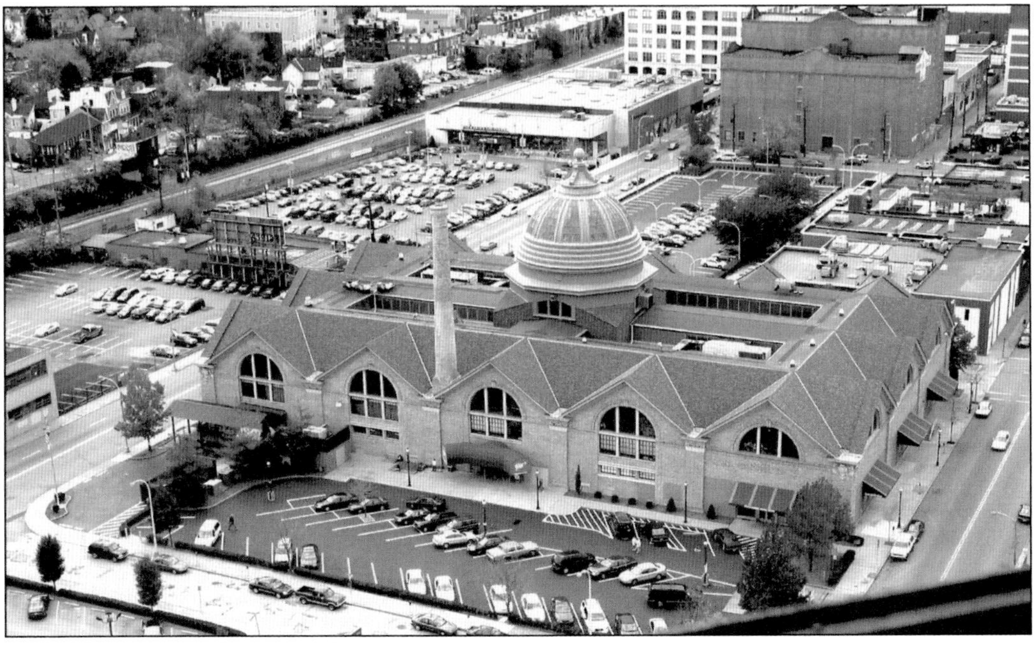

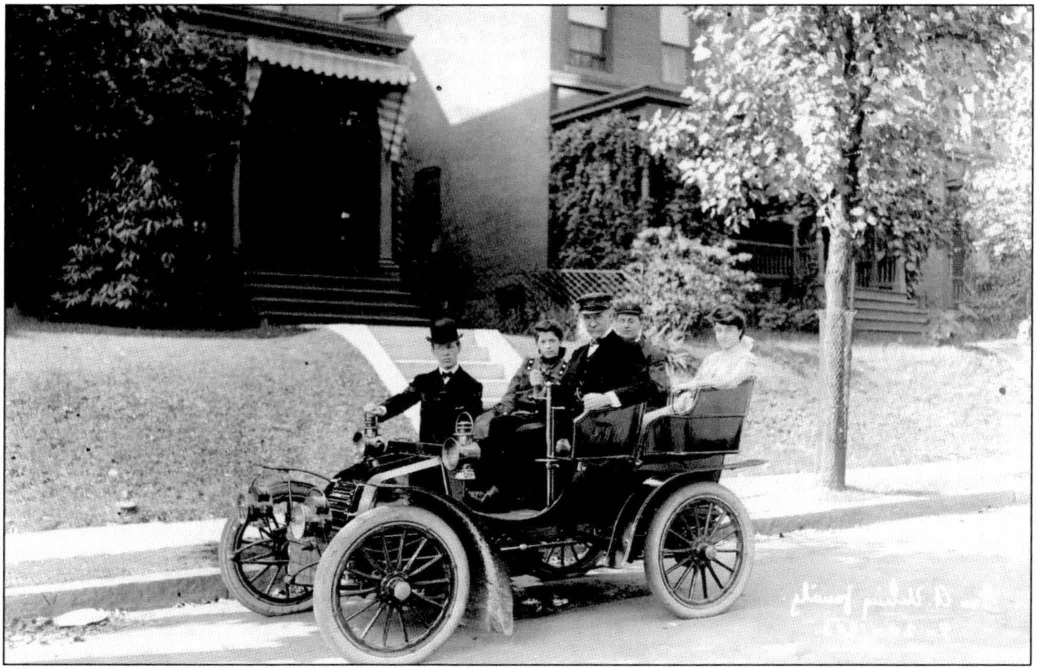

AUTOCAR, 1903. The Urling family has been out for a drive in their Autocar and is parked in front of their home at 218 South Euclid Avenue. Cars soon became popular in the wealthy East End. Descendant George Clark lives in the community of Highland Park.

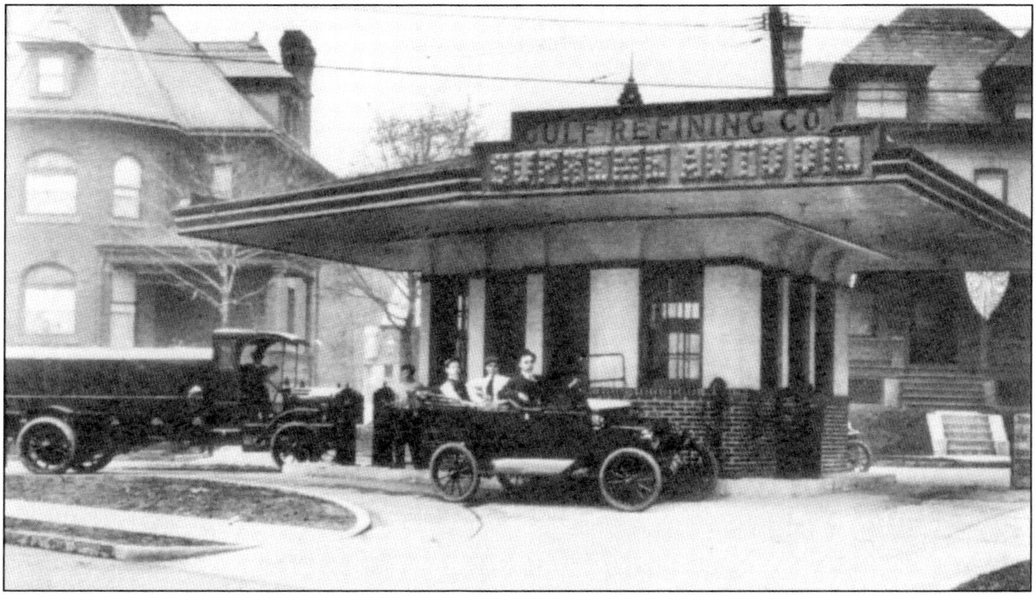

GASOLINE STATION, 1913. Gulf Oil, founded in 1901 and headquartered in Pittsburgh, opened the world's first drive-in station at Baum Boulevard and St. Clair Street to serve the growing number of cars in the wealthy East End. Previously gasoline pumps were located at curbs and automobiles parked on the street for service. A Pennsylvania Historic Commission marker commemorates this event.

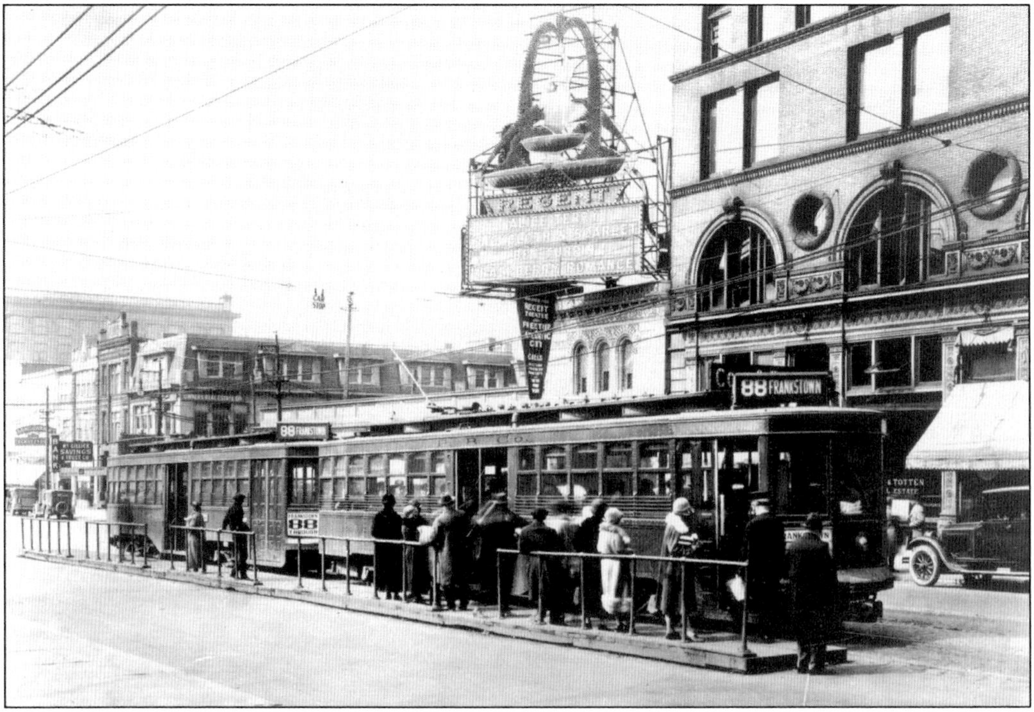

STREETCARS, 1930S. Two No. 88 Frankstown streetcars in tandem are stopped on Penn Avenue opposite the Regent Theatre.

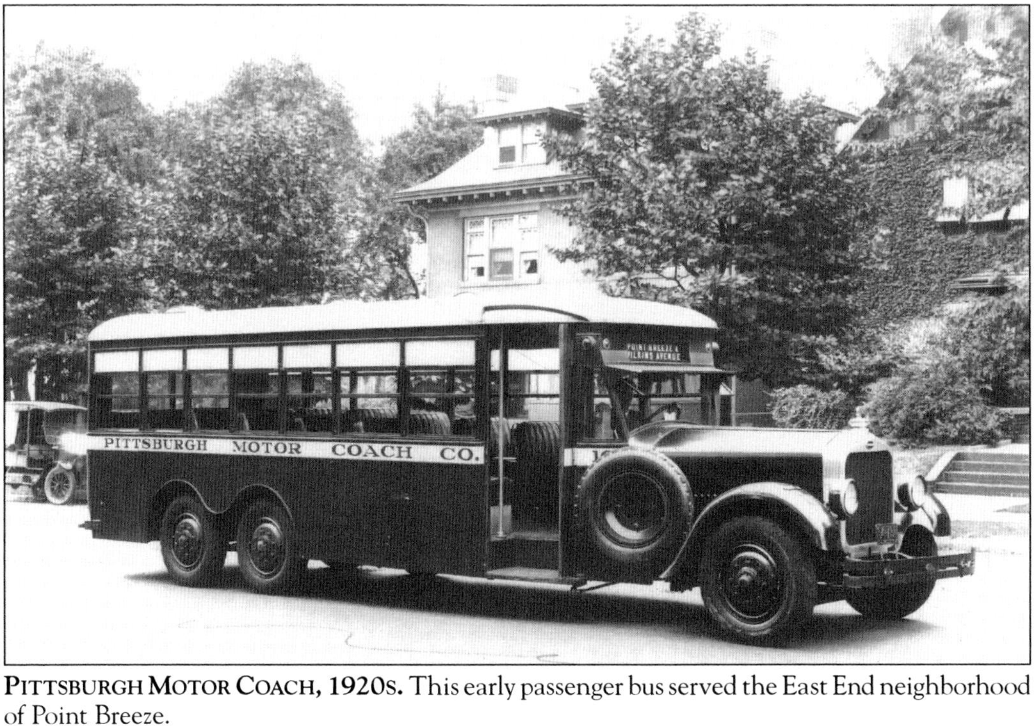

PITTSBURGH MOTOR COACH, 1920S. This early passenger bus served the East End neighborhood of Point Breeze.

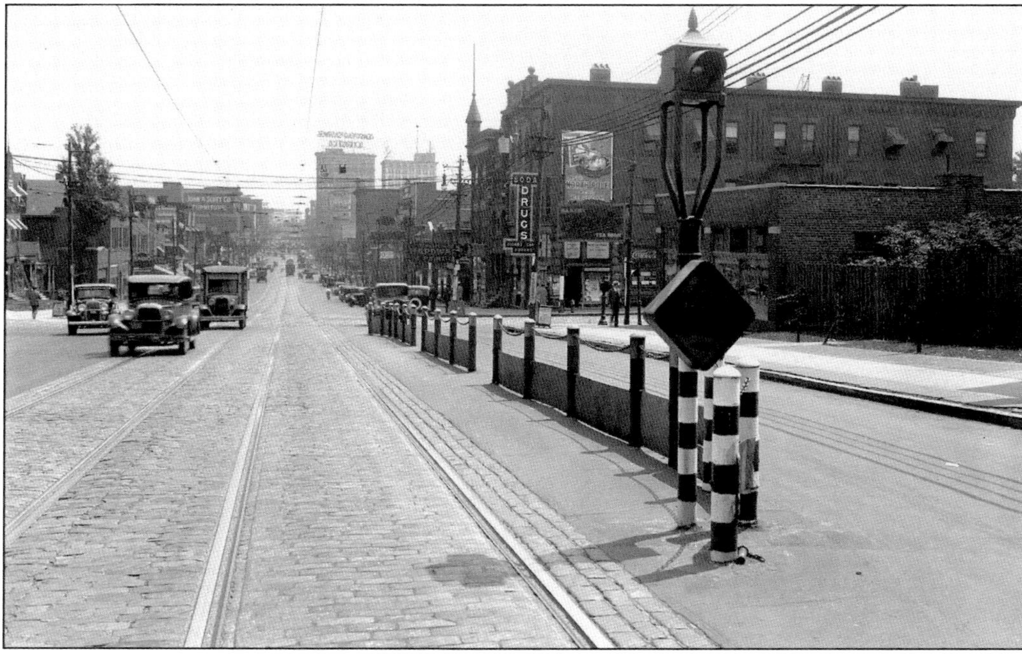

TRAFFIC SAFETY ZONE, 1931. This picture at Penn and Negley Avenues looking east shows a safety island to accommodate streetcar passengers. In the background are the East End Savings Building (on the left) and the Highland Building (on the right). To the right are Fishel's Bakery and Tea Room, a large advertisement for "North Pole Real Ice Cream," a drug store, and beyond it, Pennsylvania Hardware and Paint.

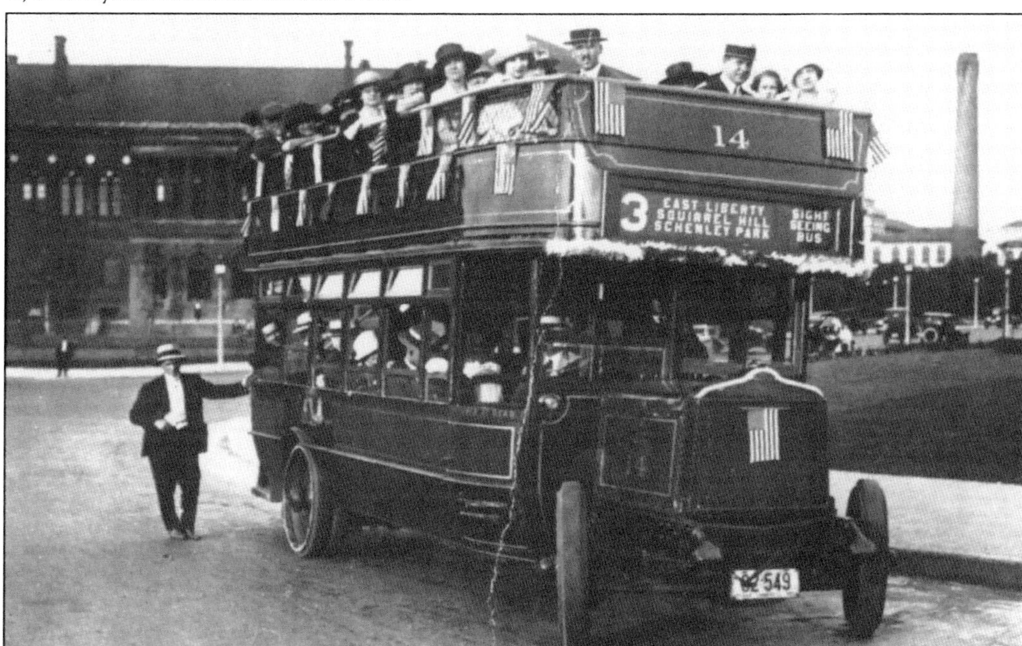

SIGHTSEEING BUS, 1922. This No. 3 double-decker bus leaves the Carnegie Library in Oakland to visit the upscale East End neighborhoods of the day, including East Liberty, Squirrel Hill, and Schenley Park.

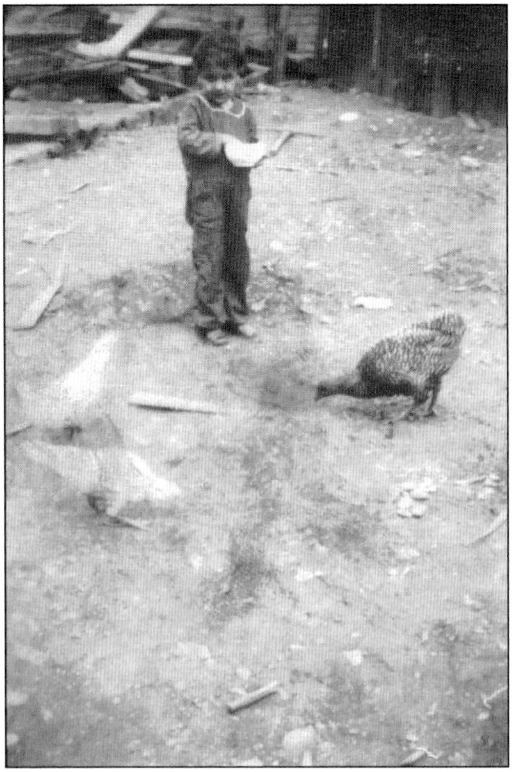

Boy Feeding Chickens, 1930s. This young man is doing his chores on the family farm, which was located on Washington Boulevard near the Pennsylvania State Police barracks. The family still lives in the area.

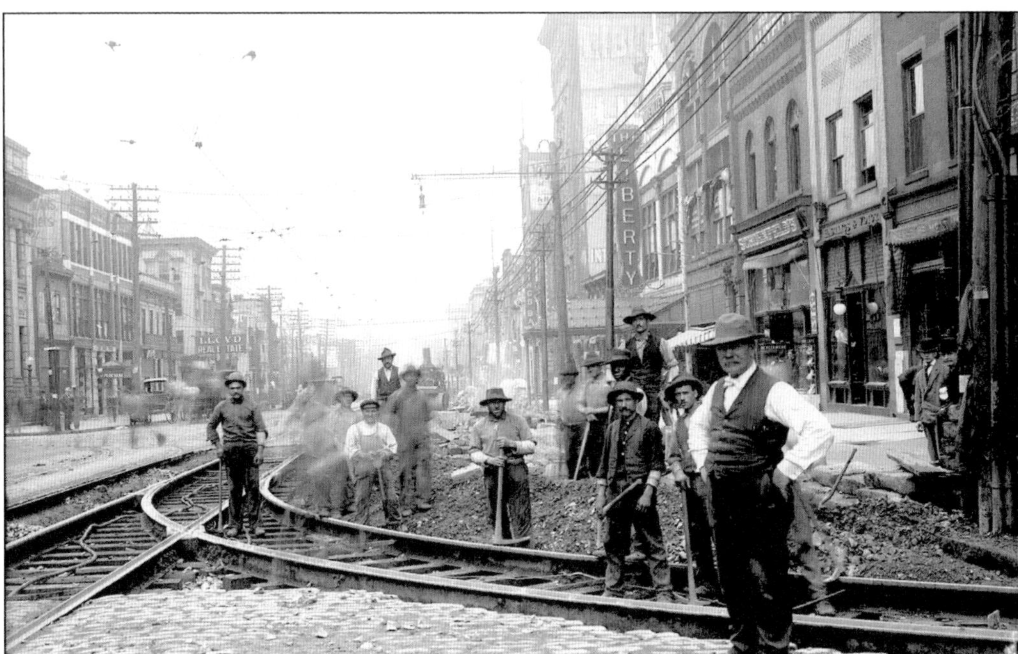

Street Workers, 1907. City workers are on Penn Avenue and Collins Street, looking west, laying or repairing tracks. The Liberty Theatre can be seen at the right center. Moving to the right of it are W. J. Spahr, Schoenfeld's, Hastings and Voigt, and M. Denholm Brothers Meats.

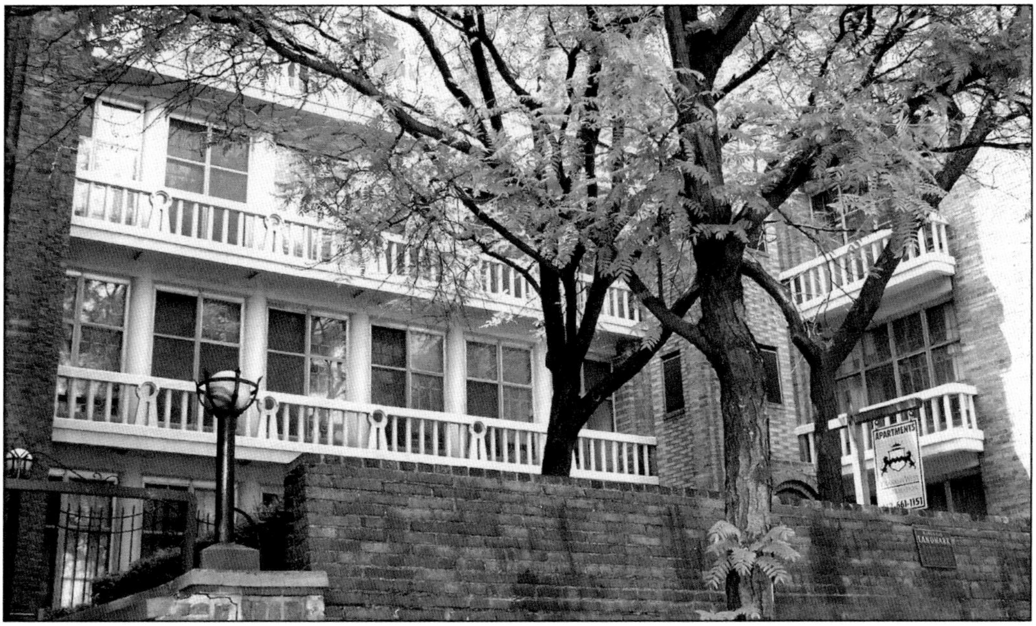

HIGHLAND TOWERS, 1913. Frederick Scheibler designed this four-story concrete and brick apartment building at 340 South Highland Avenue in the Modernist style. Its two towers with colorful panels, landscaped courtyard, and balustrade porches are both functional and spacious with 36 apartments. Interiors include stained glass and safes. It is recognized on the National Register of Historic Places and by the Pittsburgh History and Landmarks Foundation.

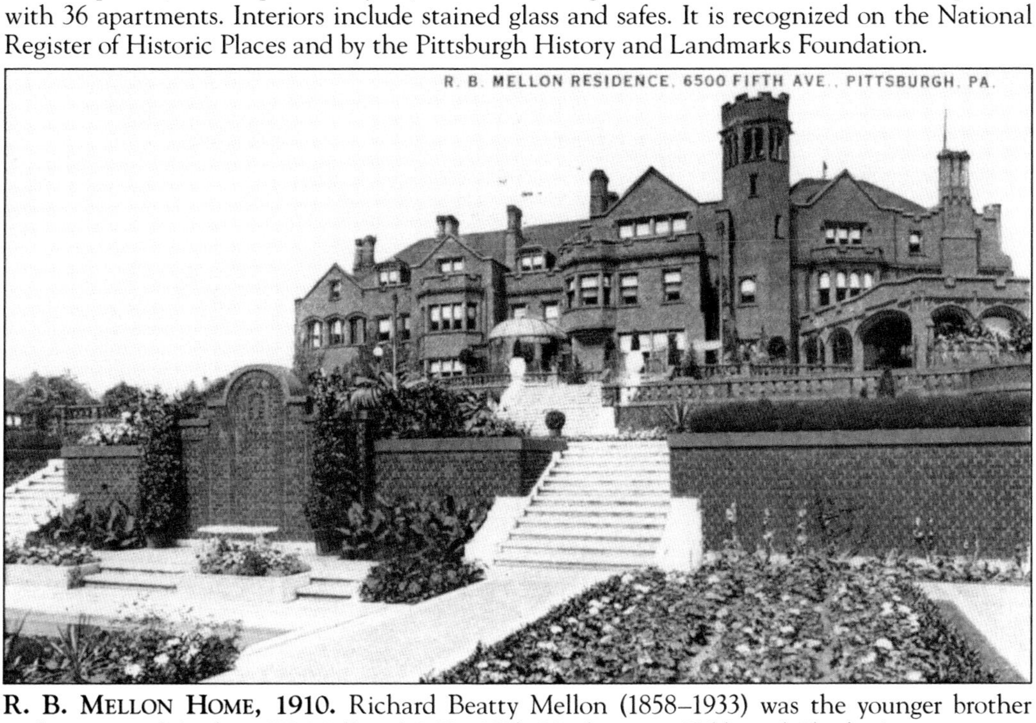

R. B. MELLON HOME, 1910. Richard Beatty Mellon (1858–1933) was the younger brother and partner of Andrew W. Mellon (1865–1937). His home at Fifth and Shady Avenues was a three-story, ivy-covered brownstone of some 60 rooms, with a basement bowling alley and landscaped gardens. It was razed in 1941, and the 10-acre property was given to the city for use as a park.

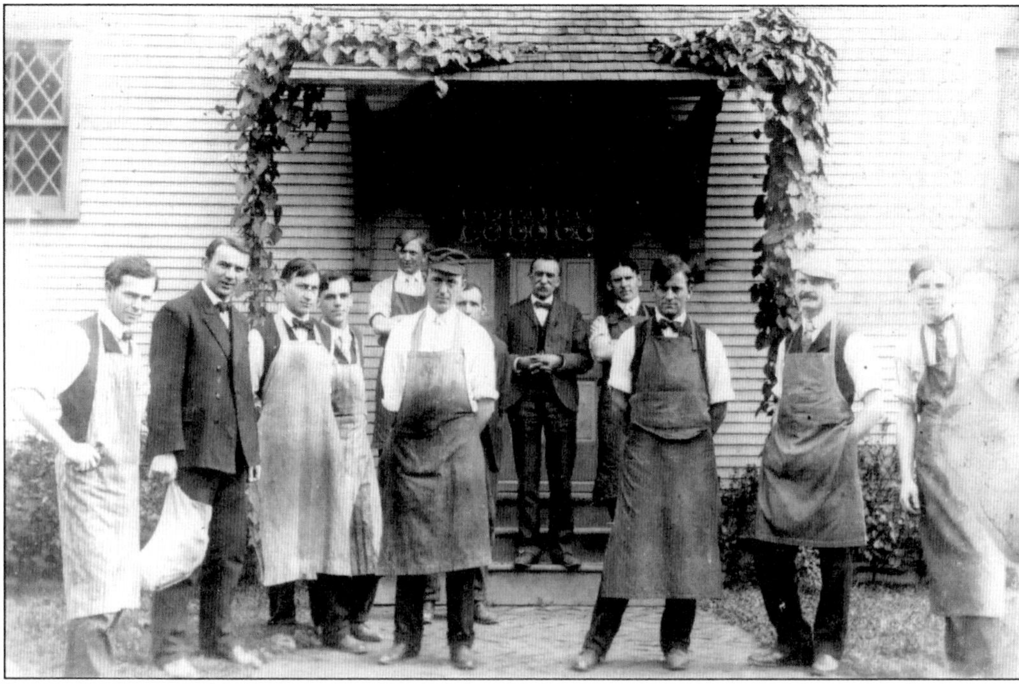

RUDY BROTHERS STUDIO, 1901. One of the first stained glass shops in the United States was operated in East Liberty by the famous Rudy Brothers from 1843 until 1932. The brothers John, Jesse, Horace, and Frank trained many apprentices, including the acclaimed George Sotter. Many public buildings here and abroad hold their works. Examples can be seen at Peabody High School and private homes in the area.

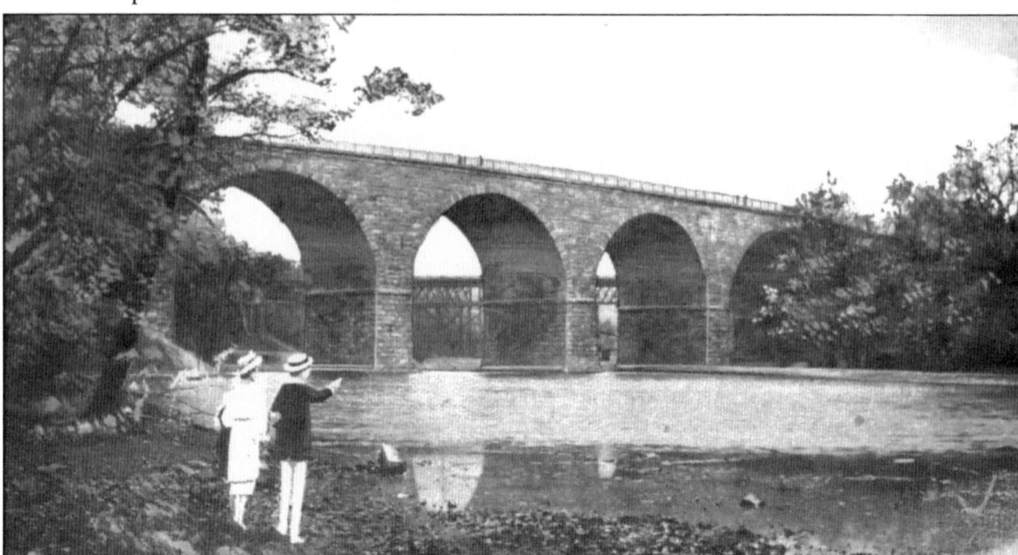

SILVER LAKE, 1904. Once a popular spot for swimming and ice skating, Silver Lake is now filled in and occupied by industrial firms. Frederick Law Olmsted, in a 1910 city planning report, urged that the entire Negley Run valley, including Silver Lake, be added to the park system. He predicted "unsightly development" in the narrow terrain. The handsome stone arches form the Lincoln Avenue Bridge.

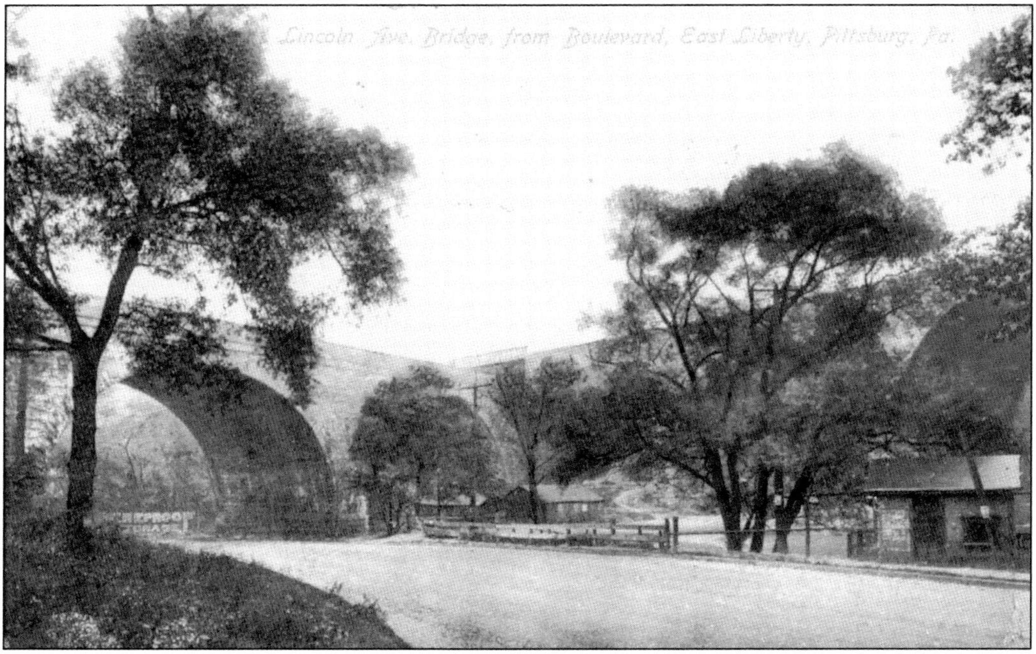

LINCOLN AVENUE BRIDGE, 1906. After five years' work, the opening of this stone-arch span was celebrated with an elaborate street parade, fireworks, cannon salutes from the nearest hilltop, floats, and bands. Mayor George Guthrie and others delivered addresses at the Lemington Avenue School. This massive Roman structure is one of the last of its kind to be built, as concrete gained favor in the construction of other East End bridges.

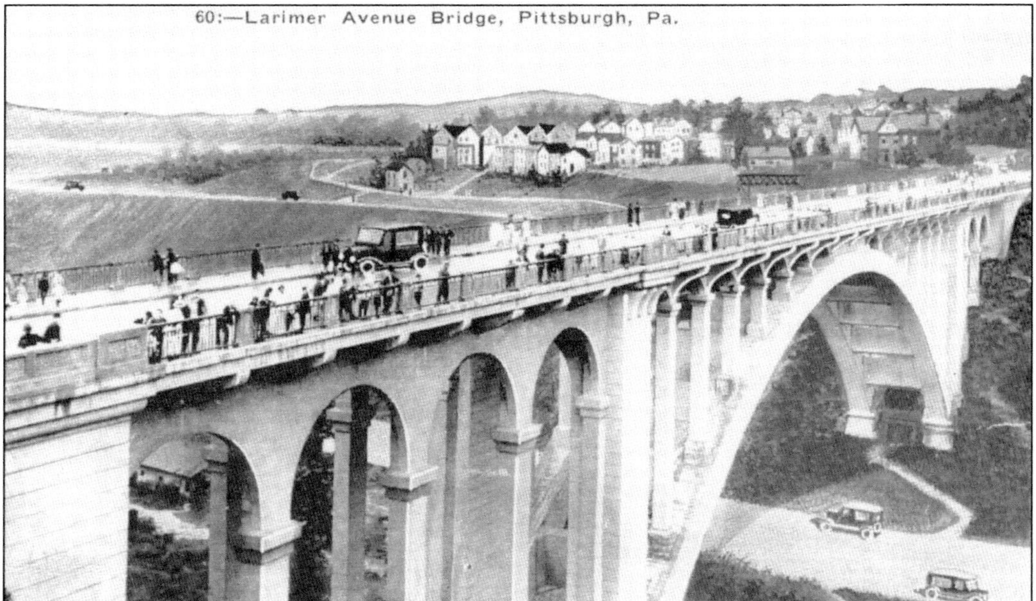

LARIMER AVENUE BRIDGE, 1912. This bridge spans Washington Boulevard to link Larimer Avenue with the Lemington Avenue hilltop. It was dedicated by Christopher Magee, followed by a parade and ribbon-cutting. The ceremonies concluded with fireworks. The street is named for Gen. William Larimer (1809–1875), who had a home here overlooking the East Liberty Valley.

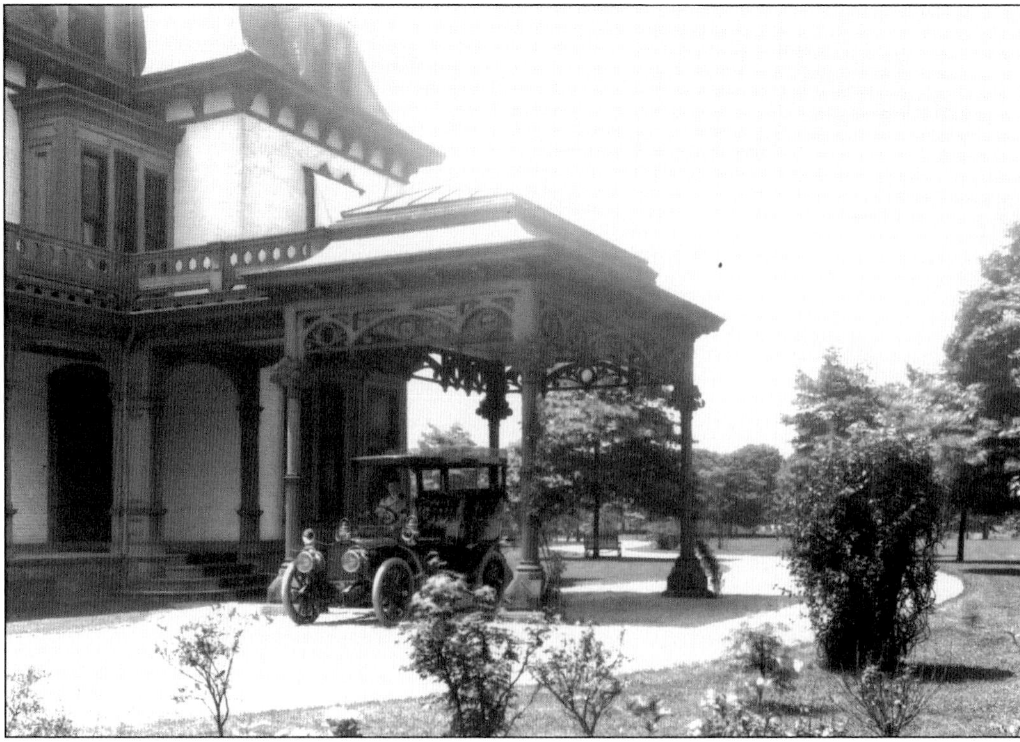

ELECTRIC CAR, EARLY 1900S. This photograph shows George Westinghouse's electric automobile parked in the driveway of his mansion.

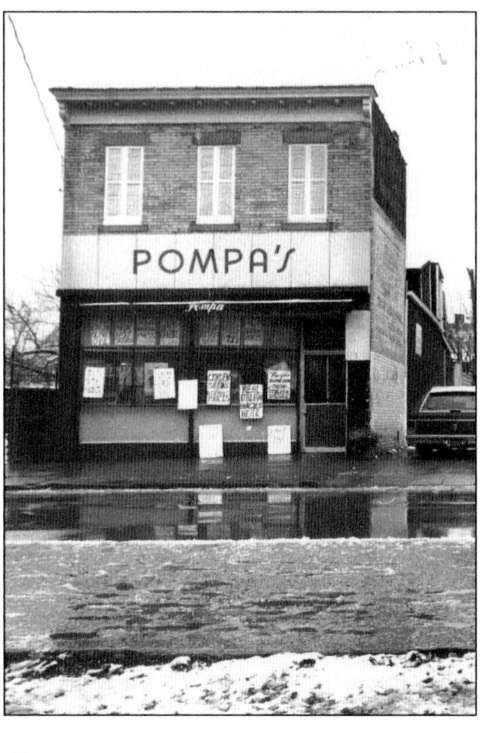

POMPA'S. This grocery store was one of many serving the Larimer neighborhood.

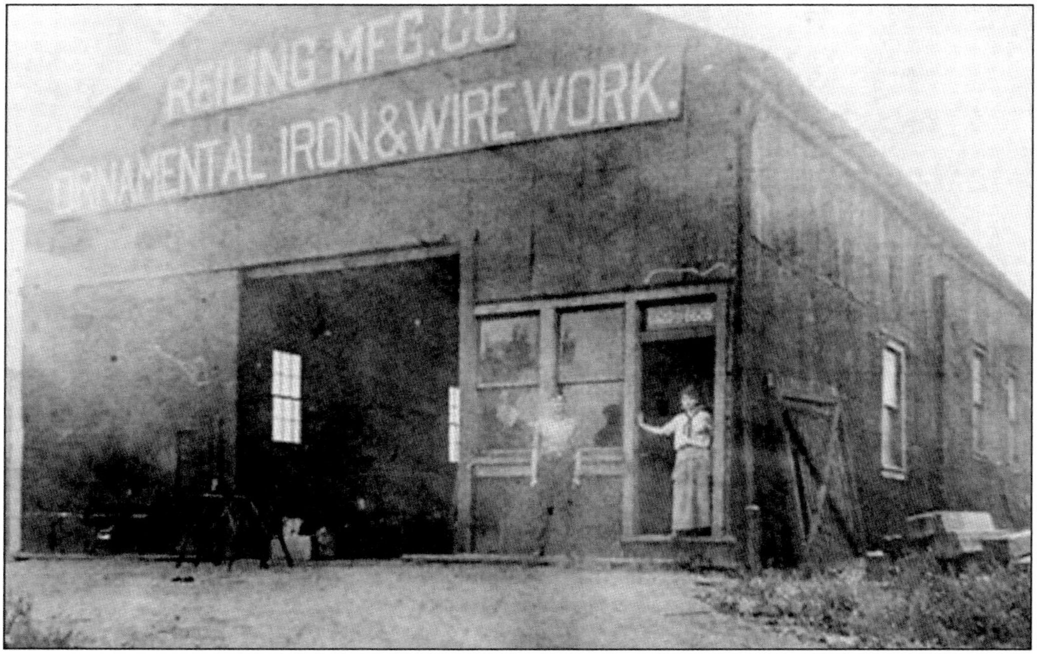

REILING MANUFACTURING COMPANY. Reiling Manufacturing Company, specializing in ornamental metal works, has been located in East Liberty for five generations. Founded by Felix Reiling in 1850, it is currently managed by Felix's great grandson Christopher Reiling Jr., whose father and aunt are shown in this 1912 photograph. In addition to the *Joy of Life* sculpture in East Liberty, the company's work is incorporated in the National Gallery of Art and Pittsburgh's David L. Lawrence Convention Center.

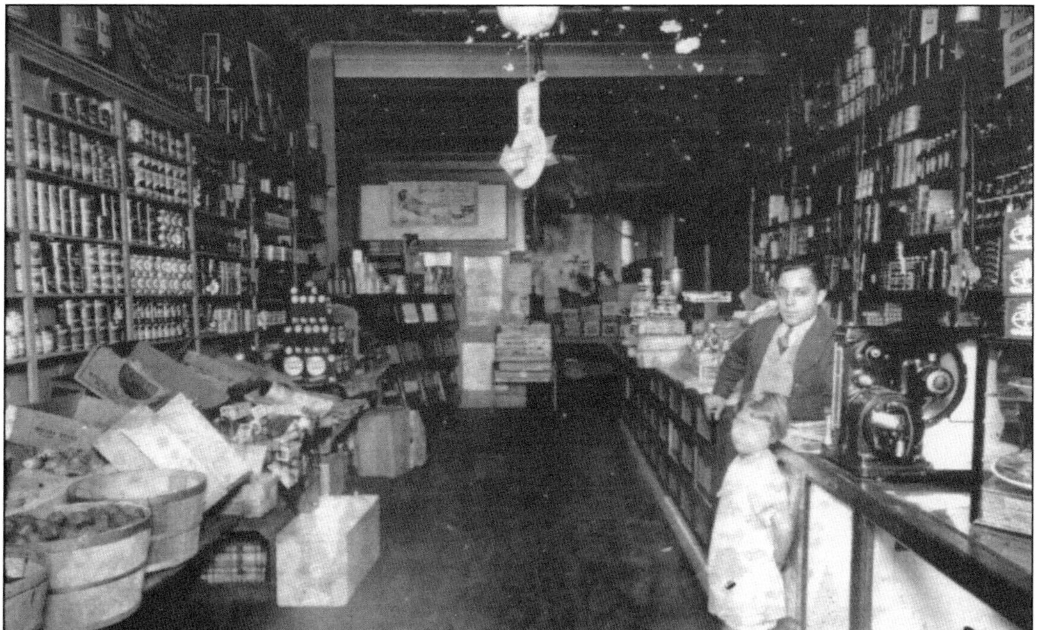

LARIMER AVENUE MARKET, 1930S. Josie Nozzolillo is waiting for a sale. Members of this family were involved in the foundation of Our Lady Help of Christians Catholic Church.

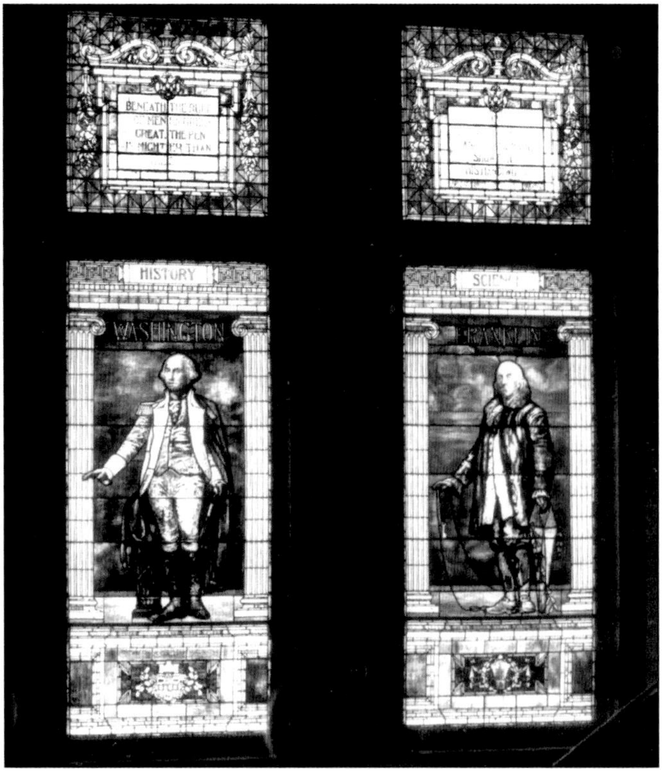

STAINED GLASS WINDOWS AT PEABODY. This photograph shows two of the five windows originally installed in 1902 in the Margaretta Elementary School, which was incorporated into Peabody High School in 1911. Crafted by the renowned Rudy Brothers Studio, they are examples of extraordinary beauty. The windows depict literature, geography, nature, history, and science, and include portraits of William Shakespeare, Christopher Columbus, Mother Nature, George Washington, and Benjamin Franklin.

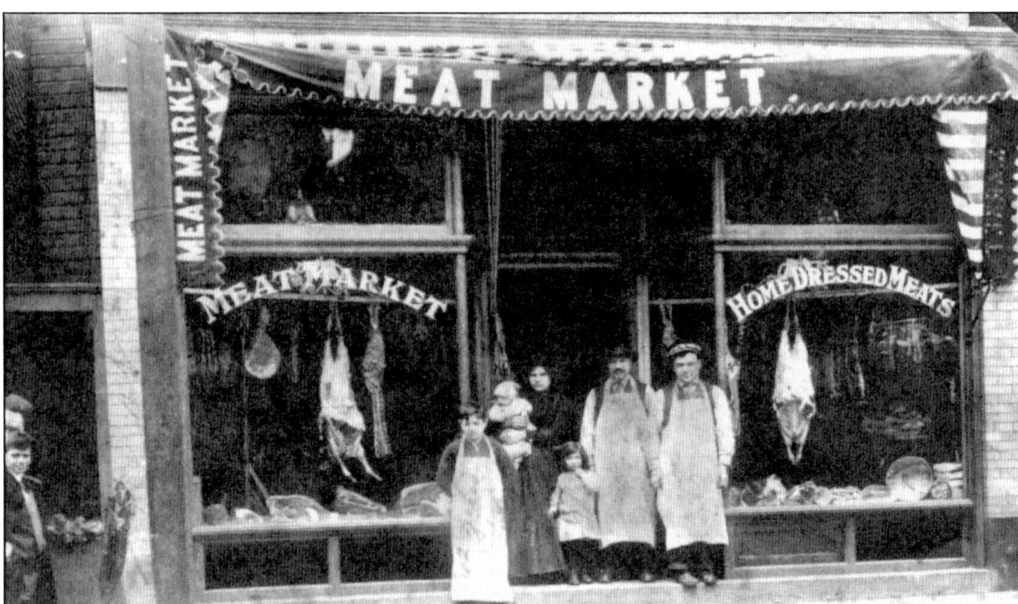

FIORE'S MEAT MARKET. This store, located at 413 Larimer Avenue, was founded in 1903 by Teodosio Fiore, who bought the property from the Mellon family. It incorporated a butcher shop in the front of the store and a slaughterhouse in the rear. Fiore descendants now operate meat markets in other sections of Pittsburgh.

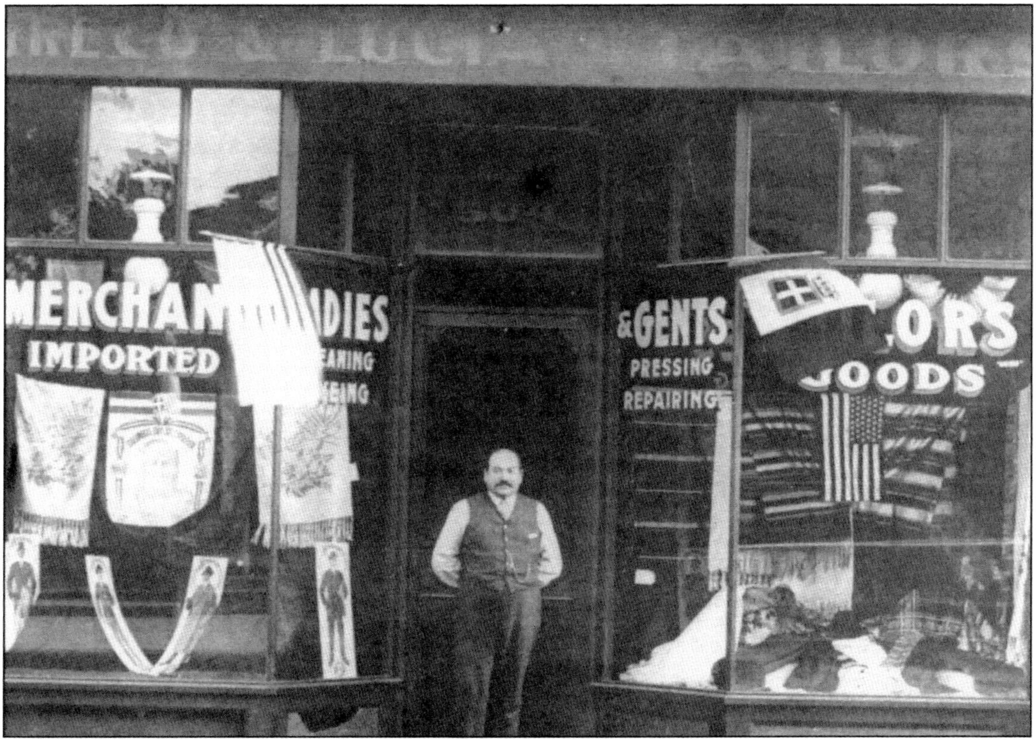

Tailor Shop, c. 1930s. Raffaele Greco stands in front of Greco and Lucia's tailor shop at 504 Larimer Avenue serving "Ladies & Gents."

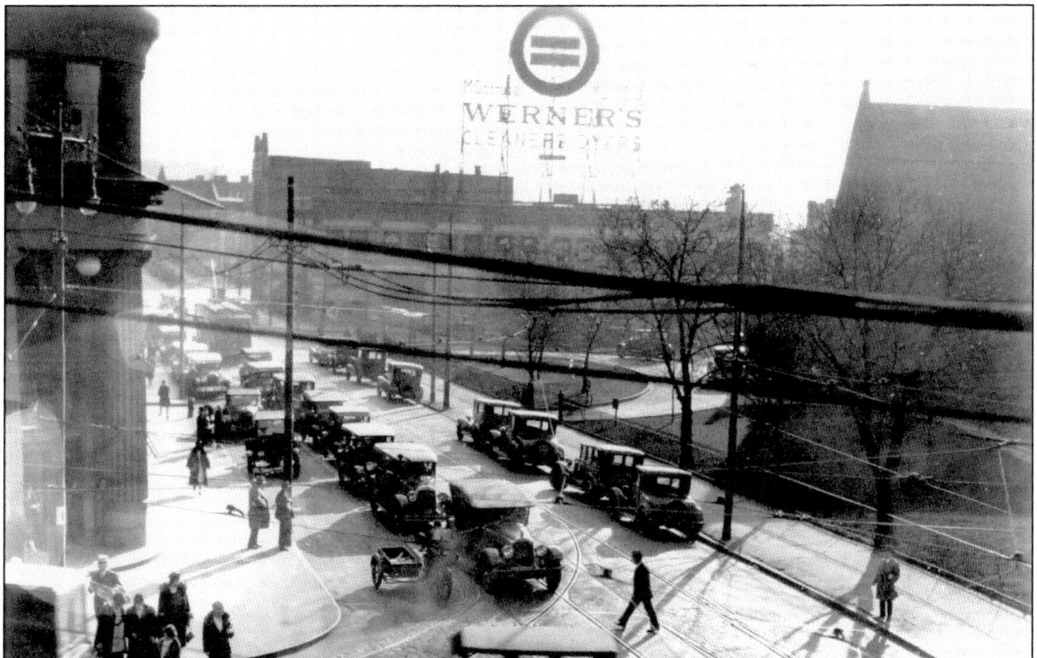

South Highland Avenue at Penn, c. 1920. At this busy intersection, the large sign advertising Werner's Cleaners is prominently shown.

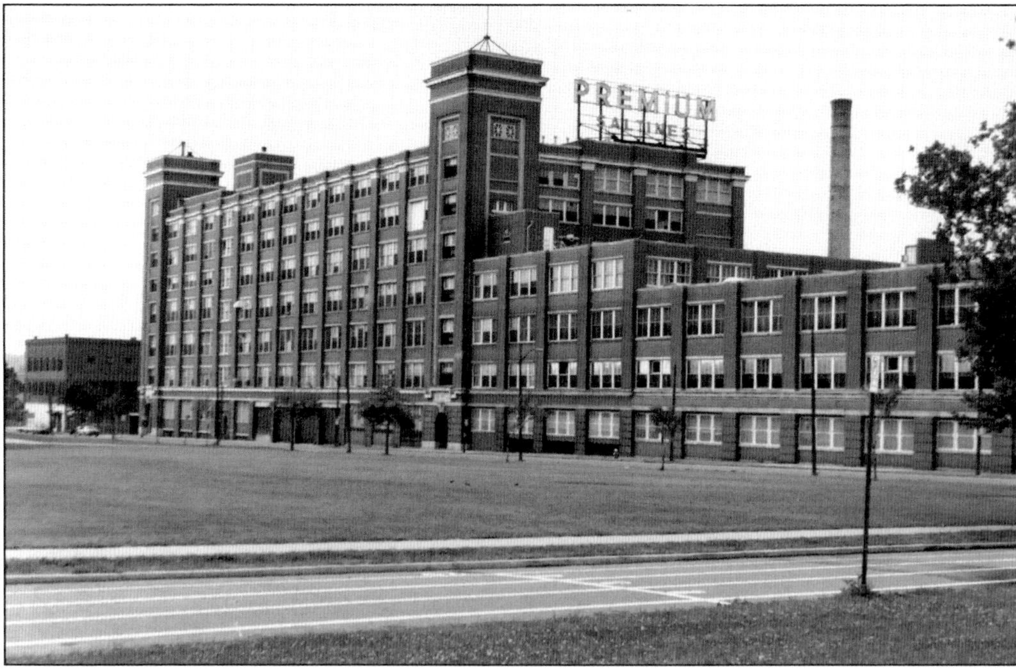

NABISCO BAKERY, 1917. This landmark facility, located at Penn Avenue and Dahlem Street (now East Liberty Boulevard), produced Premium Saltines, Ritz Crackers, and Chips Ahoy! before it closed in 1986. The building currently is being remodeled for commercial use, including a hotel, retail shops, and condominiums.

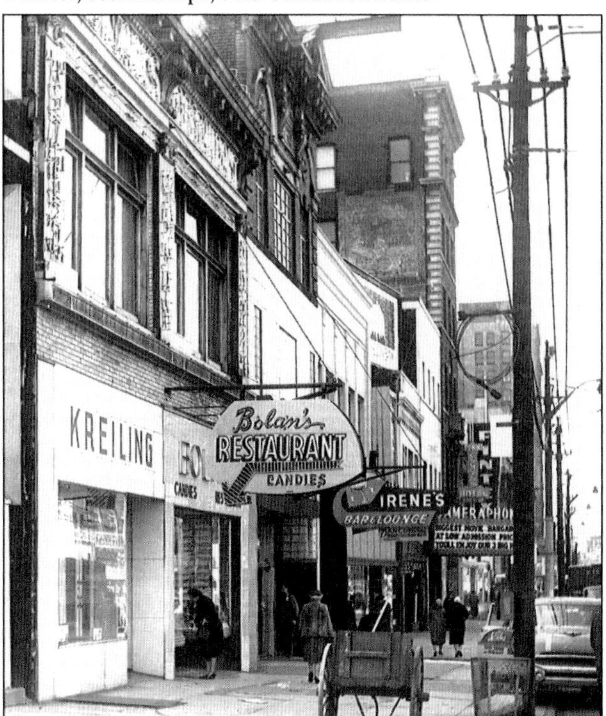

BOLAN'S CHOCOLATES, 1918. Founded by George Bolanis, who emigrated from Greece in 1914, this company was long known for its fine hand-dipped candies and homemade ice cream. The main store, which included a popular restaurant, was on Penn Avenue, with branch stores in Oakland, station square, and downtown. The retail stores have closed, but the business is being restructured by a third-generation family member.

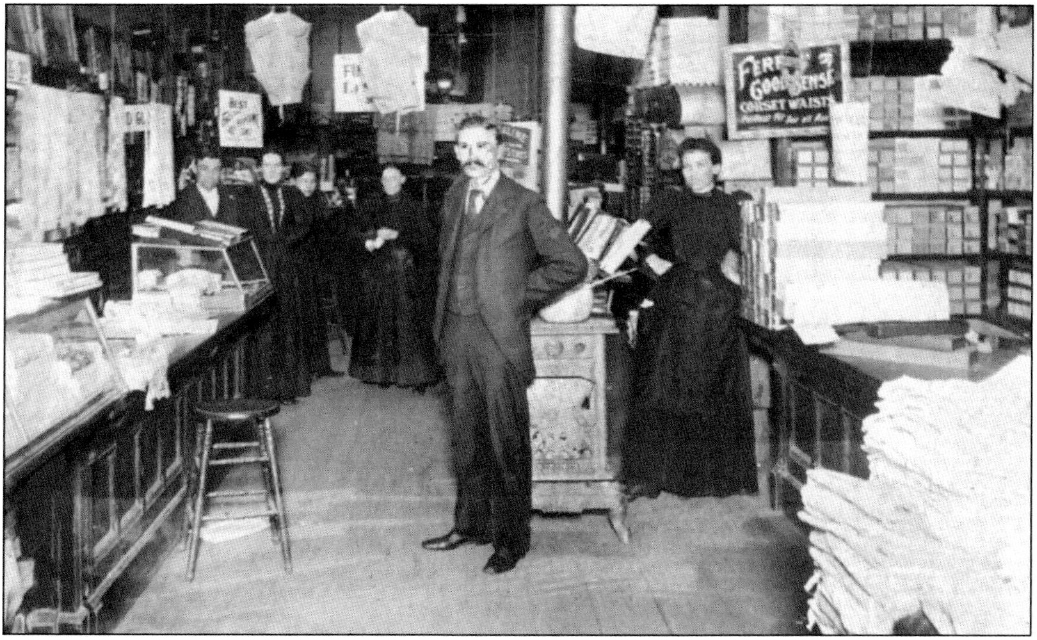

MANSMANN'S DEPARTMENT STORE, C. 1890. Before redevelopment, the 5900 block of Penn Avenue was one of the busiest shopping areas in East Liberty, and Mansmann's was a landmark. Founded by Albert Mansmann in 1888, it closed in 1978. Longtime residents remember the friendly service as well as the pneumatic tube system for sending money to and from the central cash register.

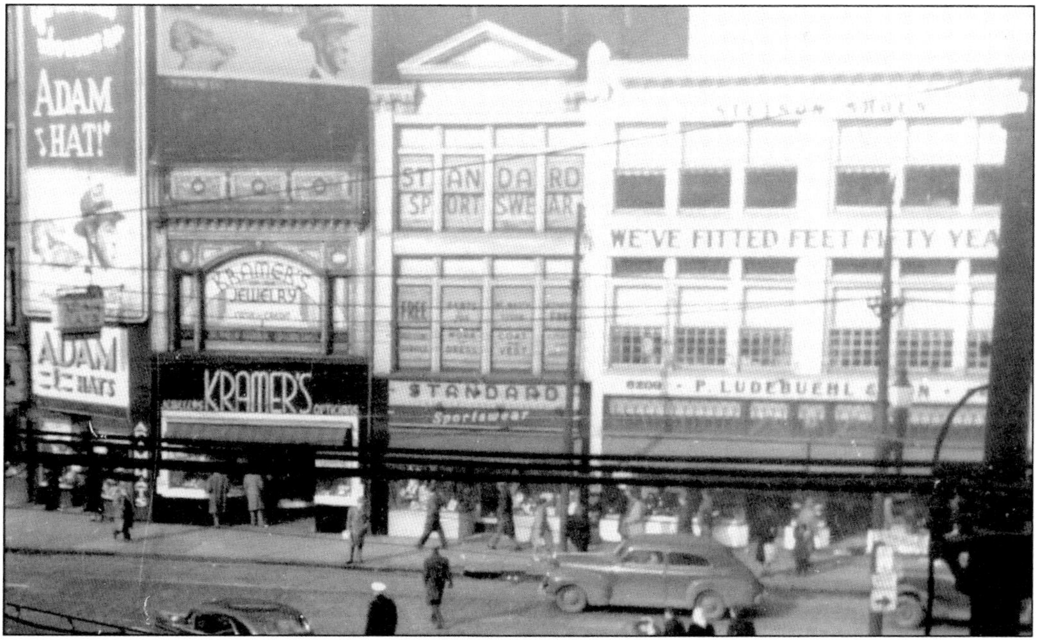

LUDEBUEHL'S SHOE STORE, 1950. John Ludebuehl, who was born in Germany, started his shoe business downtown in 1867, employing as many as 35 shoemakers. This store at 6209–6211 Penn Avenue was opened about 1890. The business was sold in 1965 after 98 years of operation. Ludebuehl's had a community-wide reputation for its high quality shoes.

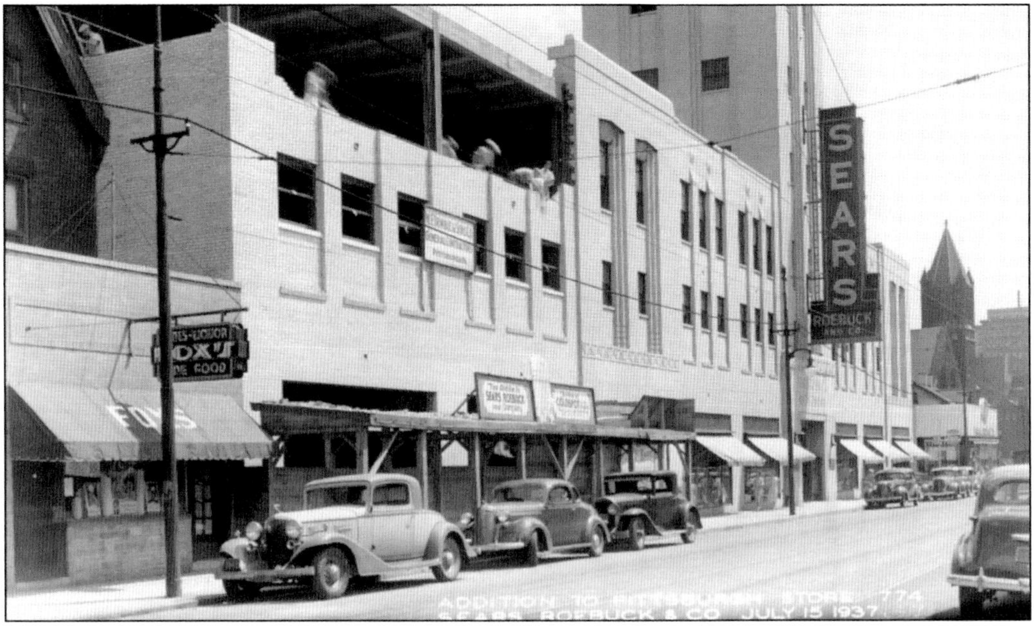

SEARS ROEBUCK AND COMPANY, 1937. By the 1920s, East Liberty had become one of the major retail centers of Pittsburgh. In 1929, Sears opened their first Pittsburgh store at North Highland Avenue and Station Street (now Penn Circle North). This photograph shows an addition made in 1937. Sears closed in 1992 and was demolished along with several shops. Home Depot built a new store at this location in 2004.

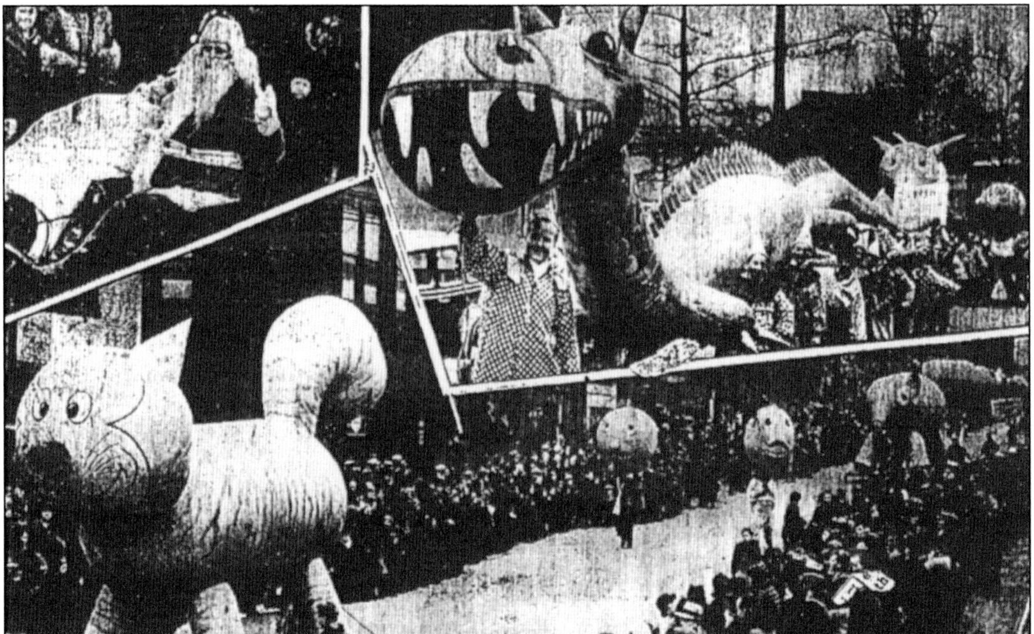

CHRISTMAS SCENE, 1936. This Christmas parade on Penn Avenue was described by local newspapers as one of the largest in the United States. Featured were 40 of the largest balloon figures made at the time. According to newspaper accounts, a blimp from which Santa Claus made parachute jumps flew over the community.

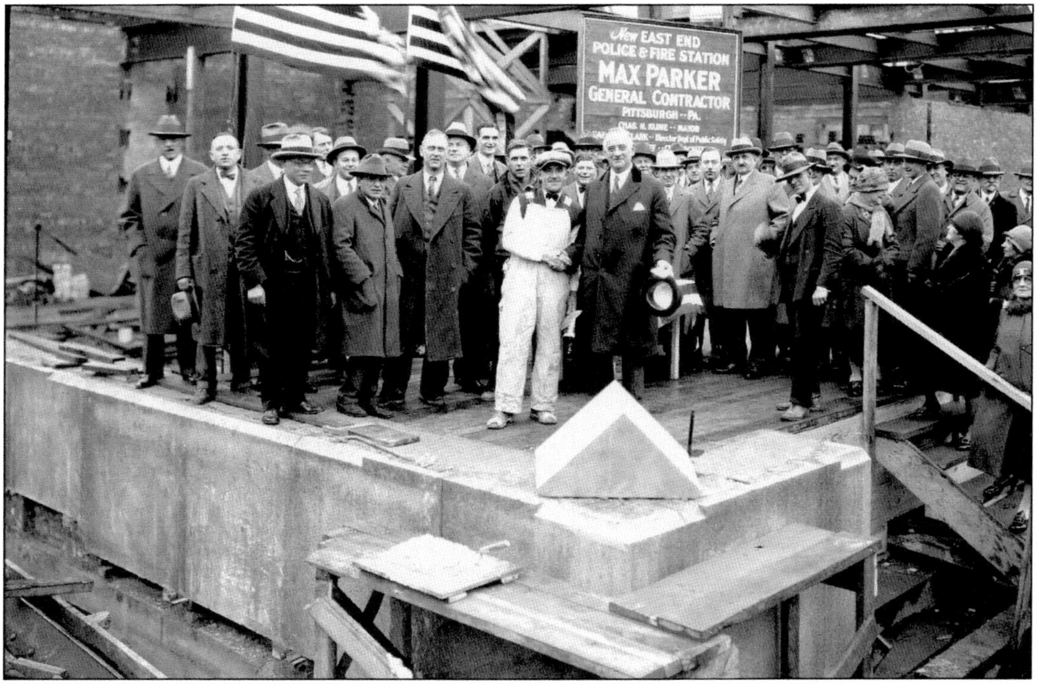

POLICE AND FIRE STATION, 1928. The cornerstone for No. 5 Station is being laid, with Mayor Charles Kline and others officiating at the ceremony. This station is slated to be replaced by a new one on Washington Boulevard near Negley Run Boulevard.

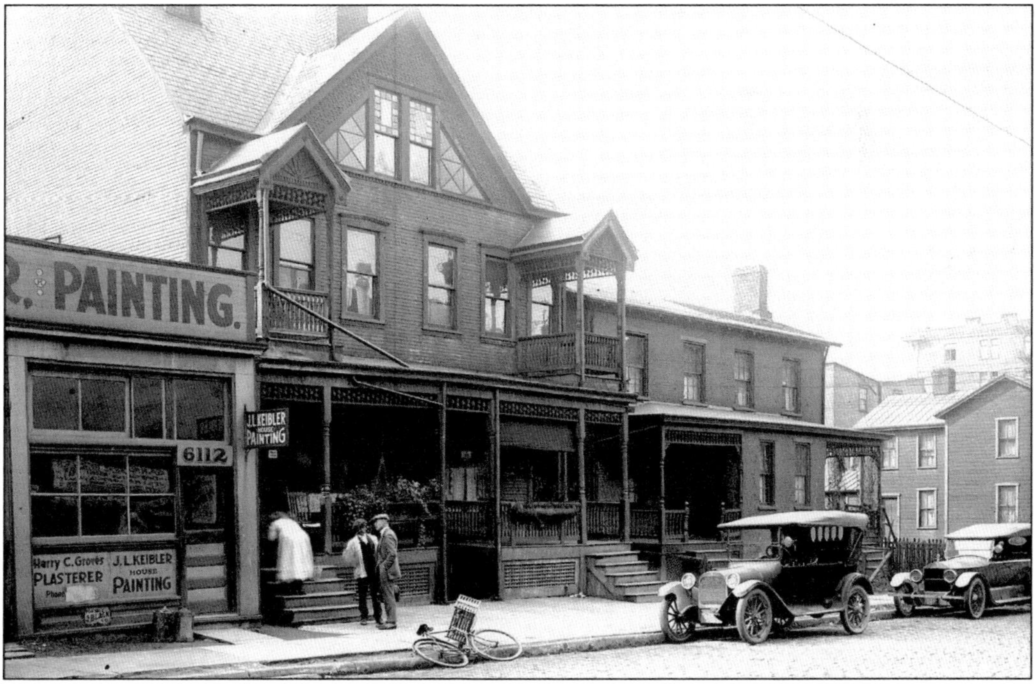

BROAD STREET AT SHERIDAN AVENUE, 1921. The store in this building at 6112 Broad Street was headquarters for J. L. Keibler, house painting, and Harry Groves, plastering. The adjacent building, with the bicycle lying on the curb, appears to have been residential.

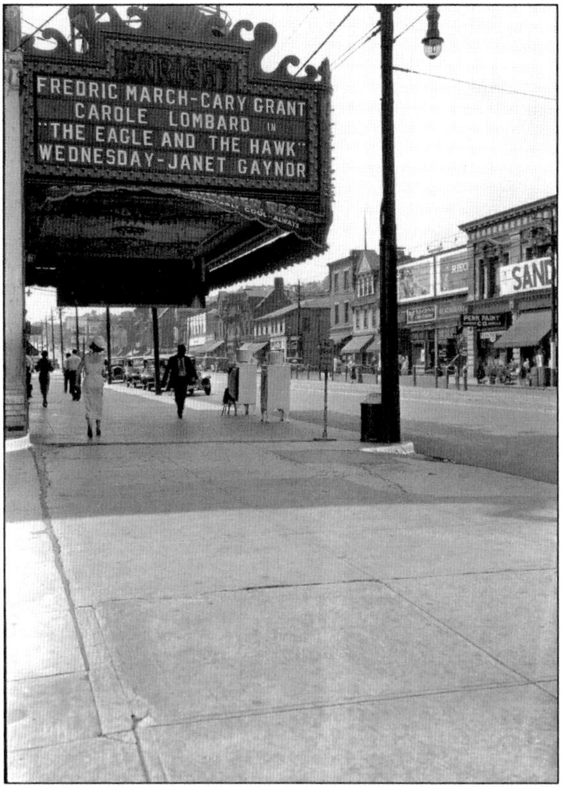

ENRIGHT THEATRE, 1933. On the Enright Theatre at Penn Avenue at Beatty Street, the marquee reads, "Frederic March–Cary Grant, Carole Lombard in 'The Eagle and the Hawk.' Wednesday–Janet Gaynor."

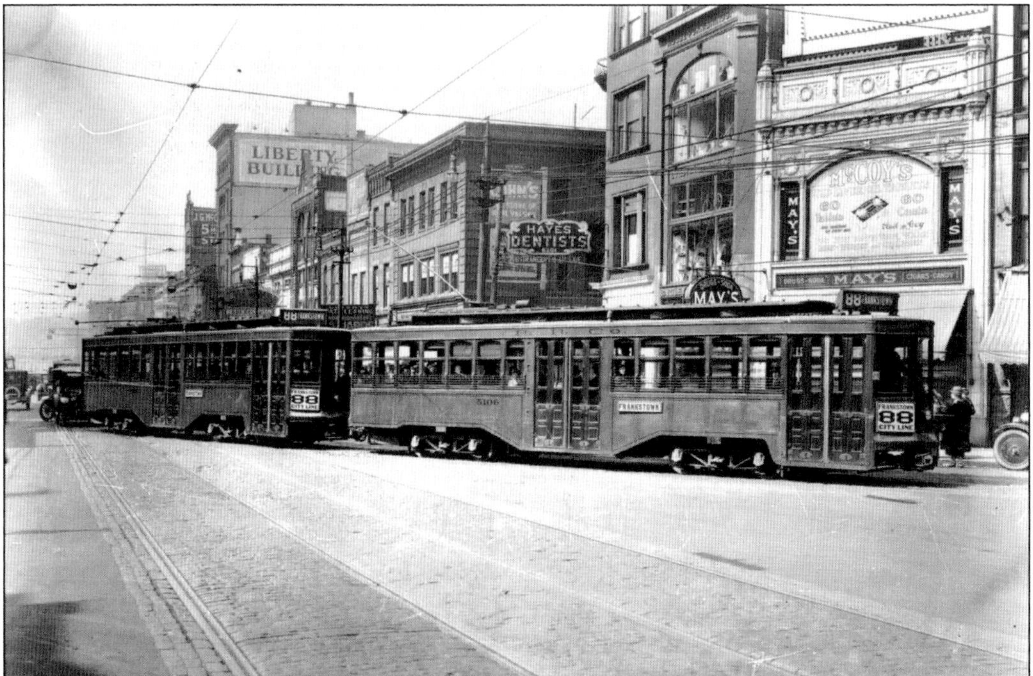

STREETCARS, 1930S. Two No. 88 Frankstown streetcars in tandem are turning at the busy intersection of Penn and Frankstown Avenues.

LIBERTY THEATRE, 1915. Henry Hornbostel designed this tall rectangular theater with street marquee on Penn Avenue beside the Pennsylvania Railroad tracks. It featured a decorative terra-cotta front and a central panel with an illuminated American flag. Moviegoers often heard trains passing. It was razed in 1968 by the Navarro Corporation, which saved and mounted the theater medallion above its new offices on Baum Boulevard beside the new Carnegie Library.

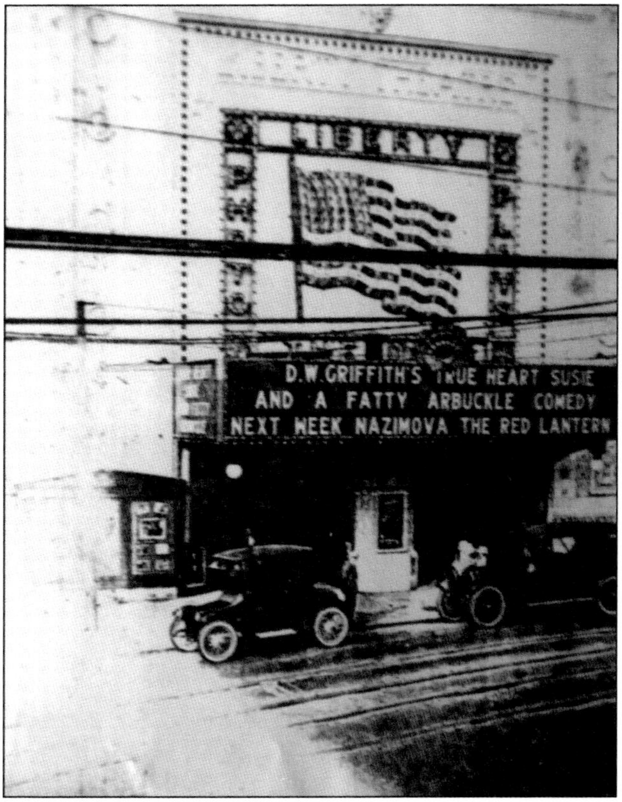

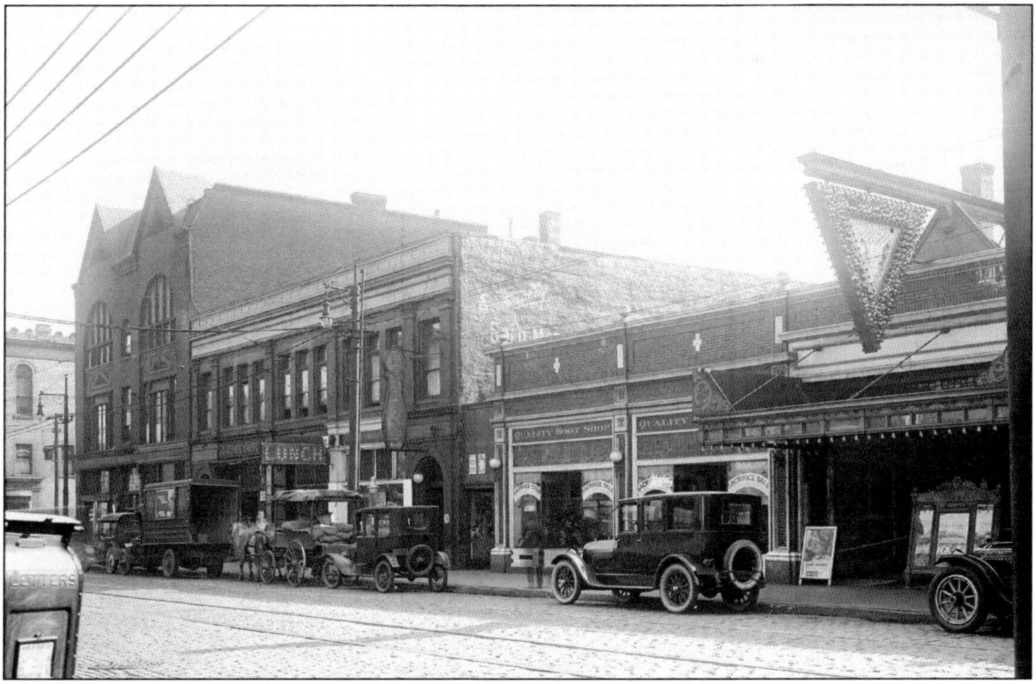

TRIANGLE THEATRE, 1921. This photograph of Broad Street, looking toward Station Street, shows the Triangle Theatre, a bowling alley, and the Greater Pittsburgh Lunch.

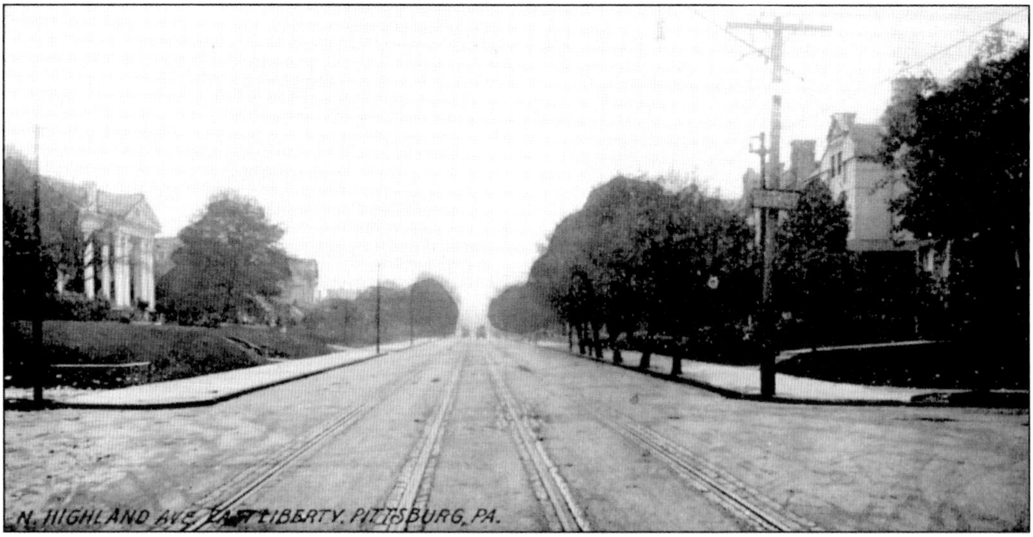

RESIDENTIAL NORTH HIGHLAND AVENUE, EARLY 1900S. This tranquil scene shows the North Highland Avenue residential area beginning around Stanton Avenue and ending at the entrance to Highland Park. The tracks show streetcar service, which was replaced by buses in 1967. Many of the larger homes in this neighborhood still stand, although some have been demolished and replaced with smaller structures.

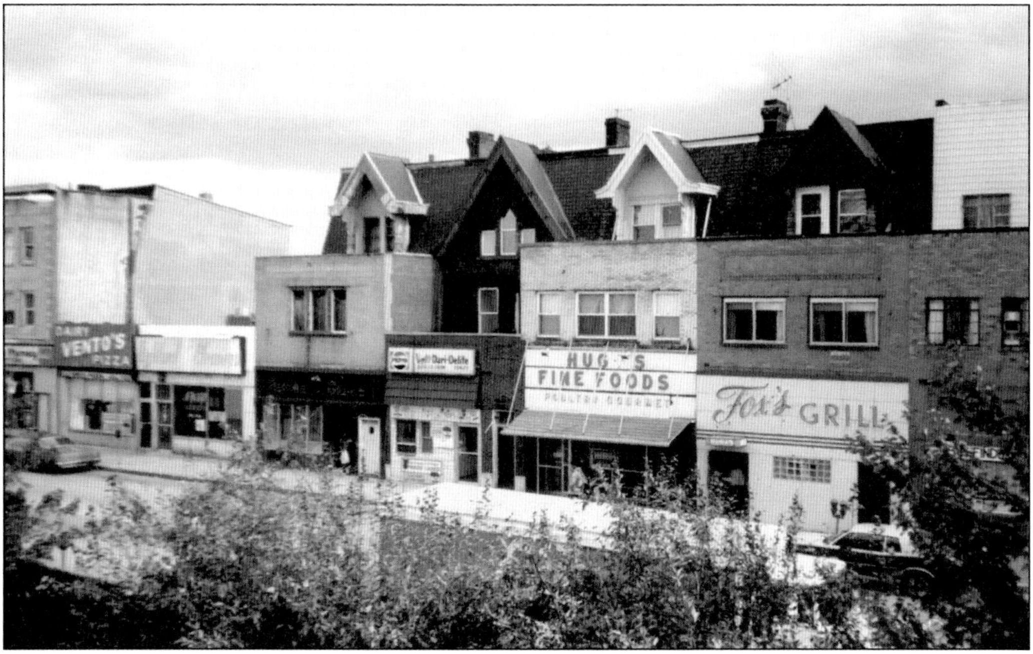

NORTH HIGHLAND AVENUE BUSINESS DISTRICT, 1980S. Since the 1920s, Highland Avenue north of Penn Avenue was a shopping street. This photograph of the 400 block shows businesses active at the time. Hugo's Fine Foods catered to the German population in the area. Sears is outside the picture to the far right. This stretch was demolished and is presently occupied by a Home Depot store and its parking lot.

Five

THE PATRIOTS

The cause of freedom from Great Britain in the 18th century found many supporters from western Pennsylvania and the East Liberty Valley. There were few people in the valley during the Revolutionary War, but participation in the cause is well documented.

John Conrad Winebiddle Sr. was a soldier and supporter of the colonists. Capt. Peter Parchment was captain of a Virginia regiment and fought under George Washington at Princeton and other locations. Maj. George Croghan served in the 4th Regiment of the Virginia Line. Alexander Negley joined Samuel Moorhead's Rangers and was sent by Washington on a mission to Fort Pitt. Henry Heth was captain of an independent Virginia company, and James Ross was a Revolutionary War soldier. Recognizing its beauty and fertile lands, all returned to the rich valley to start farms and businesses.

James Scott Negley fought in both the Mexican-American War (1846) and the Civil War (1861–1865). During the Civil War, patriotic citizens in the area supported the conflict with contributions of men, money, meals, and medical care. In June 1863, during Gen. Robert E. Lee's invasion of Pennsylvania, several forts were hastily built at high vantage points. They contained rifle pits with commanding views of the terrain to stop advancing Confederate troops. Because of Lee's defeat at Gettysburg, they were never used.

Hunt Armory was built in 1911 and honored Capt. Alfred Hunt, who died in 1899 of complications from malaria contracted during the Spanish-American War. The armory is still used today for the training of military personnel.

East Liberty's 107th Field Artillery served with distinction in Belgium and France during World War I. On the home front, the East Liberty branch of the American Red Cross was organized in 1917. The 107th Field Artillery again served with further distinction in World War II in the Battle of Normandy and the Battle of the Bulge.

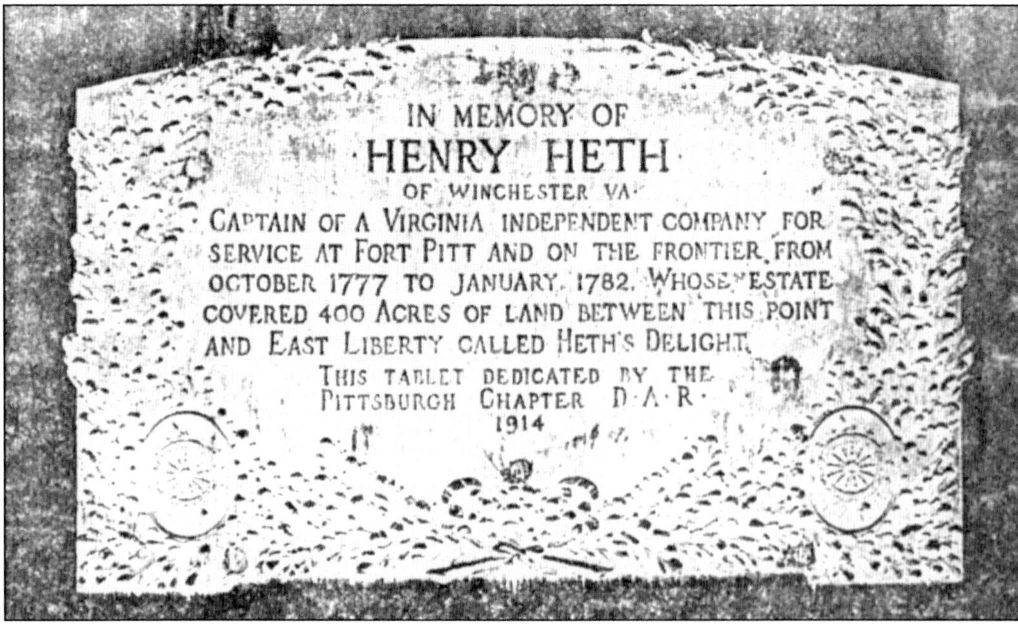

HETH MARKER, 1914. This plaque, placed on Heth's Run Bridge by the Daughters of the American Revolution, commemorates Henry Heth, captain of an independent Virginia company in the Revolutionary War who served on the frontier from October 1777 to January 1782. In 1789, he purchased over 400 acres near the present site of the bridge from George Croghan, calling it Heth's Delight.

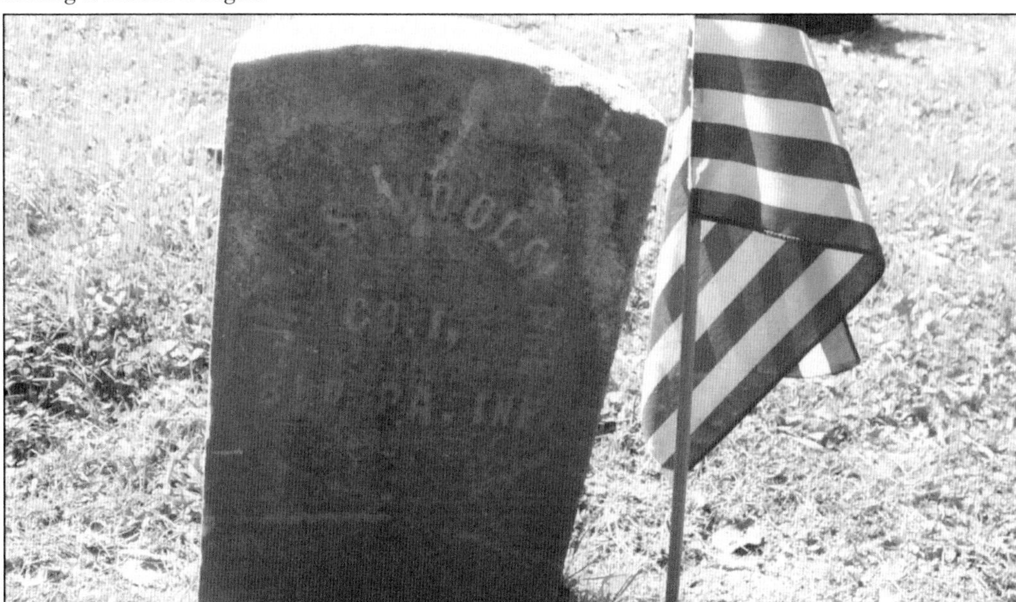

WOOLSLARE MARKER, 1861. Private James C. Woolslare, Company I, 3rd Regiment, Pennsylvania Infantry Volunteers, died July 11 at age 24 at Chambersburg. He was first interred in the burial ground of East Liberty Presbyterian Church. When its third church was replaced by the fourth church in 1888, his grave and others were removed to the Homewood Cemetery, where he became the first burial in their Grand Army of the Republic lot.

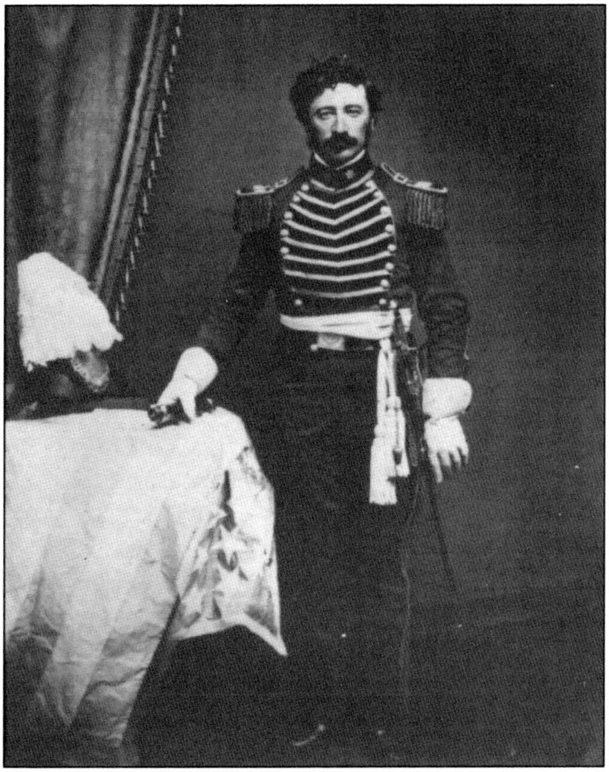

James Scott Negley (1826–1901). A descendant of Alexander Negley, James Negley served in the Mexican-American War and the Civil War. He served four terms in Congress. James became vice president of the Pittsburgh, New Castle and Lake Erie Railroad in 1879 and president of the New York, Pittsburgh and Chicago Railroad in 1884.

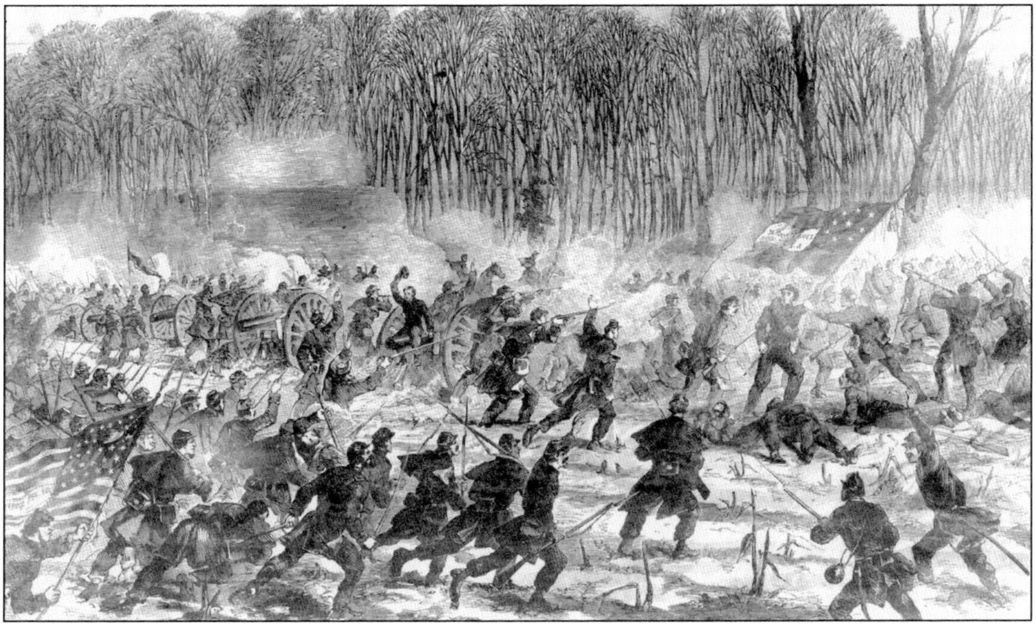

General Negley in Battle, 1863. In the Civil War, James commanded the 2nd Division of the 14th Corps in the Army of the Tennessee. In 1863, at the Battle of Stones River, he was promoted to major general for the skillful and effective deployment of his division leading to victory in that battle. He participated in three more major battles that led to dividing the South in half.

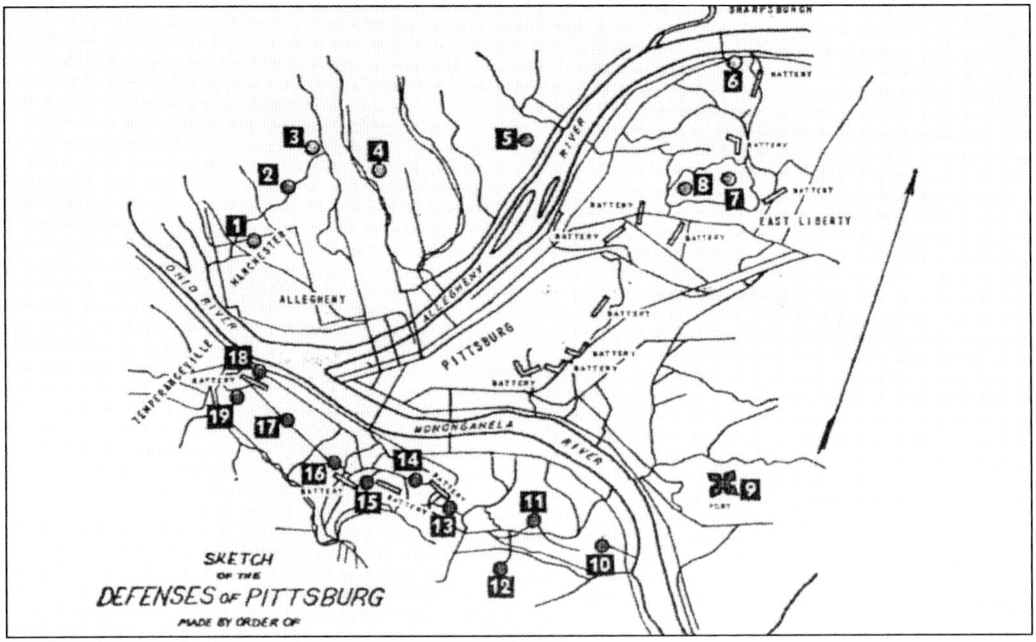

Defenses of Pittsburgh, 1863. In June 1863, the secretary of war and the governor informed Gen. William Brooks of the Monongahela Department that Gen. Robert E. Lee planned to invade Pennsylvania. Brooks lost no time in building a chain of 20 redoubts and 14 batteries on prominent heights to protect the city. This sketch by Capt. William P. Craighill shows the location of these redoubts, six of which were in the East End.

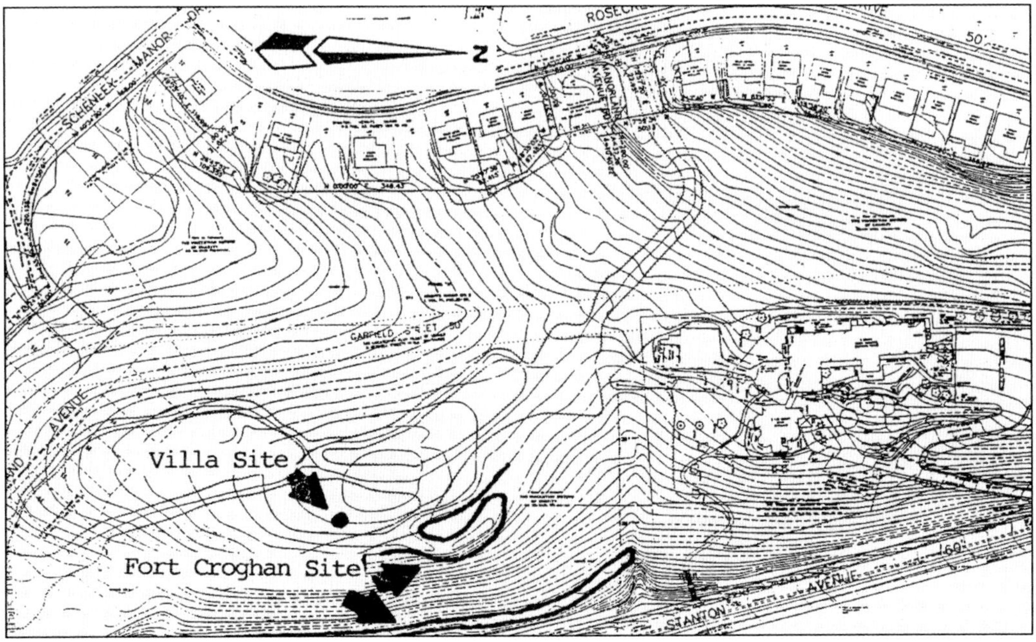

Fort Croghan Civil War Site, 1863. This fort is shown on this topographic map by Christine Davis Consultants. It was located on the Croghan-Schenley estate at Stanton and Morningside Avenues, where eroded cannon platforms and rifle pits are still visible. Its isolated location very likely accounts for the remarkable condition of this 144-year-old site.

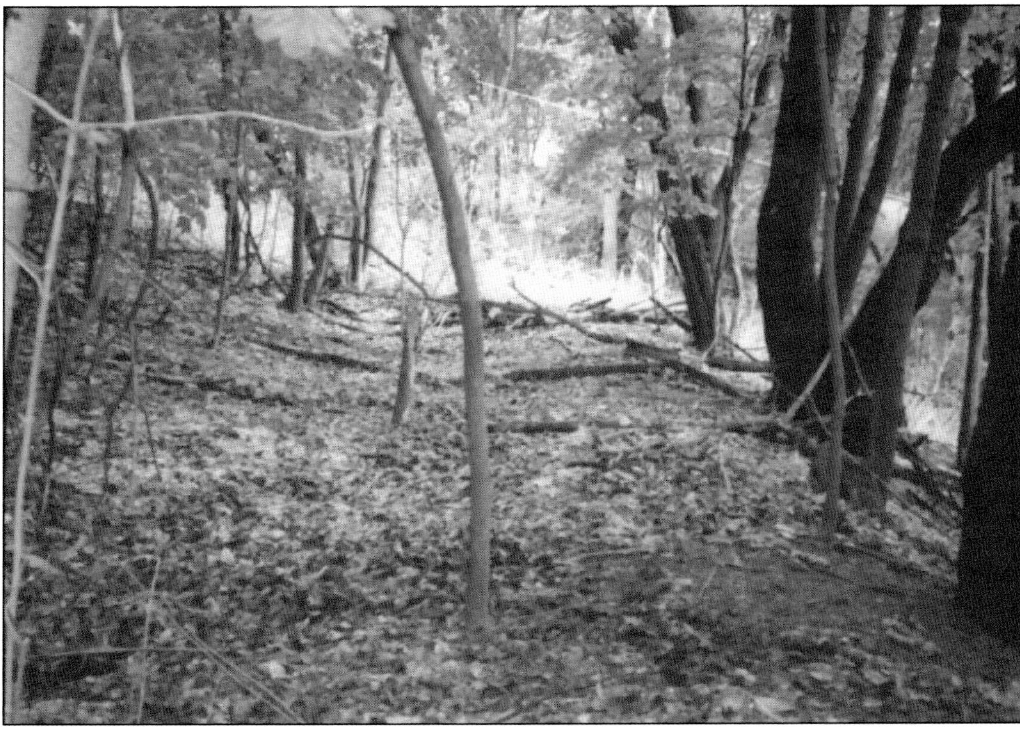

RIFLE PITS. This photograph shows traces of the rifle pits at Fort Croghan.

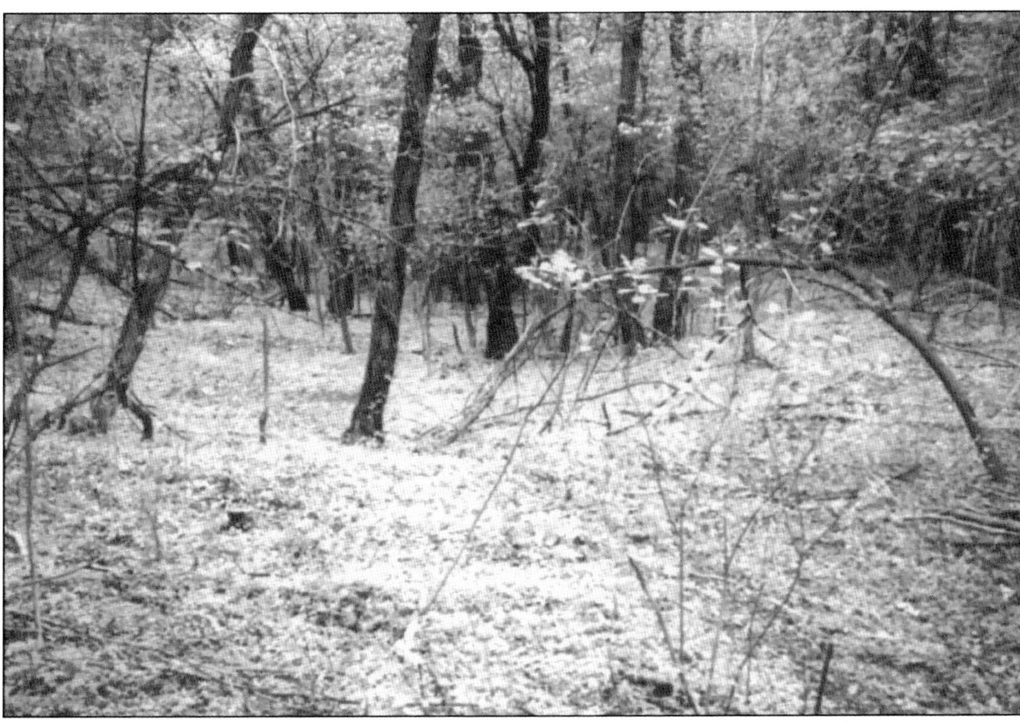

CANNON PITS. This photograph shows traces of the cannon pits at Fort Croghan.

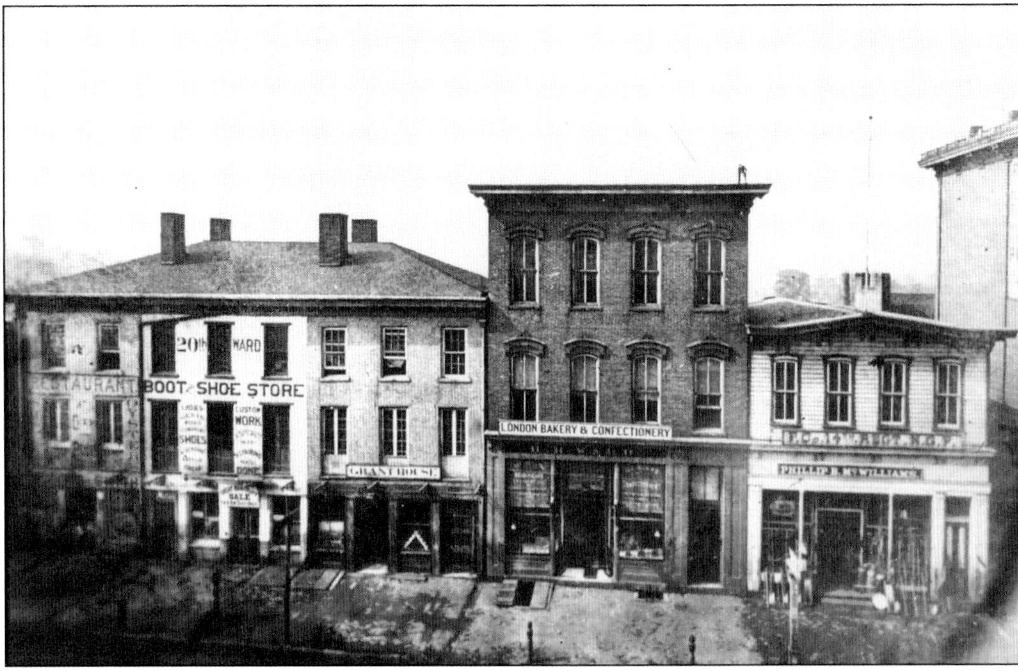

ARMORY OF COMPANY K, MID-1800S. The second floor of the building on the right housed the armory of Company K, 14th Regiment, Pennsylvania National Guard. This company was formerly known as the "Armstrong Zouaves."

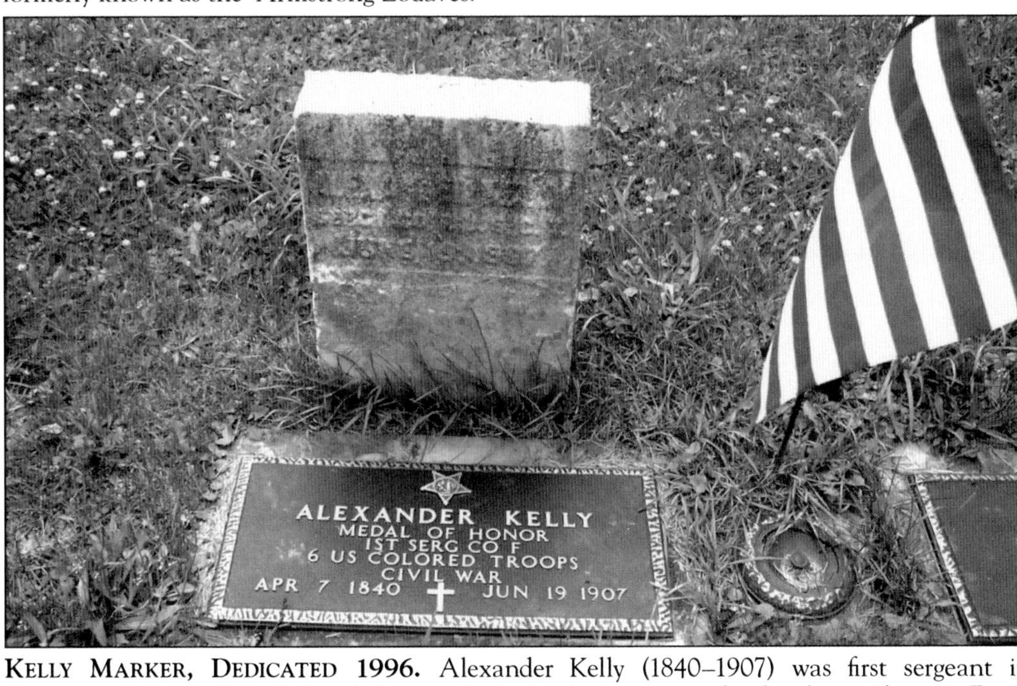

KELLY MARKER, DEDICATED 1996. Alexander Kelly (1840–1907) was first sergeant in Company F, Sixth U.S. Colored Troops. In 1864, during a two-day battle at Chapin's Farm, Virginia, with most of his company either killed or wounded, he seized the fallen colors, raised them, and led his men to victory. He received the Congressional Medal of Honor. He lies buried in Saint Peter's Cemetery on Lemington Avenue.

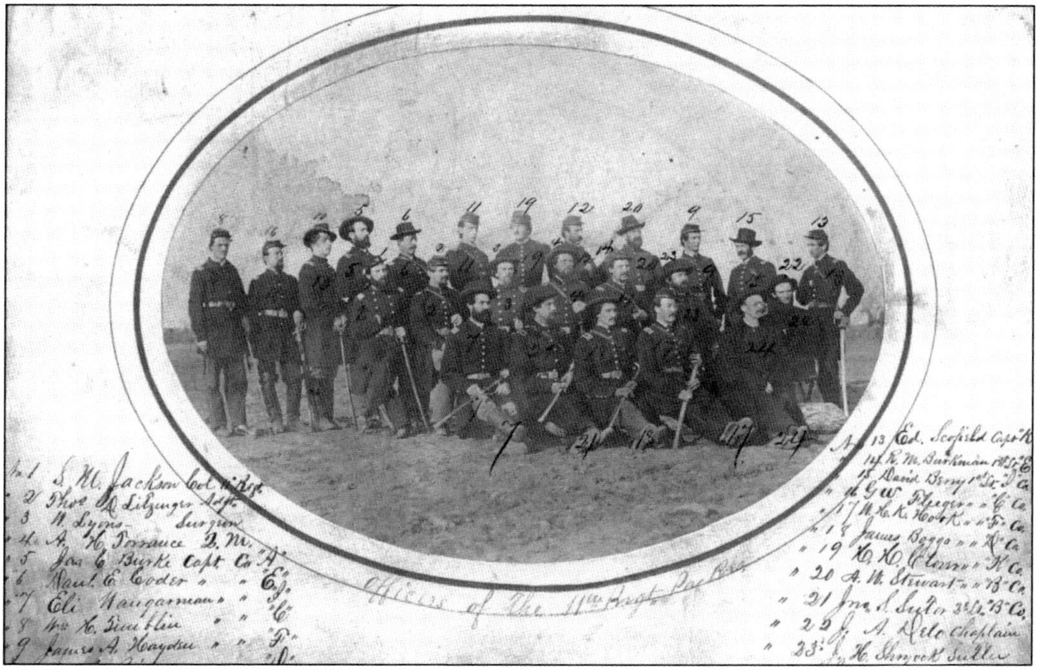

OFFICERS OF THE 40TH REGIMENT, 1863. This regiment was organized in 1861 from various western Pennsylvania counties. Recruits were assembled in camps located in East Liberty, as well as Wilkinsburg, Shadyside, Verona, and the Strip District.

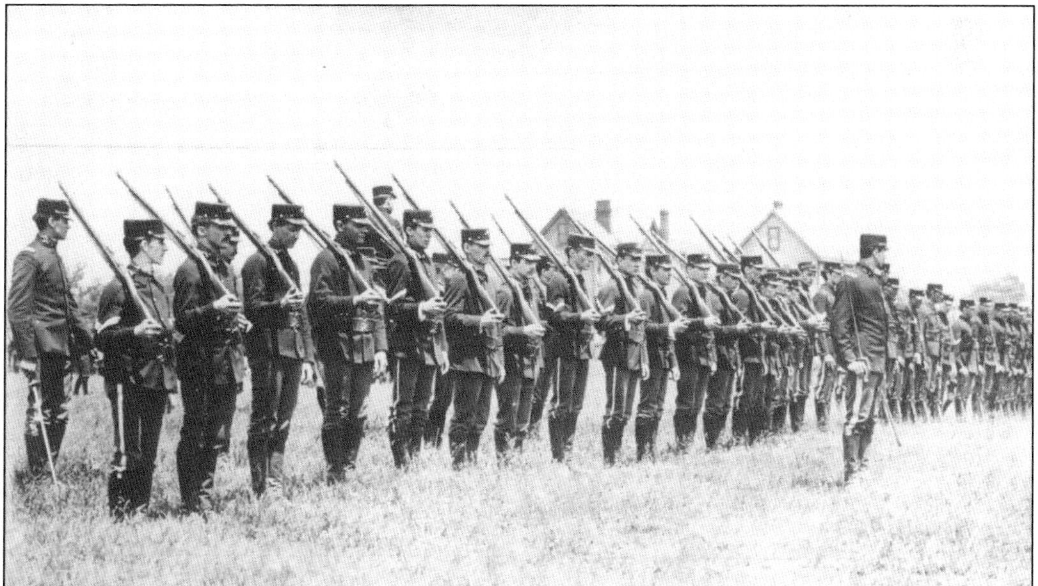

NATIONAL GUARD, 1877. The F Company of the National Guard had their armory in East Liberty.

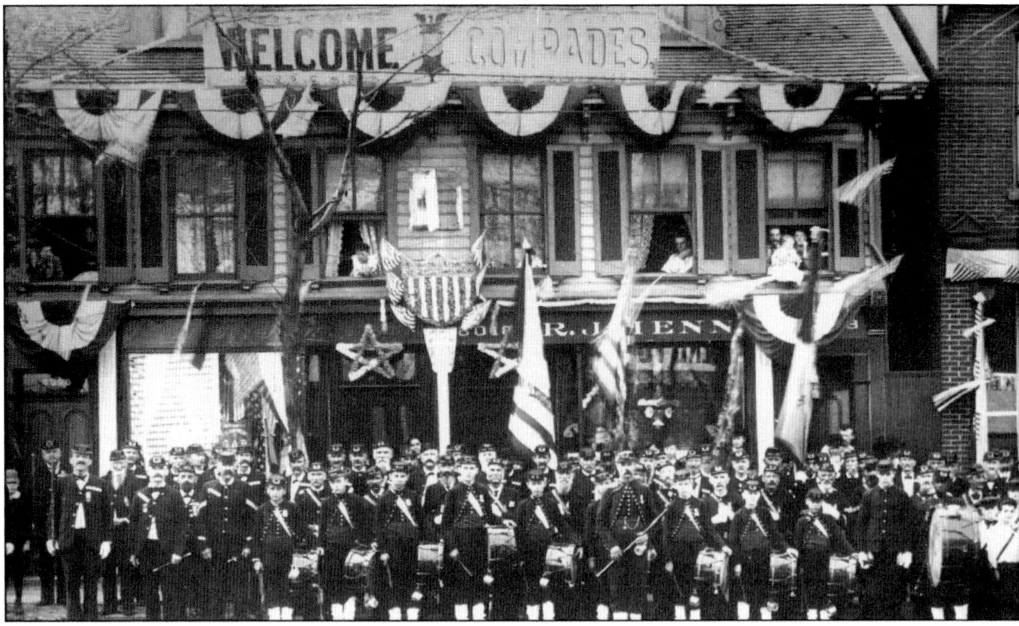

CIVIL WAR VETERANS, C. 1890. This picture shows a celebration, including a drum band, honoring veterans of the Civil War. It was held in front of R. J. Henne's jewelry shop at 6018 Centre Avenue (now Penn Circle South). This structure still stands, one of the oldest buildings in the heart of East Liberty in use today. The banner reads Welcome Comrades.

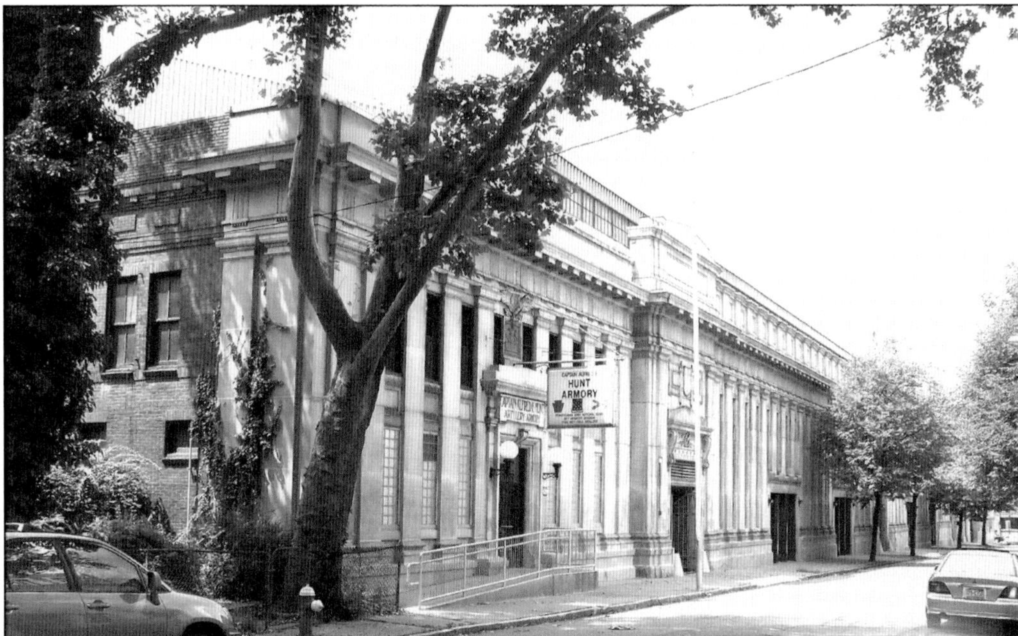

HUNT ARMORY, 1911. This block-long structure on Emerson Street continues to be used for training military personnel, currently about 250 soldiers. It was named for Capt. Alfred Hunt, who died in 1899 due to ill health incurred during the Spanish-American War. The armory has also been used for numerous events including a visit and address by Pres. Dwight Eisenhower in 1956.

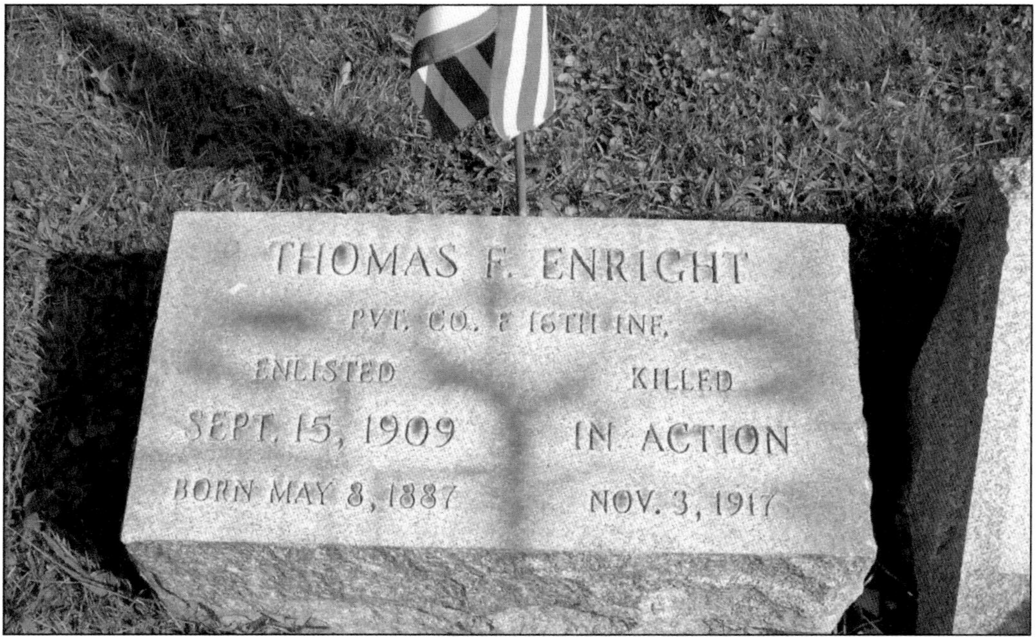

THOMAS ENRIGHT (1887–1917). A native Pittsburgher, Thomas Enright joined the U.S. Army in 1909. He died in France, one of the first American soldiers killed in World War I. He was awarded the Croix de Guerre posthumously. This marker was placed in 1920 at Enright's grave in St. Mary's Roman Catholic Cemetery on Penn Avenue in the Lawrenceville section of Pittsburgh.

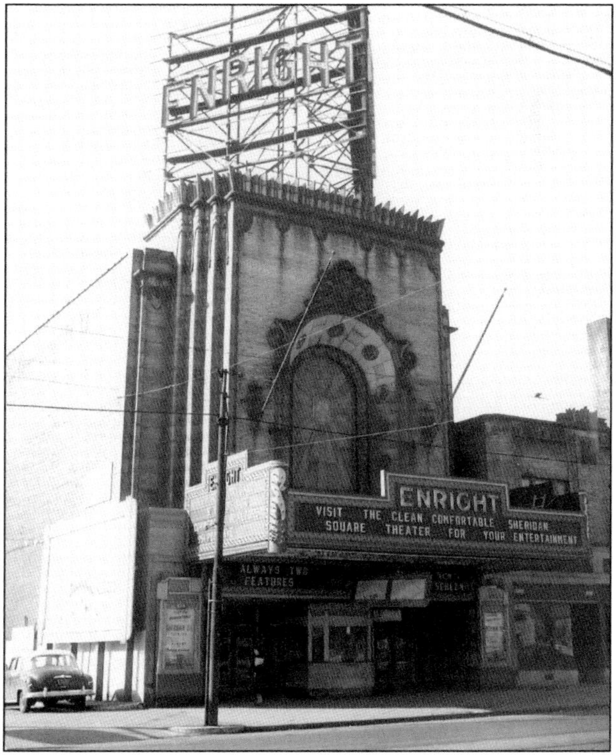

ENRIGHT THEATRE, 1928. Located on Penn Avenue at Beatty Street, it was the largest East End movie theater, seating 3,200. It was named in honor of World War I–hero Enright. Dick Powell of Hollywood renown was the master of ceremonies at the dedication and for some years afterward. Many traveling musical shows and headliner stars performed on its stage. It was torn down in 1960.

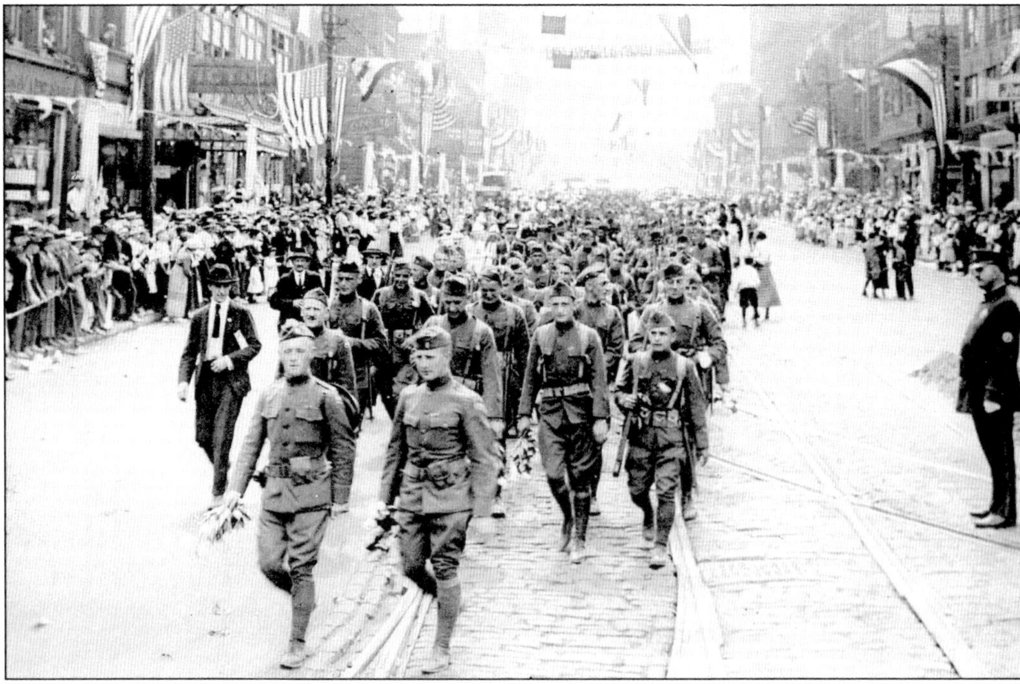

VICTORY PARADE, JUNE 1919. Men of the 310th and 320th Infantry Regiments of the 18th Division marched in this parade on Penn Avenue, commemorating the end of World War I.

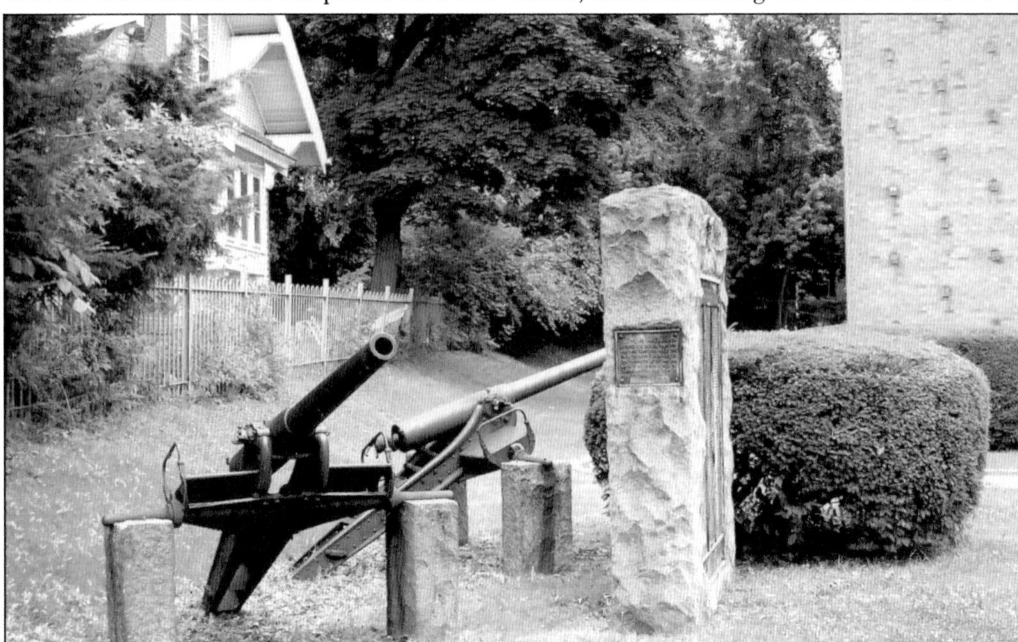

LEMINGTON HONOR ROLL MEMORIAL, 1919. This rough hewn granite stone and two cannons stand across from Paulson Avenue beside Lemington Elementary School. It holds an honor roll bronze plaque of the names of soldiers who served "That Liberty Shall Not Perish from the Earth." Eight are honored from the Spanish-American War, 13 from the Civil War, and over 400 from World War I, half of whom served overseas.

Peabody World War I Memorial, 1923. This Frank Vittor monument was commissioned by the students and alumni of Peabody High School. The figures in the group, which once held a 200-foot flagstaff, represent "Columbia calling her sons to defend humanity and liberty . . . the figure of grief shows the nation mourning for those who did not return." Beneath are panels showing 17 boys who died and 600 alumni who served.

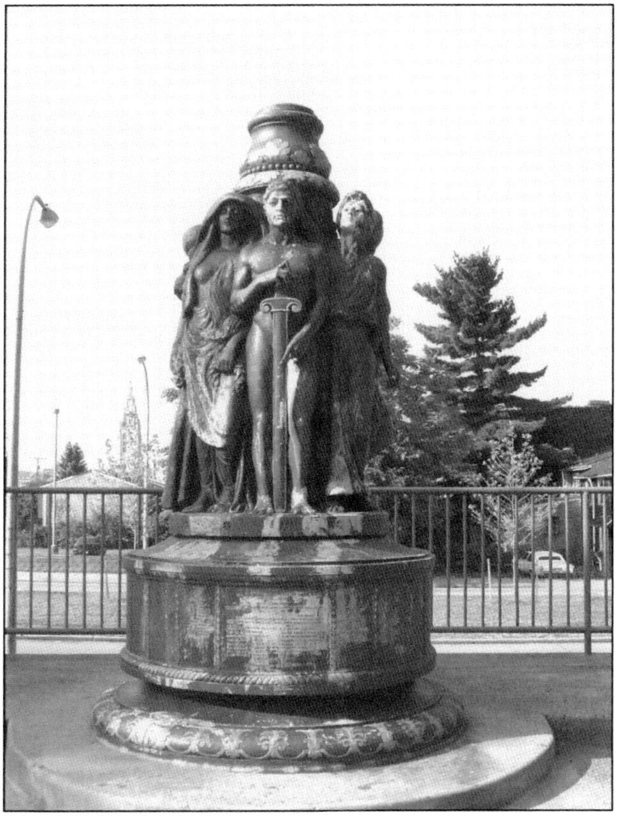

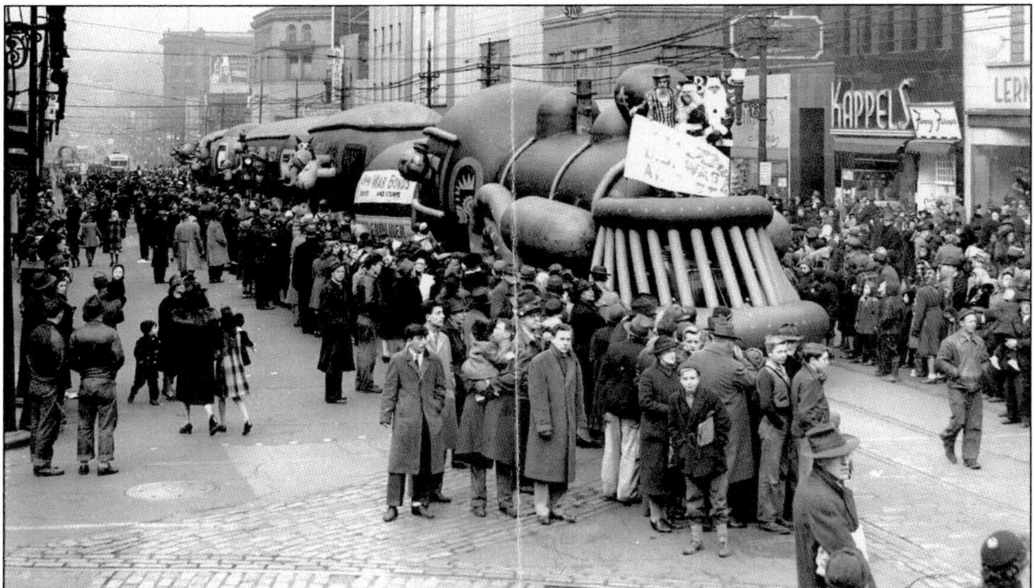

War Bond Parade, c. 1942–1943. This parade in East Liberty features a balloon locomotive train representing the "Buy U.S. War Bonds" campaign. The numerous parades that followed the United States' entry into World War II inspired patriotism, as well as the selling of war bonds to support American troops.

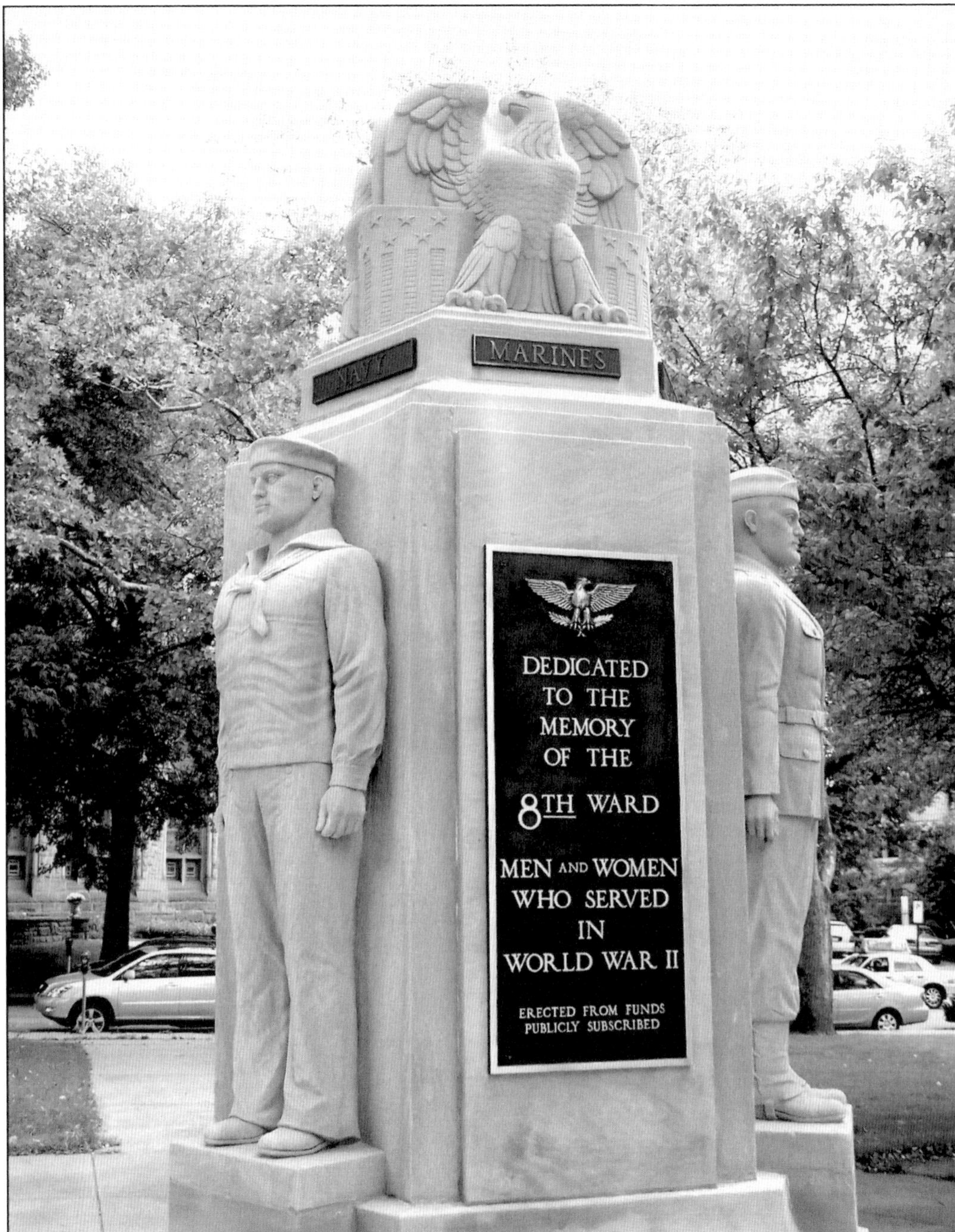

WORLD WAR II MEMORIAL, 1949. This monument, in Morrow Park at South Aiken and Liberty Avenues, was unveiled by the Gold Star Mothers after an elaborate flag parade and address by Pennsylvania State judge Michael A. Musmanno. It commemorates the 5,000 men and women who served from the 8th Ward. Designed by sculptor Frank Vittor, the figures on the faces of the hexagonal form represent the three branches of the service.

Six

Community and Institutions

Jacob Negley built a school in 1809 at what is now the intersection of Penn and Highland Avenues. He laid out the village of East Liberty in 1817. Two years later, he built the first church on land that he donated. Since that time to the present, community needs have been met by individuals and groups that have established churches of many denominations, schools, hospitals, and other public and social institutions.

East Liberty organizations and institutions have developed from diverse cultures. Ethnic churches and social groups were formed to help in both assimilation and the preservation of traditions. Larimer Avenue was settled by Italians in the early 1900s who were successful as concrete contractors and commercial bakers. A German neighborhood developed on the now-extinct streets near the double-spired German St. Peter and Paul Roman Catholic Church and, later, an African American population occupied the area. Each group provided commercial and social institutions to meet their needs.

The contributions of individuals are also evident. The Rev. George Hodges, rector of Calvary Episcopal Church, was an early leader and advocate of the social gospel and founded Kingsley House in 1893. Renamed the Kingsley Association, it has continued its mission for over 100 years and is now in a new facility at Frankstown Avenue and East Liberty Boulevard. Andrew Carnegie gave East Liberty a public library in 1905. Razed in the 1960s redevelopment, the library carries on its public work in its new location on South Whitfield Street.

The Negley legacy remains still. The East Liberty Presbyterian Church at Highland and Penn Avenues, carrying on a mission of help to its neighbors, physically dominates East Liberty with its great spire. It is the fifth church erected on the land originally donated for that purpose by Jacob and Barbara Negley. This current structure was built in 1935 by Richard Beatty Mellon, descendant of Thomas Mellon, who married Negley's daughter Sarah Jane.

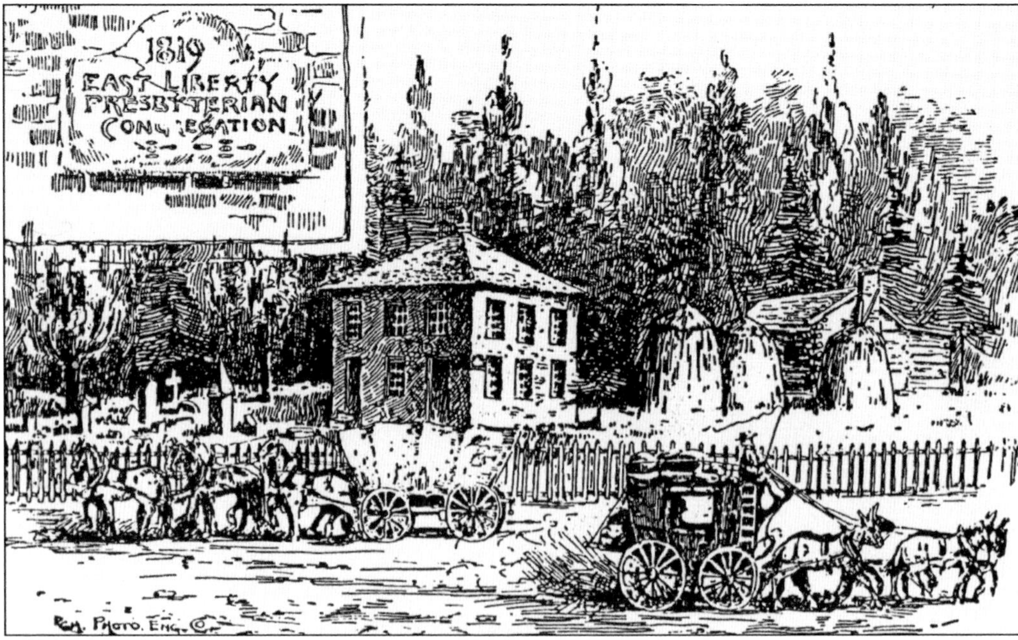

EAST LIBERTY PRESBYTERIAN CHURCH, 1819. The first church in the valley was built at Highland and Penn Avenues on land donated by Jacob and Barbara Winebiddle Negley. Subsequently, four more churches have occupied this same site in 1848, 1864, 1888, and 1935. The magnificent 1935 Gothic church, designed by Ralph Adams Cram, was the gift of the Richard Beatty Mellon family.

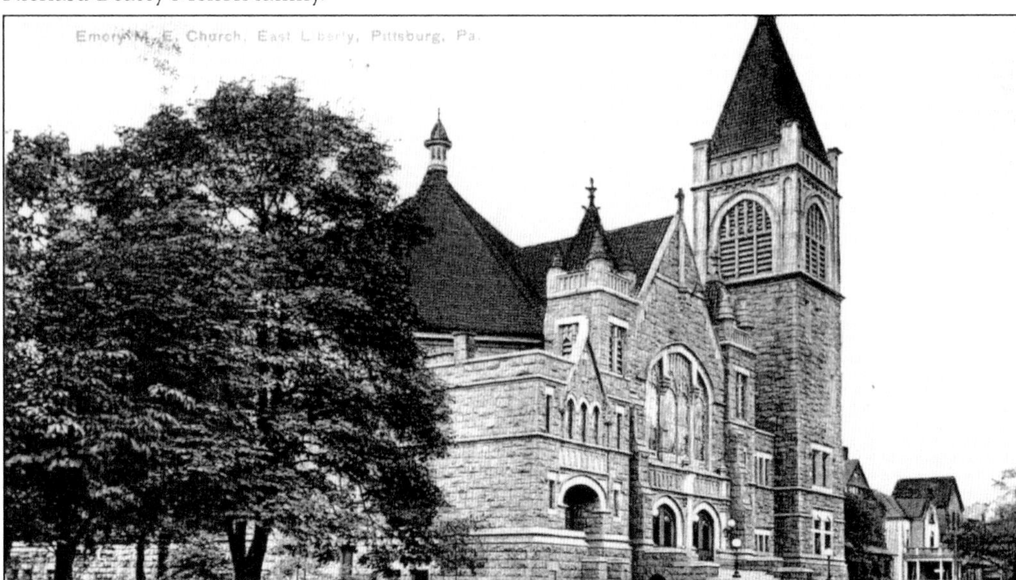

EMORY/CROSSROADS UNITED METHODIST CHURCH, 1906. The church pictured here, located at North Highland Avenue and Rippey Street, was the fourth home of this congregation. After it was destroyed by arson in 1971, it was replaced by a new church, built on the same site in 1974. The hardware on its front doors came from the razed Enright Theatre. The church has recently been renamed Crossroads.

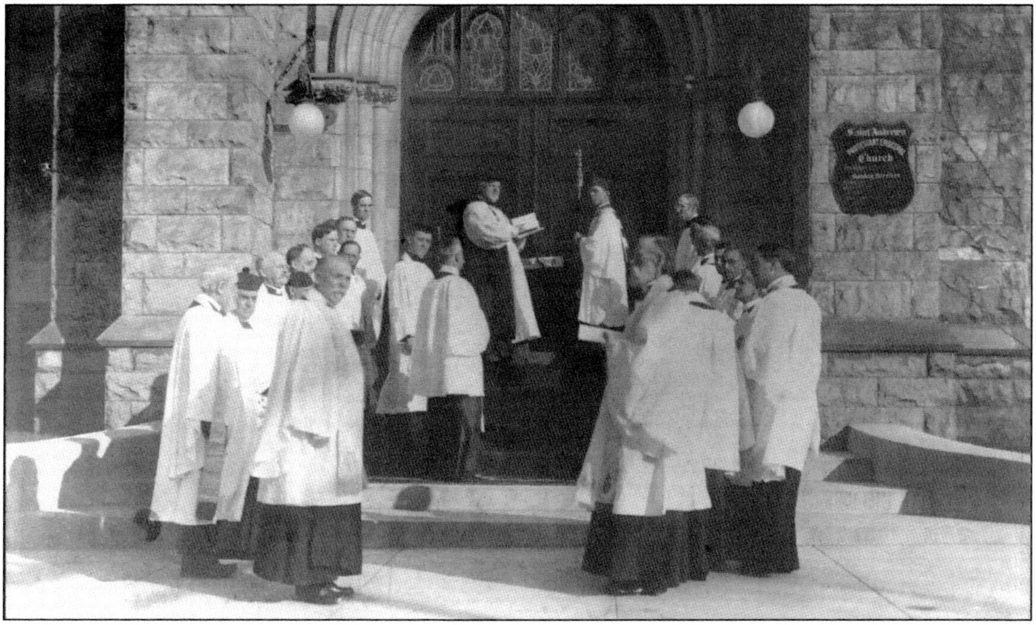

ST. ANDREW'S EPISCOPAL CHURCH, 1909. The second oldest Episcopal parish in Pittsburgh (founded 1837), St. Andrew's built its present church at Hampton Street and North Euclid Avenue in 1906. Architects Carpenter and Crocker employed a restrained form of Gothic Revival. Highlights include stained glass windows by Tiffany Studios and a handsome wrought iron interior gate by Samuel Yellin. This 1909 photograph shows Bishop Cortlandt Whitehead entering the church to perform the consecration service.

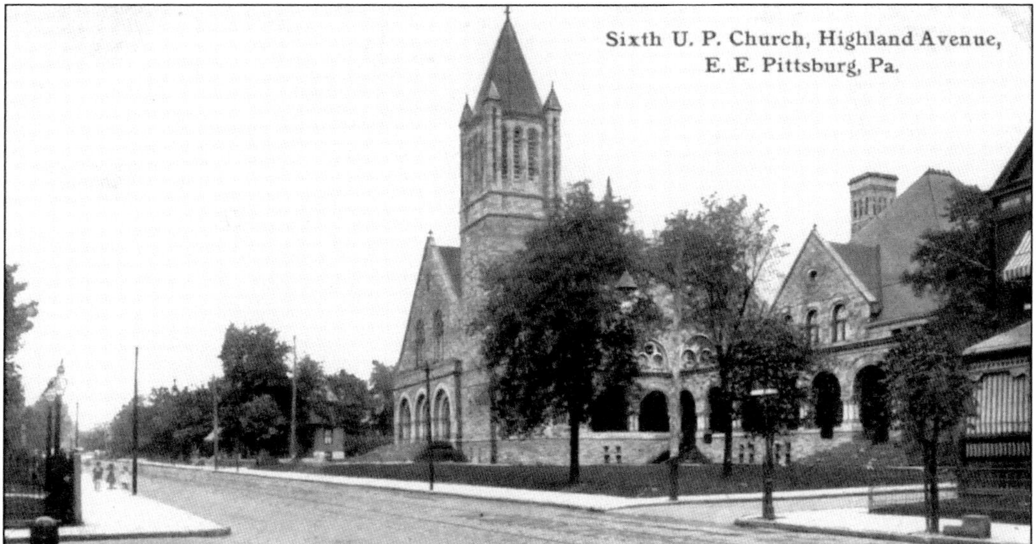

EASTMINSTER PRESBYTERIAN CHURCH, 1893. This congregation, formerly named Sixth United Presbyterian, erected its first church at North Highland Avenue and Flavel Street in 1859. The present church at North Highland Avenue and Harvard Street was built in 1893. In 1961, Sixth United Presbyterian merged with Third United Presbyterian to form Eastminster Presbyterian Church. Charles Lockhart was a major benefactor contributing to the building of this 1893 structure.

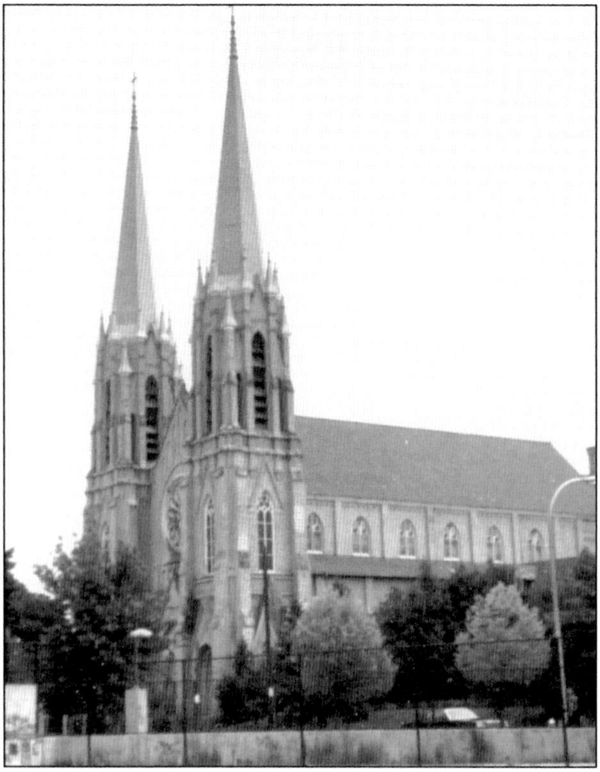

ST. PETER AND PAUL ROMAN CATHOLIC CHURCH, 1910. This handsome church served Catholic German speaking residents in the valley, who first organized the congregation in 1859. The church, built in 1890, was ravaged by fire caused by lightning in 1909, leaving only its 200-foot twin towers and altar. It was remodeled and rebuilt in 1910, containing many beautiful stained glass windows scripted in German. The church closed in 1992.

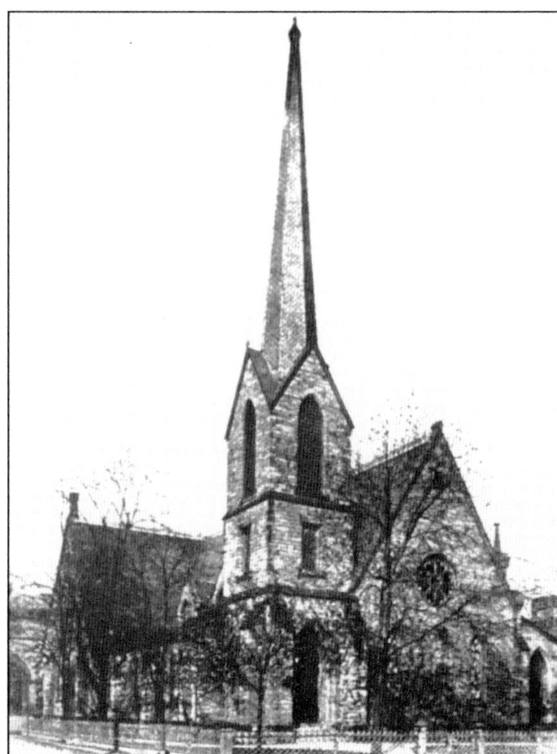

CALVARY EPISCOPAL CHURCH, 1861. The first Episcopal service in East Liberty took place in 1855, followed by construction of Calvary Episcopal Church on Penn Avenue, pictured here. This was replaced by the present Gothic church at Shady Avenue and Walnut Street in 1906. Designed by the noted architect Ralph Adams Cram with financial support from the Frick family, its spire reaches a height of 220 feet.

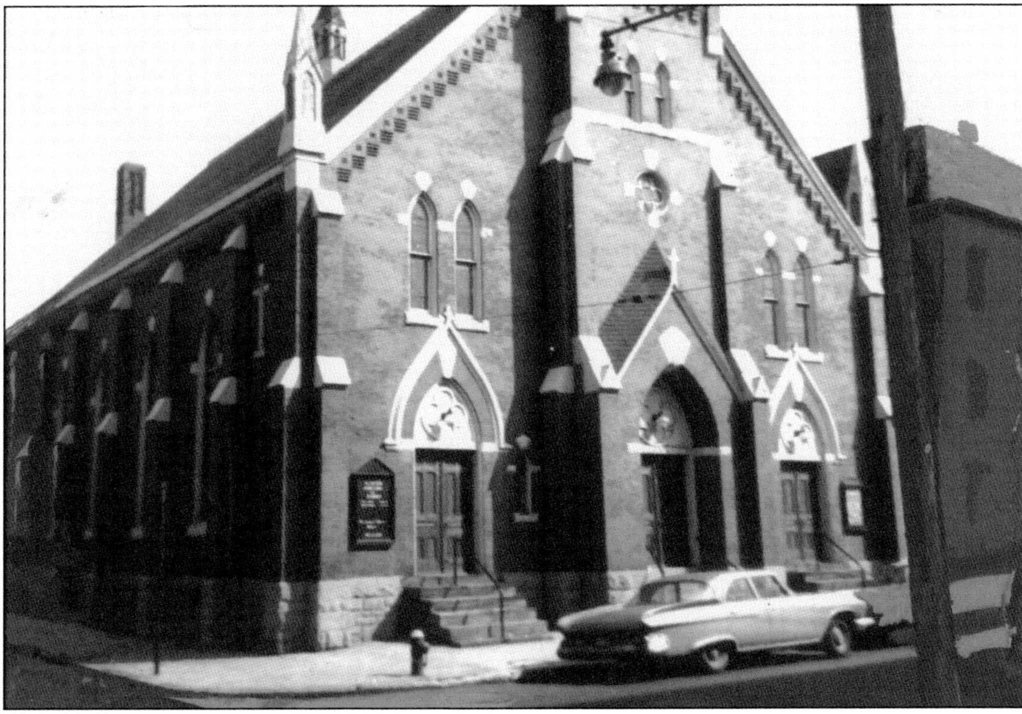

ST. PETER'S EVANGELICAL LUTHERAN CHURCH, 1889. Founded by German immigrants in 1862, this red brick church with a central bell tower was dedicated in 1889 at Collins Avenue and Station Street. The Missionary Temple Church of God in Christ began holding dual services here in 1982 and eventually purchased the building for their sole use in 1997.

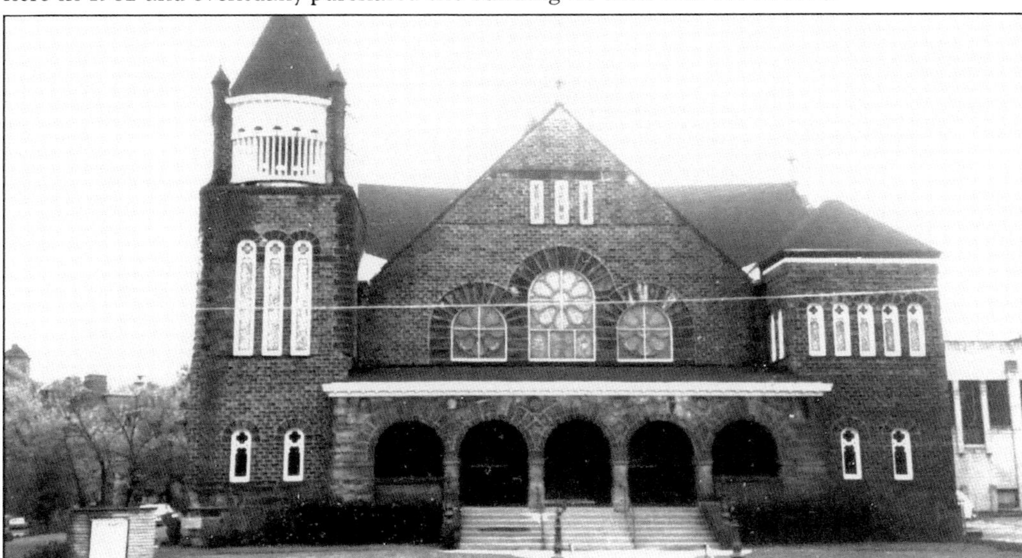

ST. JAMES AFRICAN METHODIST EPISCOPAL CHURCH. This congregation began in 1866 with informal prayer gatherings in various locations, which continued for many years. Their first church was built at North Euclid and Harvard Streets in 1891. It was damaged by fire in 1908 but was repaired and served until it was torn down in the 1960s. In 1966 they purchased this building at Lincoln Avenue and Meadow Street.

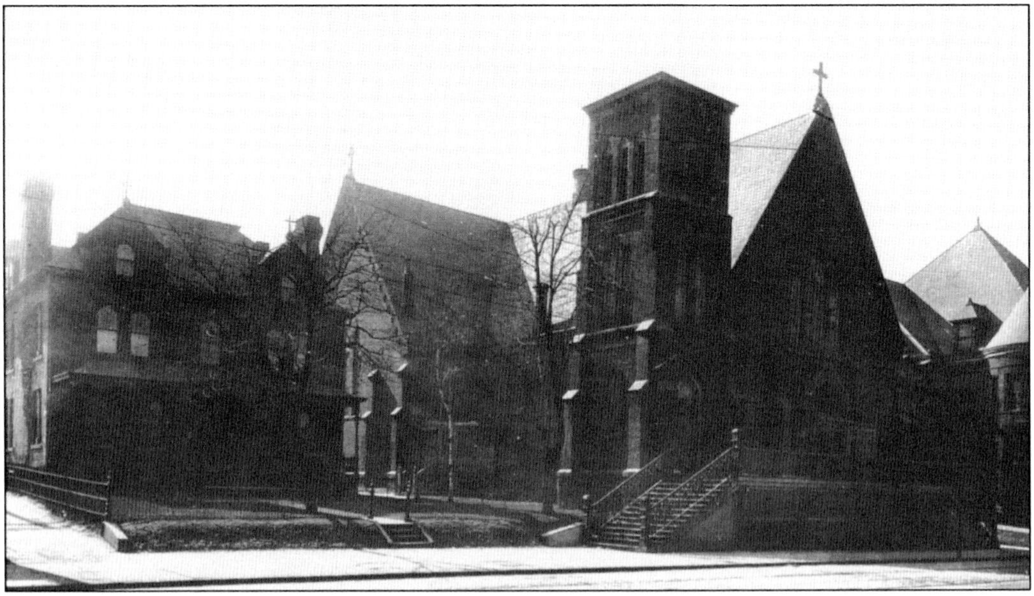

SACRED HEART ROMAN CATHOLIC CHURCH, 1873. In 1872, a wooden frame church was erected on Centre Avenue accommodating 75 families. With a growing population, the church pictured here was built in 1873 at the same location. In 1924, the present Gothic-style stone church with a front facade of stained glass windows was built at Shady Avenue and Walnut Street. The 150-foot bell tower was completed in 1954.

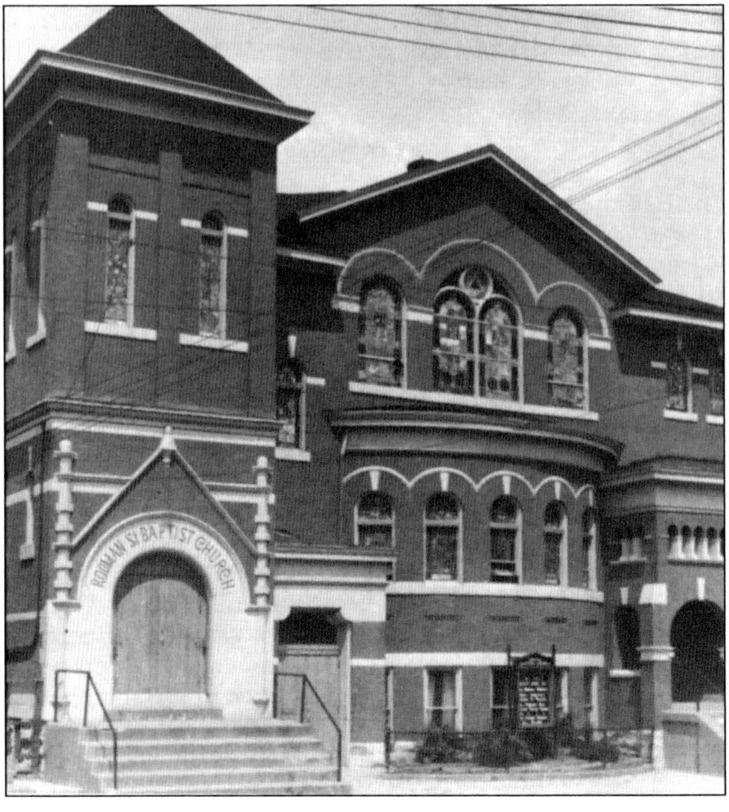

RODMAN STREET BAPTIST CHURCH, 1885. Originally founded as the Salome Baptist Church, it was renamed Rodman Street Baptist Church, which built this red brick structure at Rodman Street and Sheridan Avenue. In 1971, it was destroyed by arson. The congregation worshiped in the Pittsburgh Theological Seminary's Hicks Chapel until a new church of modern design was built on the same site. The cornerstone was laid in 1975.

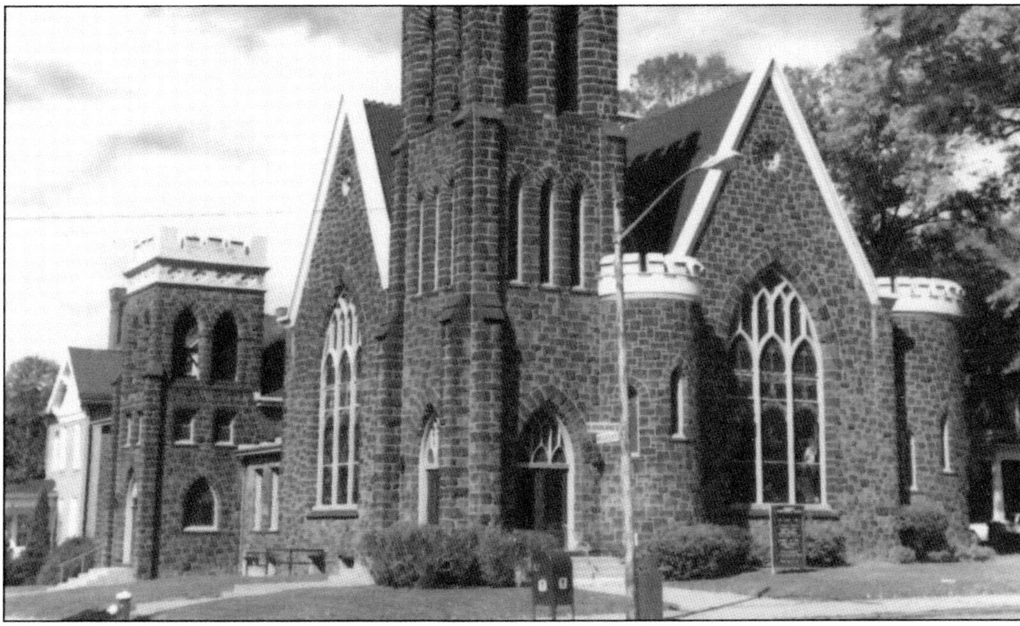

HIGHLAND PRESBYTERIAN CHURCH, 1886. After a Sunday school was established in 1886 in the McElroy home on North Highland Avenue, a frame church was built at the corner of North St. Clair Street and McCully Street (now Wellesley Avenue). In 1900, the congregation built a new Gothic-style structure at Highland and Wellesley. After the congregation merged with East Liberty Presbyterian Church in 1981, the church was razed.

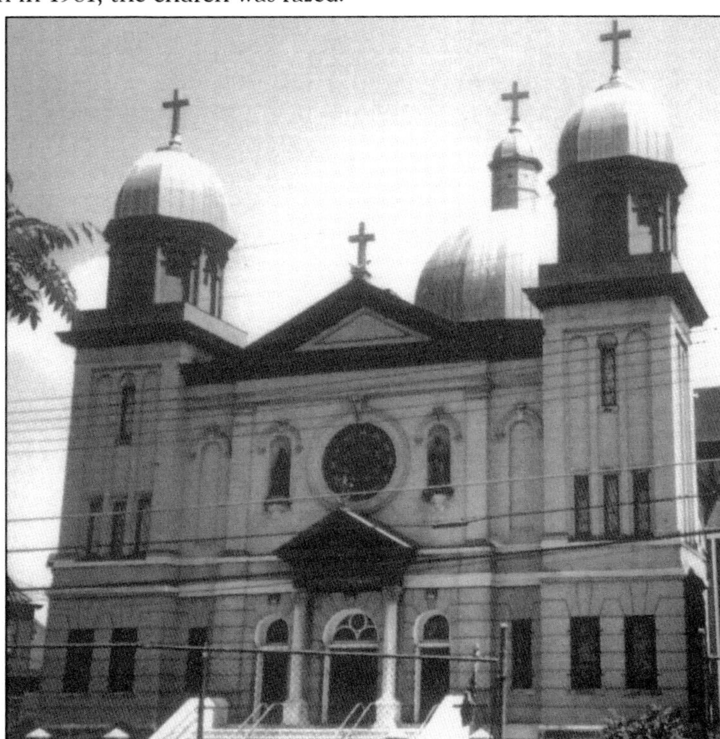

OUR LADY HELP OF CHRISTIANS CHURCH. This Roman Catholic parish church in the 6500 block of Meadow Street, founded in 1897, was the vibrant center of the Italian community of East Liberty in the area known as Little Italy. Parishioners could hear mass in familiar Italian. It closed in 1992 after almost 100 years of services.

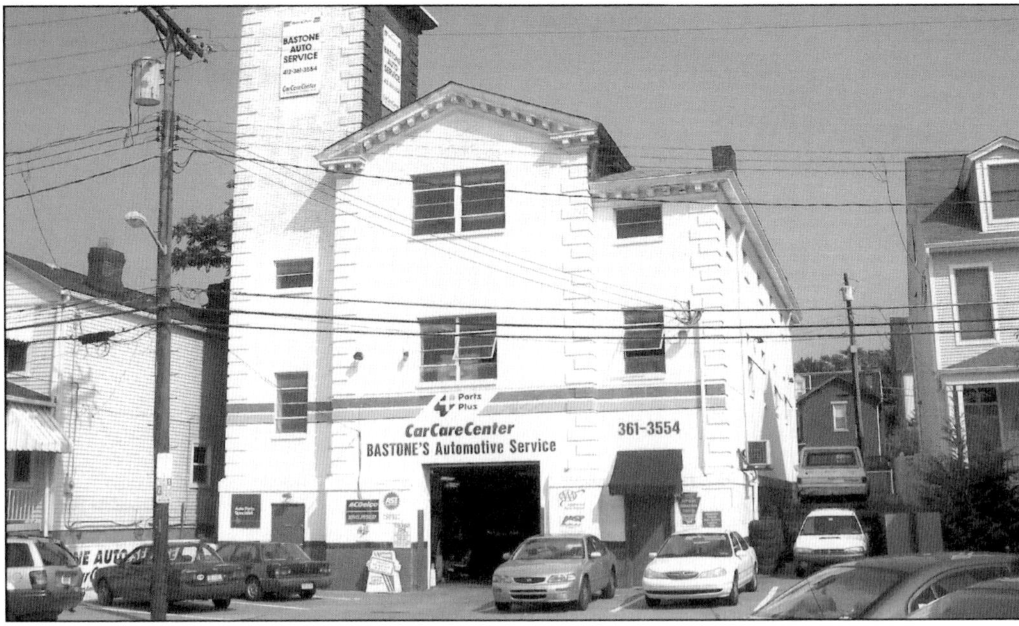

CARRON BAPTIST CHURCH, 1900. Now an automobile repair shop, this substantial brick building on Carron Street was originally the Carron Street Baptist Church, built in 1900. The congregation was initially organized as the Second Baptist Church of East End in May 1885. The church has since moved several times and is now located in an imposing structure at 7119 Frankstown Avenue.

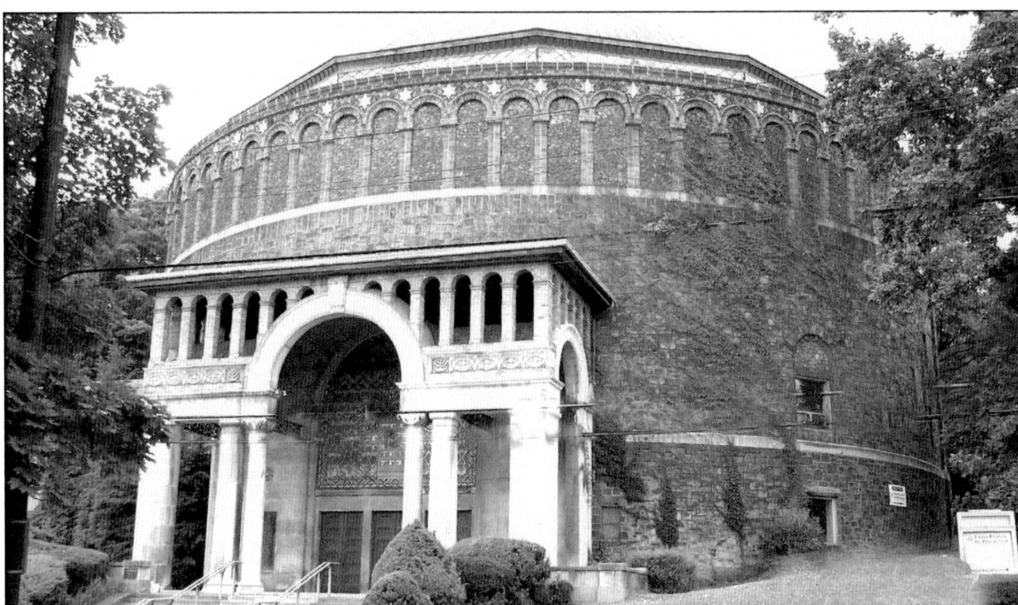

B'NAI ISRAEL, 1922. This congregation first met in 1904 and held services in several rental locations in the area before building a new synagogue to seat 1,000 on North Negley Avenue at Rippey Place. Henry Hornbostel designed a circular stone drum with a copper dome. After the congregation relocated to the suburbs in 1997, the building was sold to the Urban League of Pittsburgh.

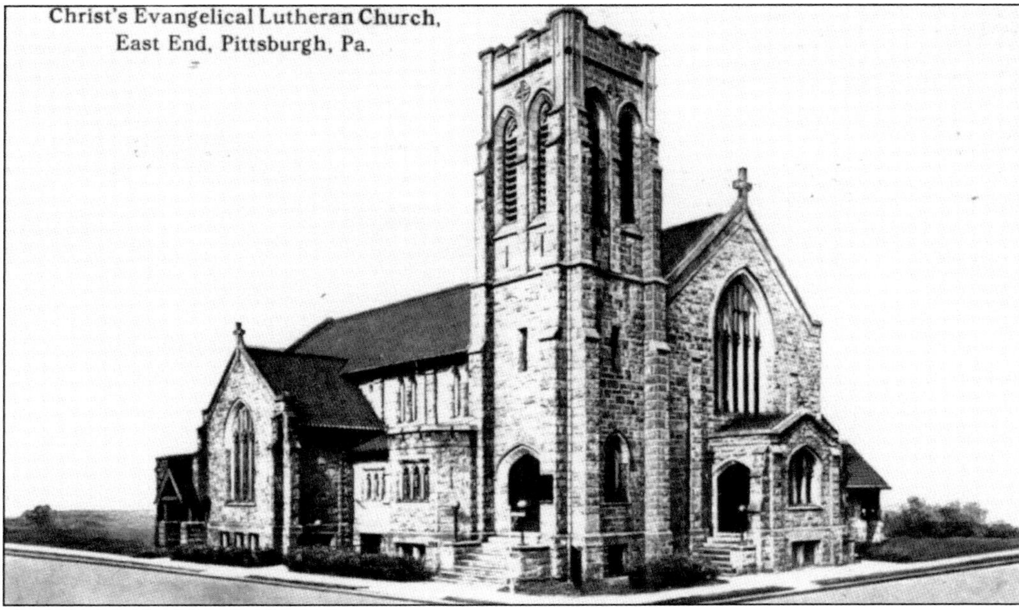

EAST LIBERTY LUTHERAN CHURCH, 1910. The congregation of Christ Evangelical Lutheran Church, founded in 1869, built this church at Beatty and Margaretta Streets in 1910. They merged with Bethany Evangelical Lutheran (founded 1888), which was located at North Highland Avenue and Kirkwood Street to form East Liberty Lutheran. A new church of modern design was completed in 1968 at Penn Avenue and St. Clair Street.

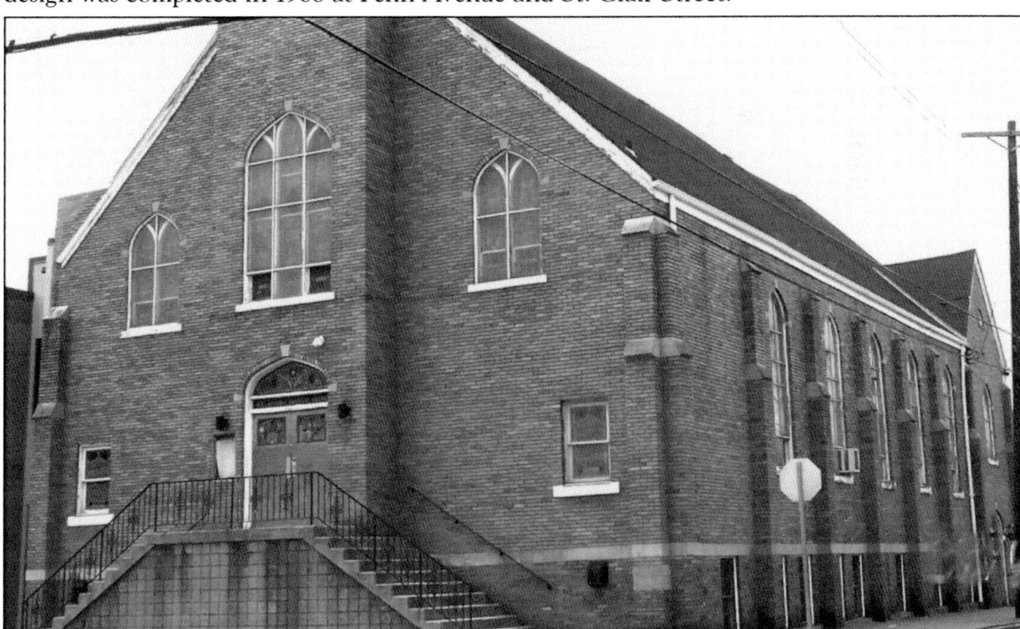

MOUNT ARARAT BAPTIST CHURCH, 1916. First located at Penn Avenue and Beatty Street, this church moved to a building on Auburn Street, which is now Gaines Funeral Home. The congregation moved to its present site, Paulson Avenue and Mayflower Street, in 1917. In 1950, a community center was begun at Paulson Avenue and Auburn Street. The present and larger adjoining church was built in 1991, and the congregation has continued to grow.

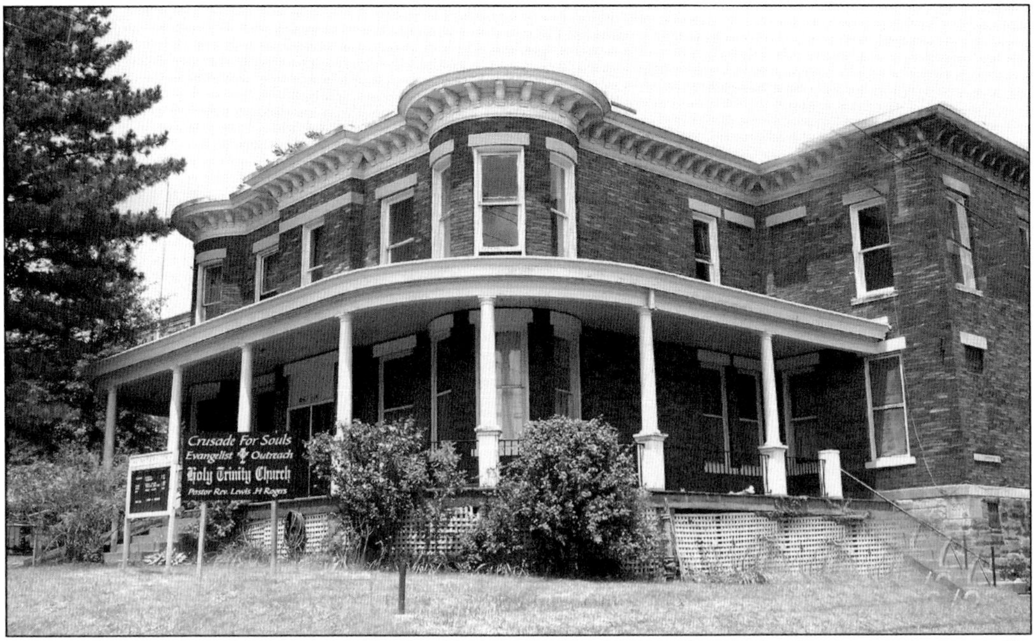

HOLY TRINITY CHURCH, 1900. This building at Lemington and Lincoln Avenues was originally the Home for Aged and Infirm Colored Women, the first home for elderly black women in western Pennsylvania. It had 21 rooms, six baths, and a hospital ward. It is now occupied by Holy Trinity Baptist Church.

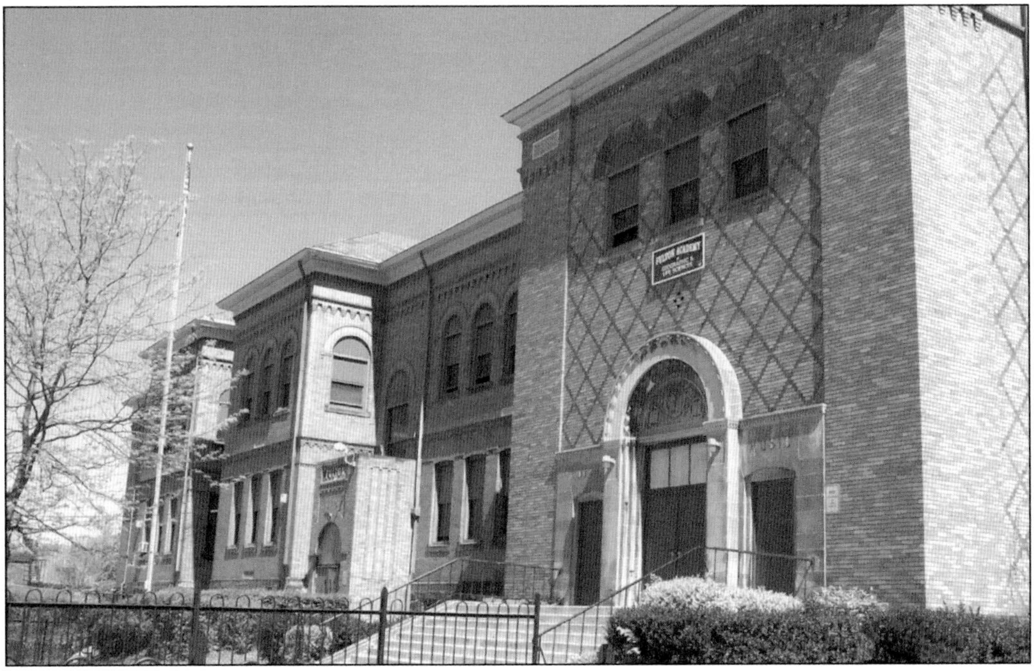

FULTON ELEMENTARY SCHOOL, 1893. This school was named for George Plumer Fulton, a member of the prominent local family who had been principal of Hiland Elementary School. Now a magnet school, it stands at Hampton and North St. Clair Streets, serving as the Fulton Academy of Geographic and Life Sciences and the Fulton French Academy.

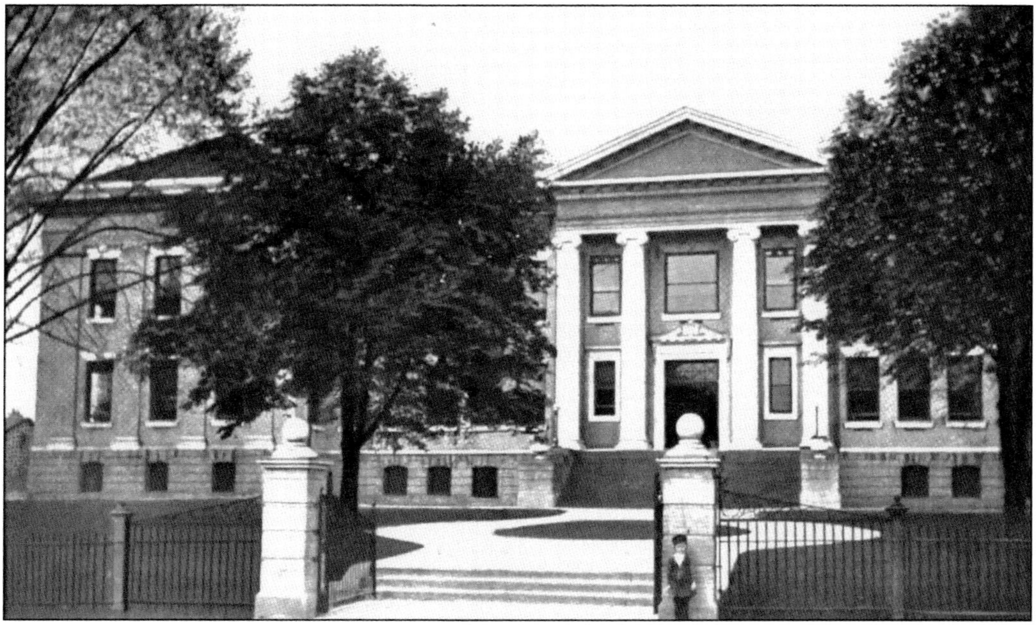

MARGARETTA ELEMENTARY SCHOOL, 1902. This school, located at Beatty and Margaretta Streets, replaced the early Hiland Elementary School, built in 1879, that stood at the same site.

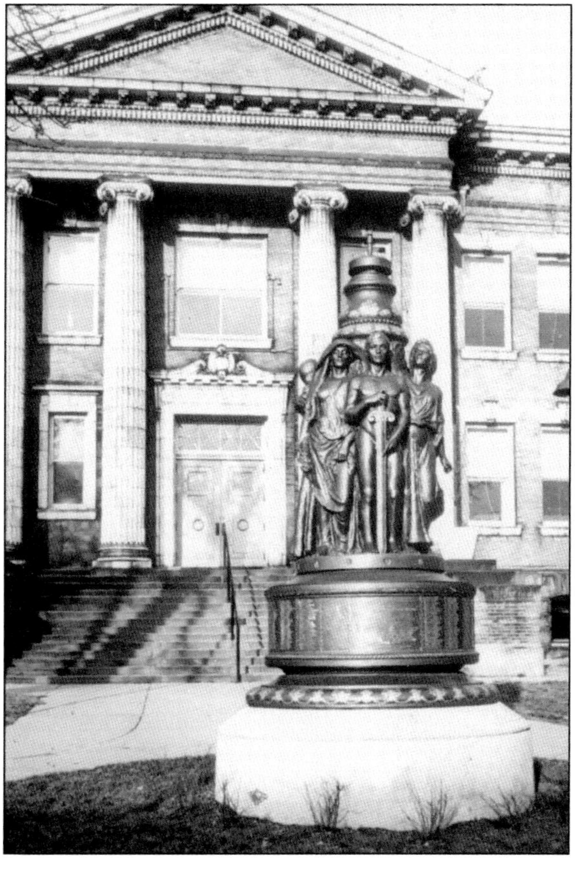

PEABODY HIGH SCHOOL, 1911. Peabody was the first high school in the East End. It is located on North Highland Avenue at East Liberty Boulevard (formerly Margaretta Street) and incorporates Margaretta Elementary School. Named for prominent physician Dr. Benjamin Peabody (1825–1910), it established an outstanding record in the quality and number of its graduates who became famous. The building was remodeled to its current configuration in 1974–1978.

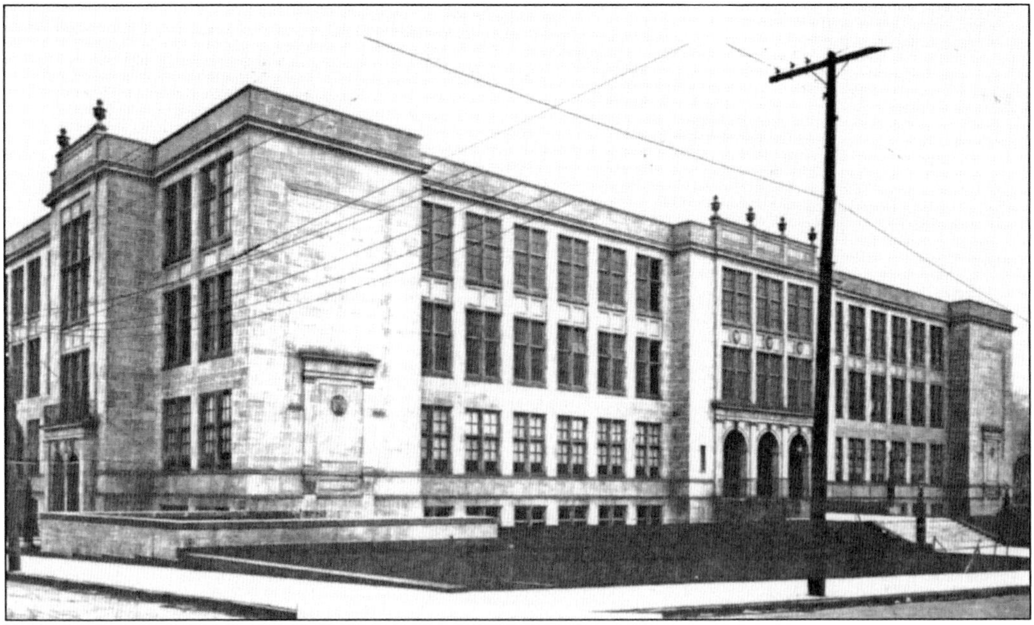

GEORGE WESTINGHOUSE HIGH SCHOOL, 1925. Faced with Indiana limestone, this school on North Murtland Avenue contains 40 classrooms on seven acres and includes a swimming pool, gymnasium, and athletic fields. Football teams coached by Pete Dimperio won the city championship 22 times and were cochampions three times.

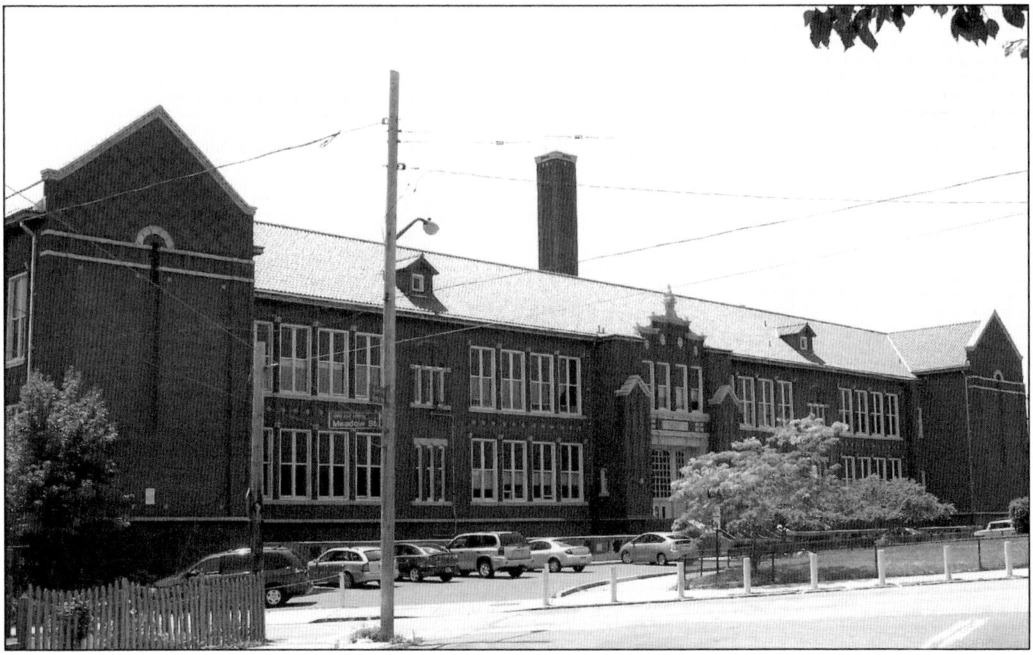

DILWORTH ELEMENTARY SCHOOL, 1915. This elegant building at Stanton Avenue at Meadow Street was designed by Vrydaugh and Wolfe, echoing European school designs of the times. It is on the National Register of Historic Places. The school is named for John and Mary Dilworth, who donated the land. It has an innovative "edible schoolyard" that provides opportunities for children to grow vegetables on school property.

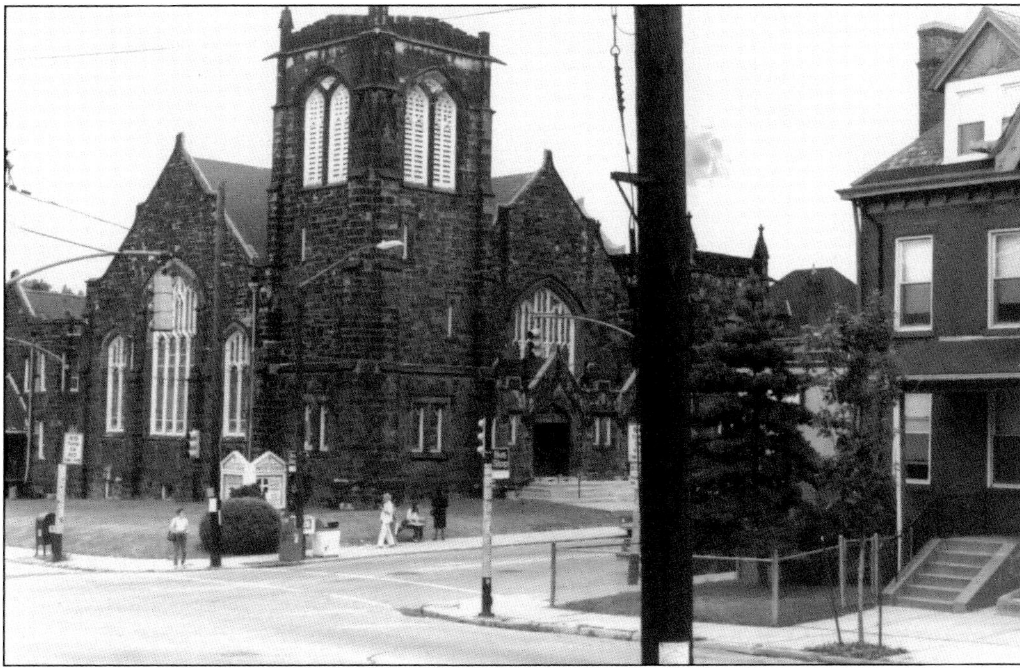

Union Project, 1903. Originally built as the Second United Presbyterian Church of Pittsburgh and subsequently housing the Union Baptist Church, this structure at Stanton and North Negley Avenues has undergone extensive renovations to serve as the home of the Union Project. Founded in 2001 by a group of faith-based young people, the project provides the East End neighborhood with a gathering and working space for artists, teachers, and community builders.

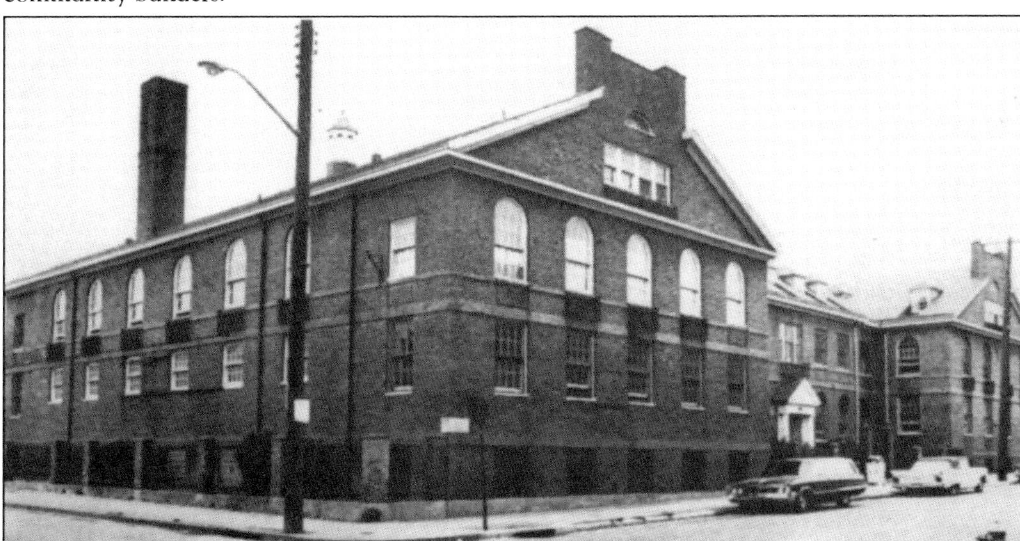

Kingsley House, 1923. Founded in 1893 by George Hodges, rector of Calvary Episcopal Church, this neighborhood center was located at Larimer Avenue and Auburn Street from 1923 to 1978. The new Kingsley Association Community Center, completed in 2005, is located at Frankstown Avenue and East Liberty Boulevard. Managed by a nonsectarian board, it continues to offer a variety of social services as well as athletic and educational programs.

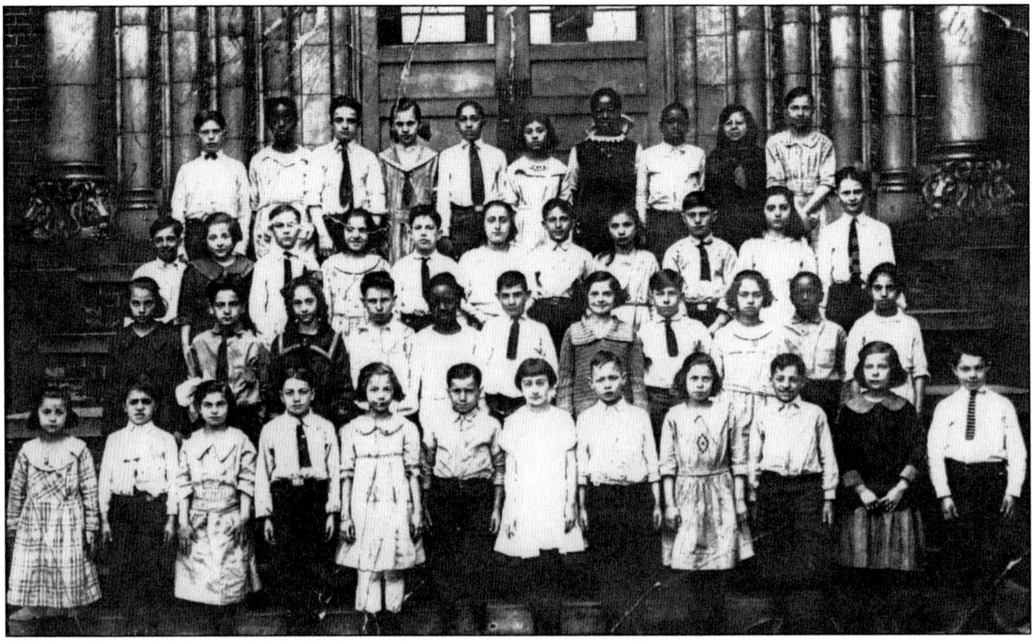

STUDENTS AT LARIMER SCHOOL, 1919. This elementary school has been closed.

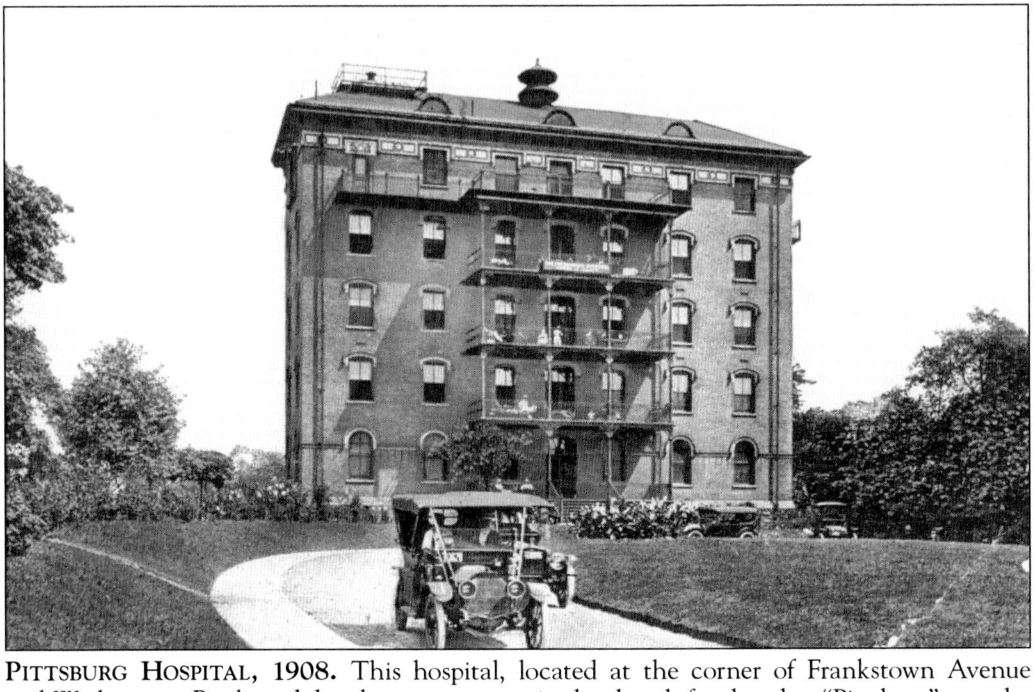

PITTSBURG HOSPITAL, 1908. This hospital, located at the corner of Frankstown Avenue and Washington Boulevard, has been a community landmark for decades. "Pittsburg" was the accepted spelling at the time of its construction. Its predecessor institution, Charity Hospital, was located on Collins Avenue. The 1908 building has been extensively expanded and remodeled.

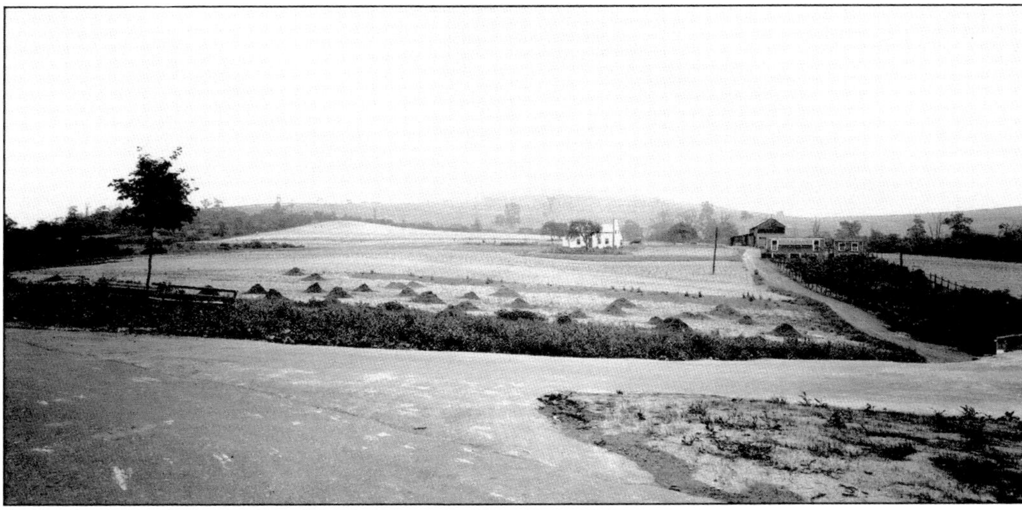

TUBERCULOSIS HOSPITAL, 1925. In 1912, deaths from tuberculosis numbered 798. This hospital complex, built on 100 acres of the former Leech Farm, had as many as 10 buildings. The main building was completed in 1915 and operated by the City of Pittsburgh for the control and prevention of tuberculosis. Great public controversy surrounded this use of the property that had been originally bought by Edward Bigelow for public park use.

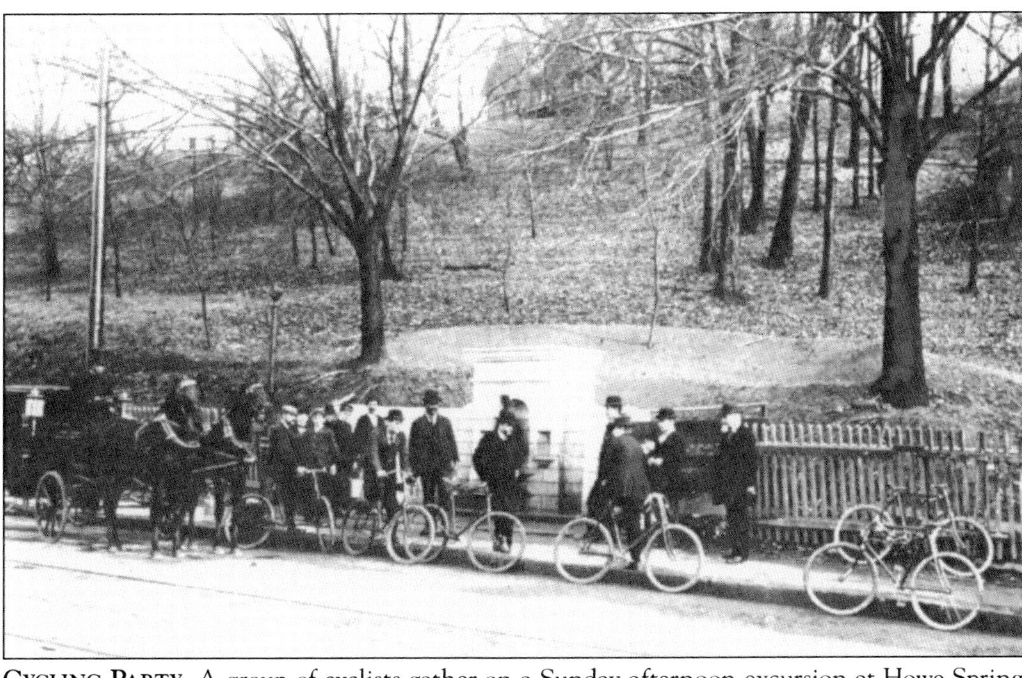

CYCLING PARTY. A group of cyclists gather on a Sunday afternoon excursion at Howe Springs on Fifth Avenue at Highland. Cycling clubs were important institutions during the cycling craze of the late 19th century and lobbied effectively for improved roads in the area.

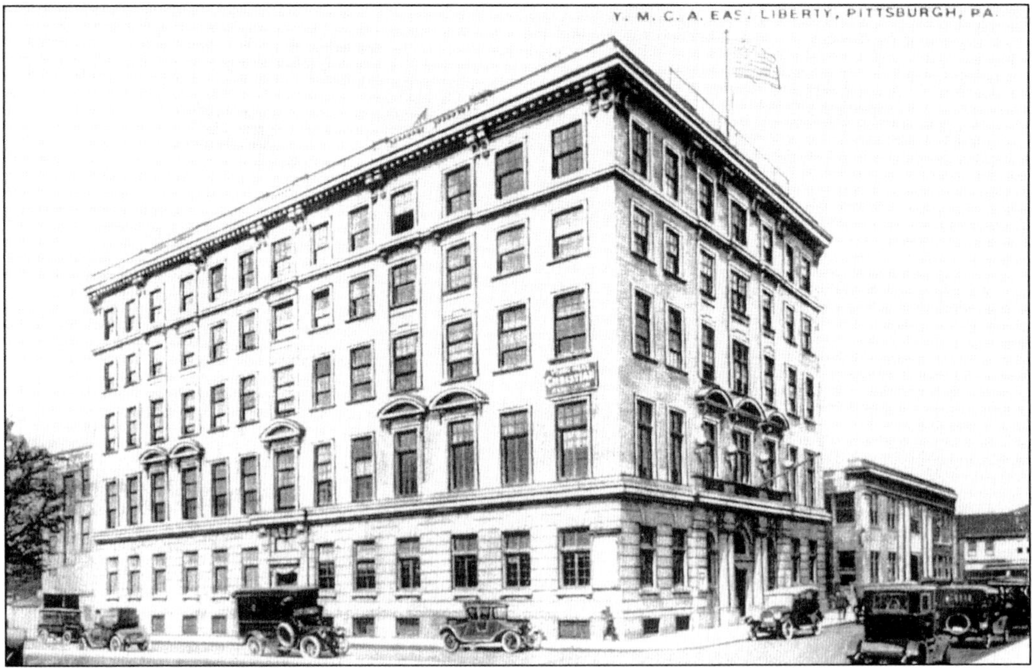

YMCA, 1910. Organized at the East Liberty Presbyterian Church in 1858, the YMCA's first permanent quarters were in the City Deposit Bank. In 1889, it was given the free use of two floors in Liberty Hall, owned by Charles Lockhart. The five-story structure on South Whitfield Street, pictured here, was dedicated in 1910. It currently houses a private charter elementary school. Plans to renovate the building are being developed.

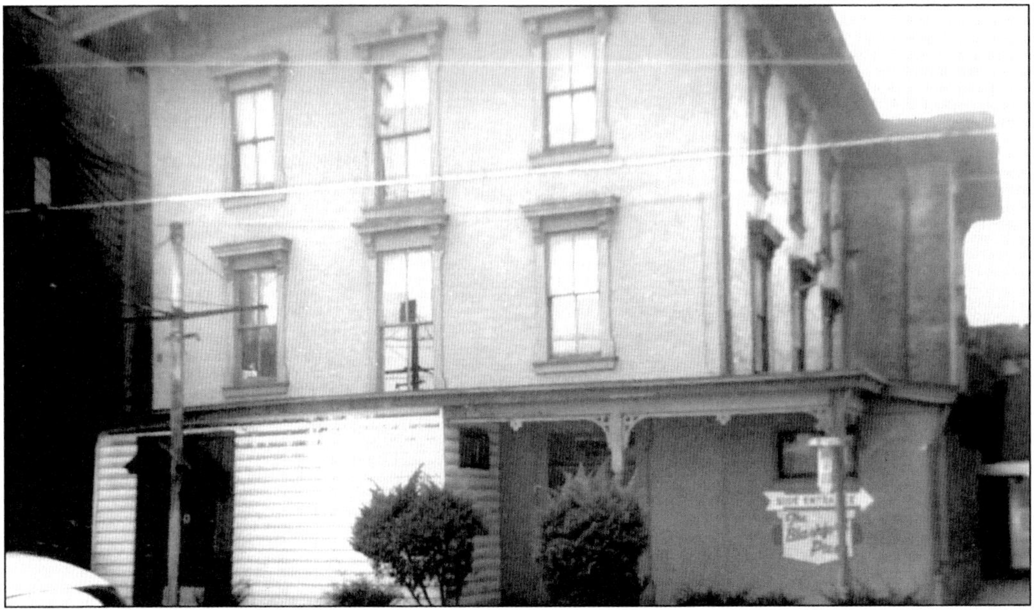

YWCA, 1893. The East Liberty YWCA, the first one in Pittsburgh, was organized in 1875 in a private home and met in various churches. In 1893, it moved to this location at Collins Avenue and Palma Way, renovating the old three-story Laclede Hotel on the site where David Kuhn's gristmill formerly stood.

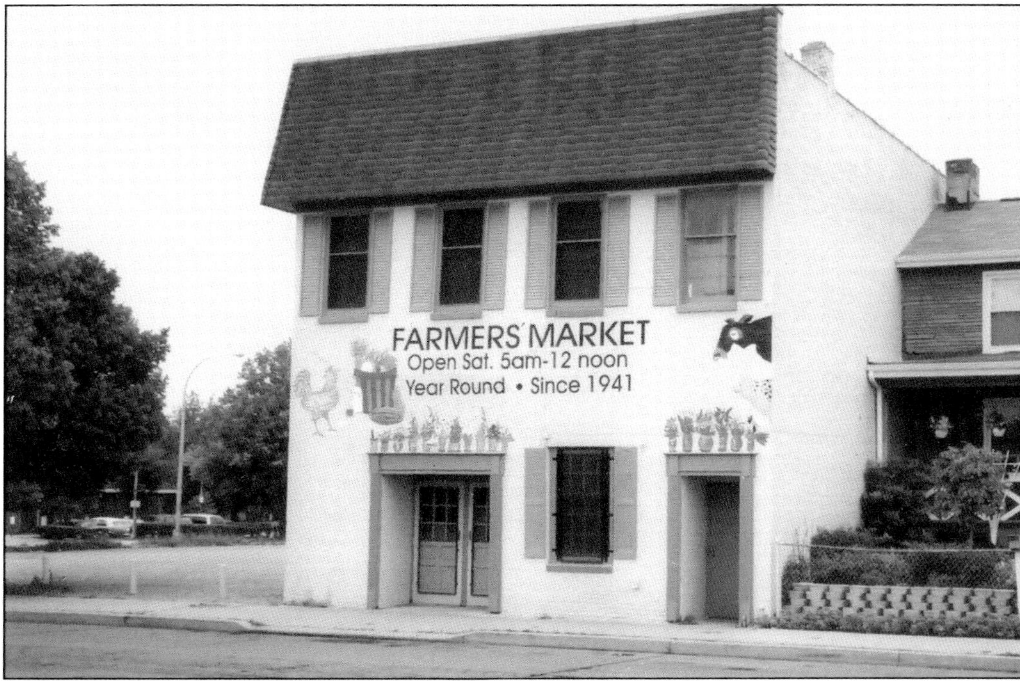

FARMERS' MARKET, 1941. This community market, which occupies its own building, has been in continuous existence since its founding by several area farmers, including some whose families continue to serve the public at this same location each Saturday morning throughout the year. Some of the farmers have been participating in the market for four generations.

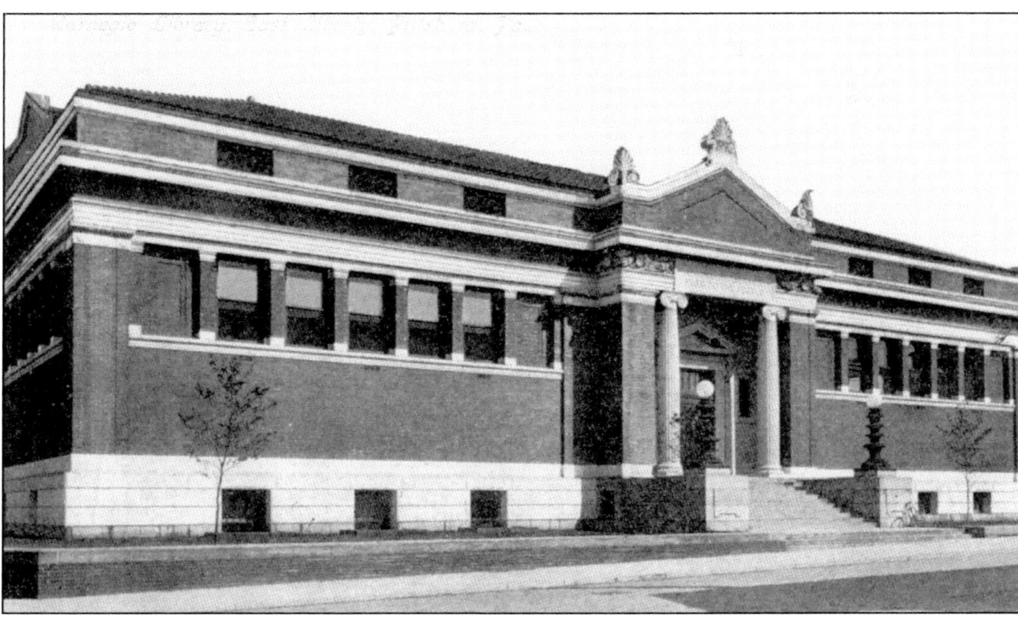

CARNEGIE LIBRARY, 1905. Located at Larimer Avenue and Station Street, this was the sixth neighborhood library branch built in Pittsburgh with funds donated by Andrew Carnegie. In 1933, Mary Shaw Mahronic painted two murals under WPA auspices. In 1969, it was demolished as part of the redevelopment project and relocated to a new building on South Whitfield Street.

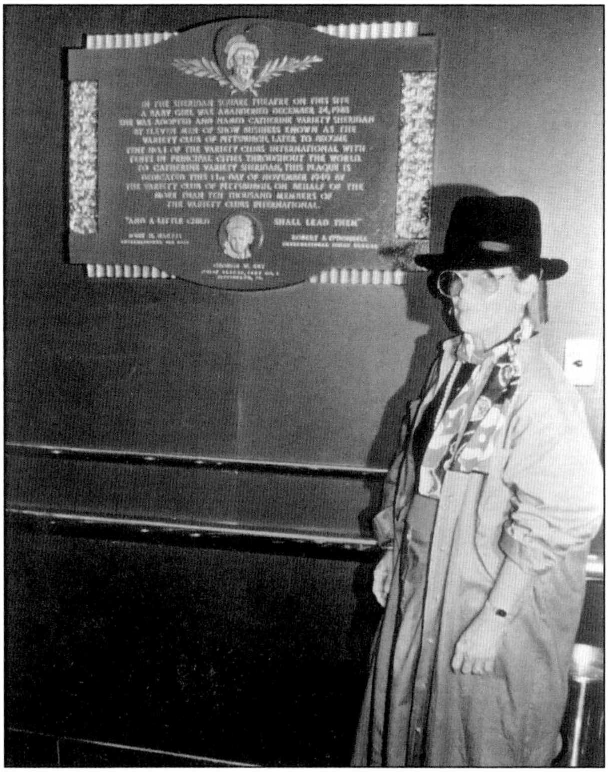

CATHERINE VARIETY SHERIDAN, 1949. A baby girl was abandoned at the Sheridan Square Theatre on Penn Avenue on December 24, 1928. Adopted by 11 men of show business known as the Variety Club of Pittsburgh, she was named Catherine Variety Sheridan. She is shown here as an adult standing in front of a commemorative plaque.

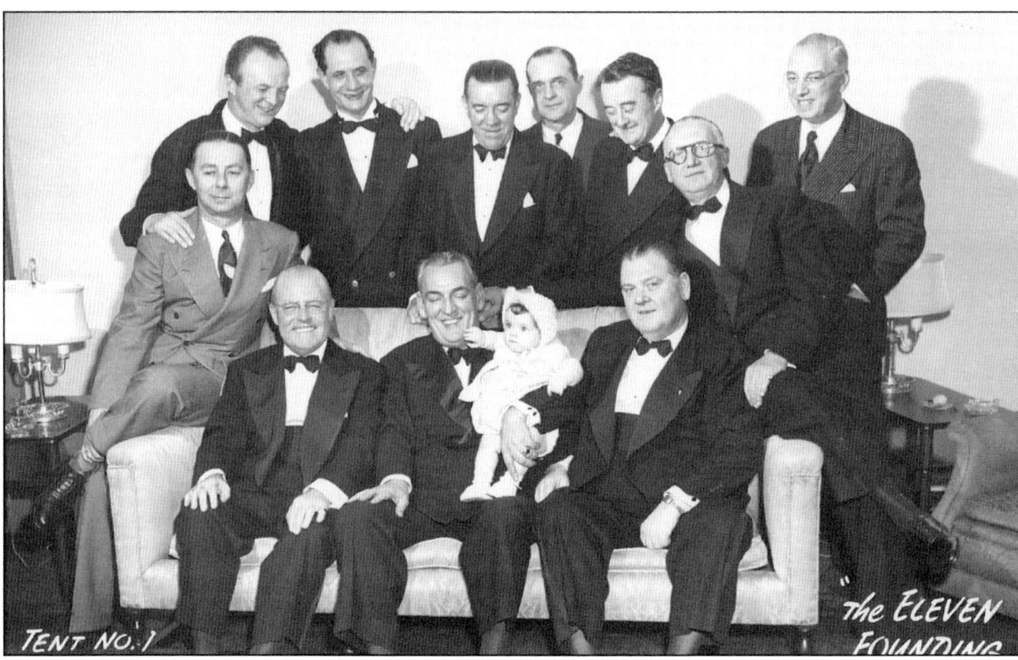

PITTSBURGH VARIETY CLUB, 1927. This photograph shows the 11 men who, as members of the Variety Club of Pittsburgh, took responsibility for Sheridan's upbringing. The Pittsburgh club has grown to Variety Club International with 57 clubs and more than 15,000 volunteers to fund clinics, hospitals, and training schools for needy and disabled children.

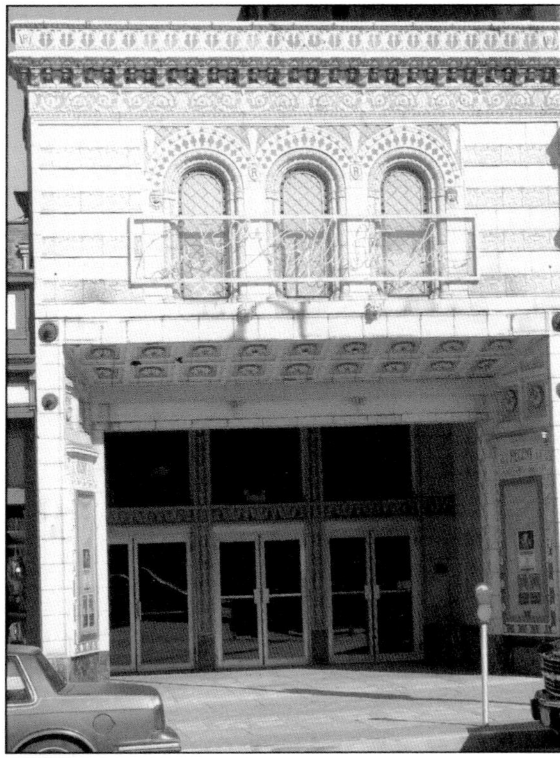

KELLY-STRAYHORN THEATRE, c. 1914. Originally called the Regent Theatre, this is the sole survivor of the eight movie houses along Penn Avenue. It reopened in 1992, after being completely refurbished as a community performing arts center and was renamed for dancer Gene Kelly and composer Billy Strayhorn. A photographic display of 67 local members of the Gallery of Stars is mounted in the lobby.

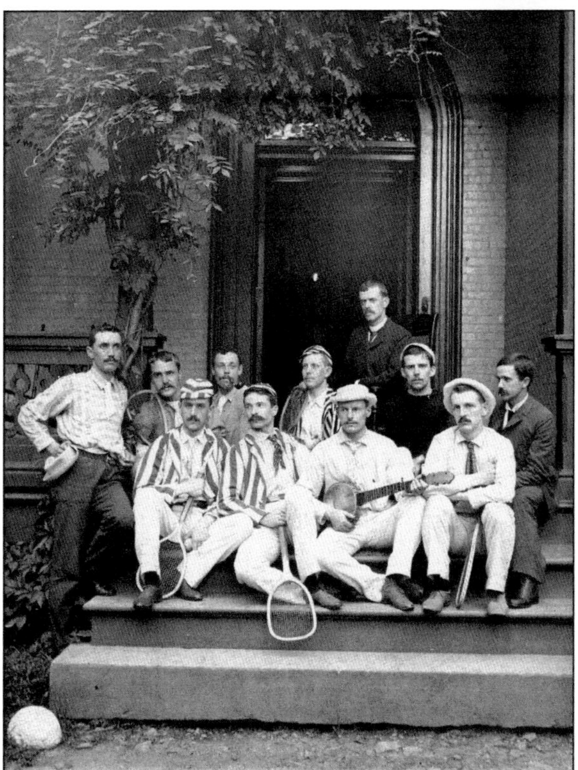

MEMBERS OF THE AMBER CLUB, c. 1900. The Amber Club was founded in 1869 by George Westinghouse to serve as a meeting place and boarding house for unmarried, male engineers employed at the Westinghouse Airbrake Company and later for unmarried professionals generally. It was located originally on Highland Avenue and later moved to Murtland and Howe Streets in the East End. The club disbanded in the 1960s.

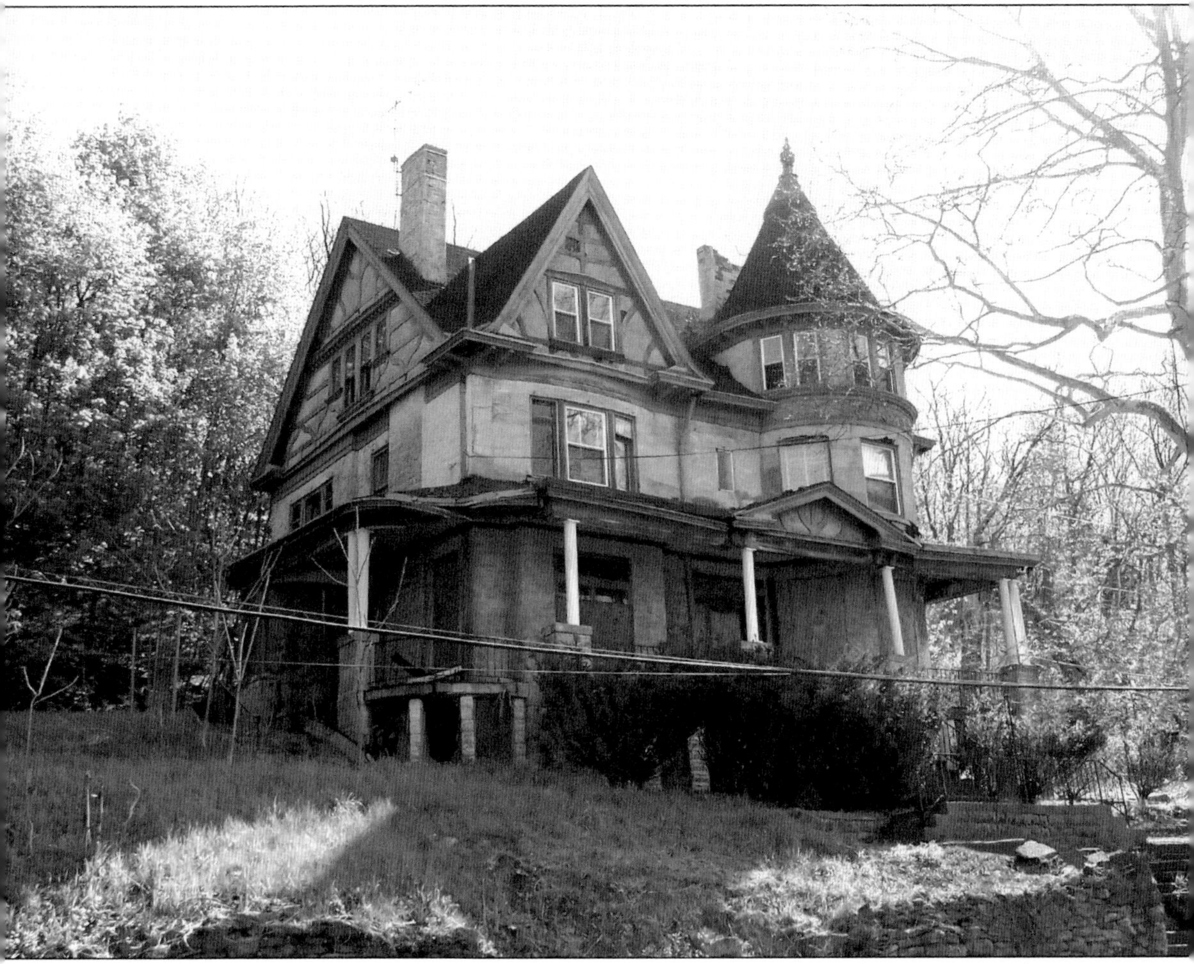

NATIONAL NEGRO OPERA COMPANY, 1941. This 13-room, 1894 house on Apple Avenue was the first home of this company. Organized in 1941 by Mary Cardwell Dawson, it ceased performances upon her death in 1962. The house has been rented to a number of prominent persons such as Roberto Clemente and Lena Horne. Plans are underway to restore it to its former beauty and reactivate its musical heritage.

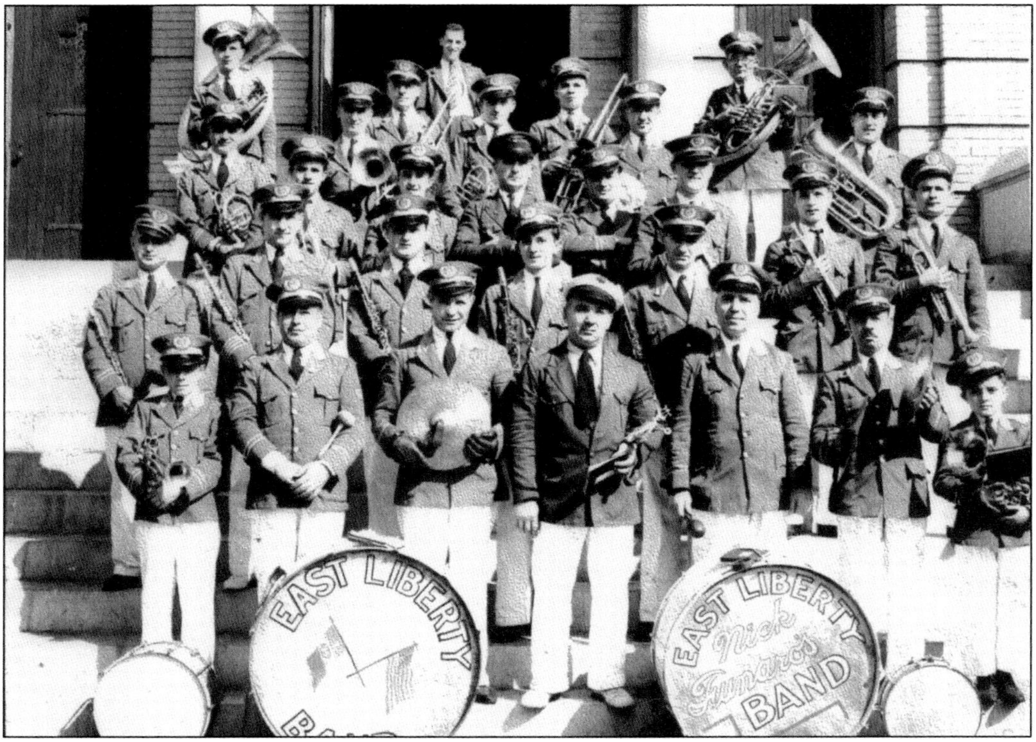

ITALIAN BAND, 1940S. This group played for all major events in the Larimer neighborhood, including festivals honoring St. Rocco, the patron saint of healing in the Italian community.

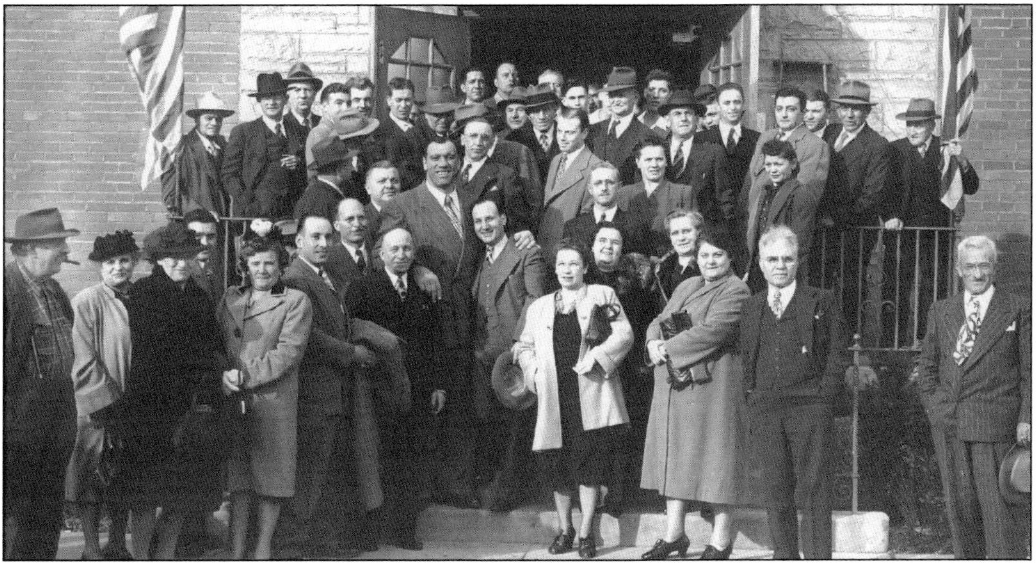

BENEFICIAL SOCIETY OF NORTH ITALY, 1947. This society was formed in 1930. Members are pictured in front of their new lodge on Nelson Street at its dedication. The Larimer district was settled by Italians from Abruzzi and elsewhere in the early 1900s. The society served to help immigrants assimilate as well as preserve their traditions. It has disbanded because of declining membership. The building is no longer occupied. The tall man at left of center is famed boxer Primo Carnera.

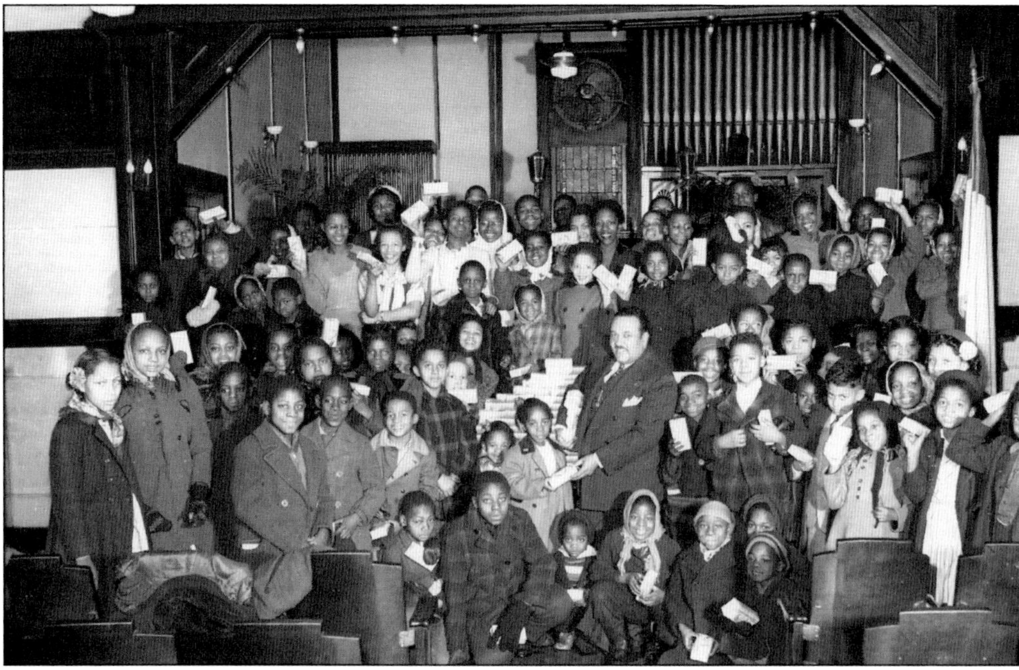

GEORGE W. GAINES, CHRISTMAS, C. 1940–1950. A major annual community event occurred at the Gaines Funeral Home on 220 Auburn Street. George Gaines passed out chocolates at a Christmas party each year for local school children. The funeral home is still in operation at the same site.

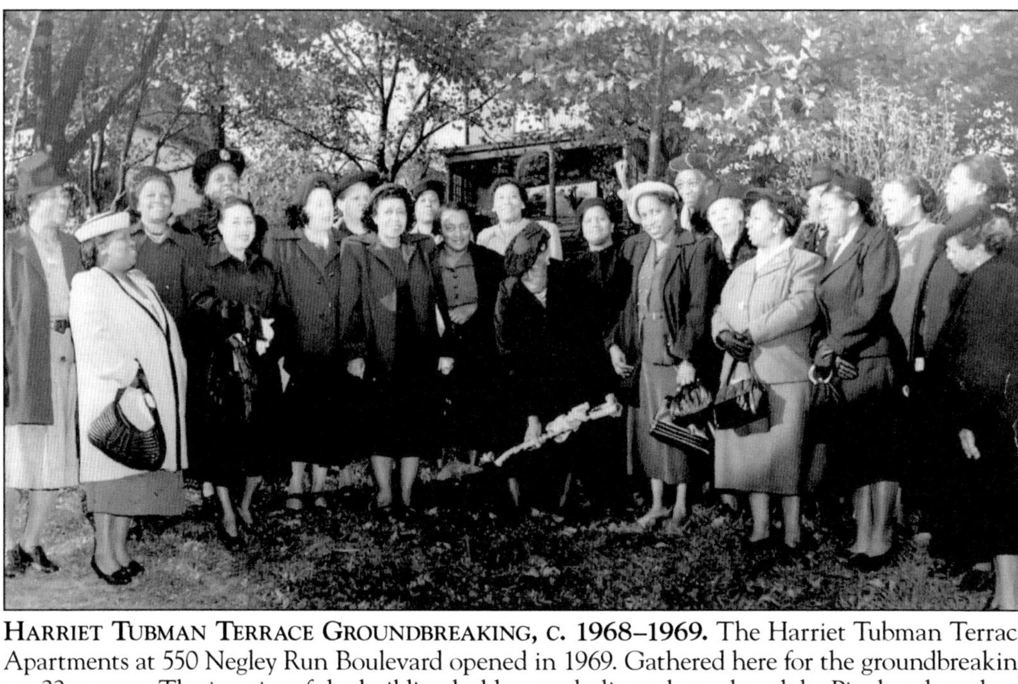

HARRIET TUBMAN TERRACE GROUNDBREAKING, C. 1968–1969. The Harriet Tubman Terrace Apartments at 550 Negley Run Boulevard opened in 1969. Gathered here for the groundbreaking are 22 women. The interior of the building holds a symbolic sculptural work by Pittsburgh sculptor Thaddeus Mosely. Harriet Tubman was a runaway slave who led hundreds of slaves to freedom along the Underground Railroad and was a formidable leader in the Abolitionist movement.

Seven

Highland Park and Zoo

Highland Park is located on the site of the 1778 land purchase of pioneer and patriot Alexander Negley, which he farmed and named Fertile Bottom. The 1850s home of James McCully stood near the Highland Avenue entrance, evidenced by the remnants of a well. Enterprising Charles Lockhart was employed by McCully and became a business partner, constructing one of the first oil refineries (1861) at the foot of Washington Boulevard with storage tanks on the bluffs near the present swimming pool—the embryo of the Standard Oil Company.

The Pittsburgh Water Commission purchased the McCully hilltop property for a reservoir, which was completed in 1879; a second reservoir was functioning by 1903. Brilliant Reservoir (now Carnegie Lake) was constructed as a halfway station to pump water from the river to the upper reservoir. When stronger pumps eliminated its need, it was converted to recreational use and named Carnegie Lake. In 1889, the city allocated the land around the reservoirs as a public park.

Pittsburgh Public Works director Edward M. Bigelow spent years, though not without controversy, in attempts to acquire land for park use. Two communities once existed in what became Highland Park and were acquired by Bigelow, piece by piece, through acquisition and condemnation.

Bigelow engaged European-trained sculptor Giuseppe Moretti to adorn the entrances at both Highland and Stanton Avenues. The layout of the drives and paths in the park is attributed to Wesley S. Wakefield; the planting and reforestation of the former farmlands were designed by William Falconer.

In an 1895 report on the newly established parks of the city, chronicler John M. Kelly describes them as "been made to blossom as the rose . . . [becoming] the pleasure grounds of thousands daily . . . [and that there] is not a prettier spot than beautiful Highland Park with its magnificent views in all directions." Today the park holds the acclaimed Kid's Kingdom and Pittsburgh Zoo and PPG Aquarium—one of only six major zoo and aquarium combinations in the country. Recreational facilities still abound in this vibrant "pleasure ground."

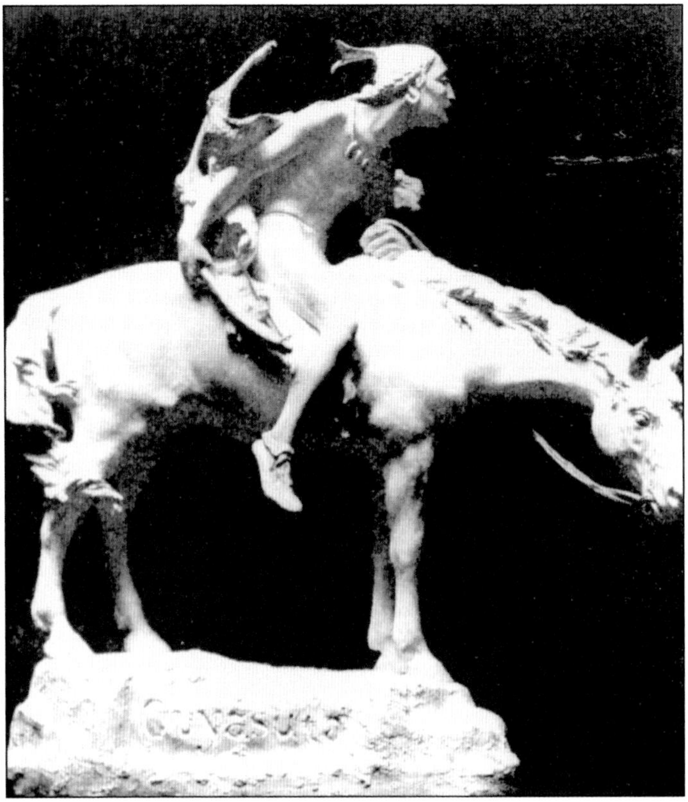

GUYASUTA, THE MINGO CHIEF. This equestrian rendition of Guyasuta, modeled by Giuseppe Moretti, was to stand on a cliff in Highland Park commanding a wide view of the Allegheny River, its pose of a scout watching the valley below appropriate for its proposed setting. In 1917, director of public works Edward Bigelow planned this tribute to the Native American leader, but did not live to carry it out.

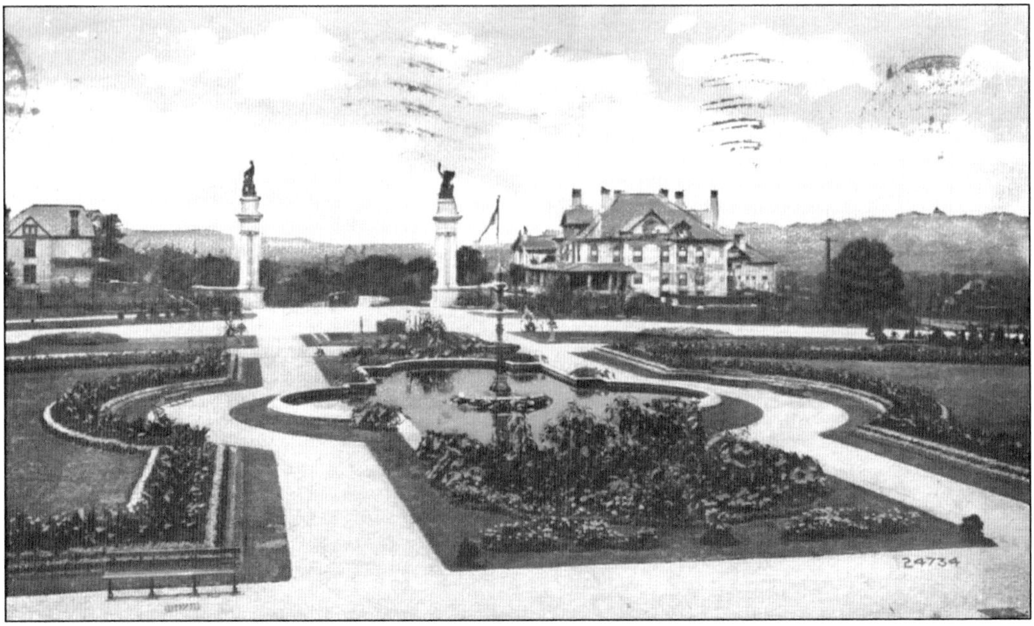

HIGHLAND AVENUE PARK ENTRANCE, C. 1899. This 465-acre park was founded in 1889 by Bigelow, director of Pittsburgh Public Works. On the right is the mansion of William Flinn, one of the leaders of the political machine that ruled Pittsburgh at the time. The mansion was demolished in 1924.

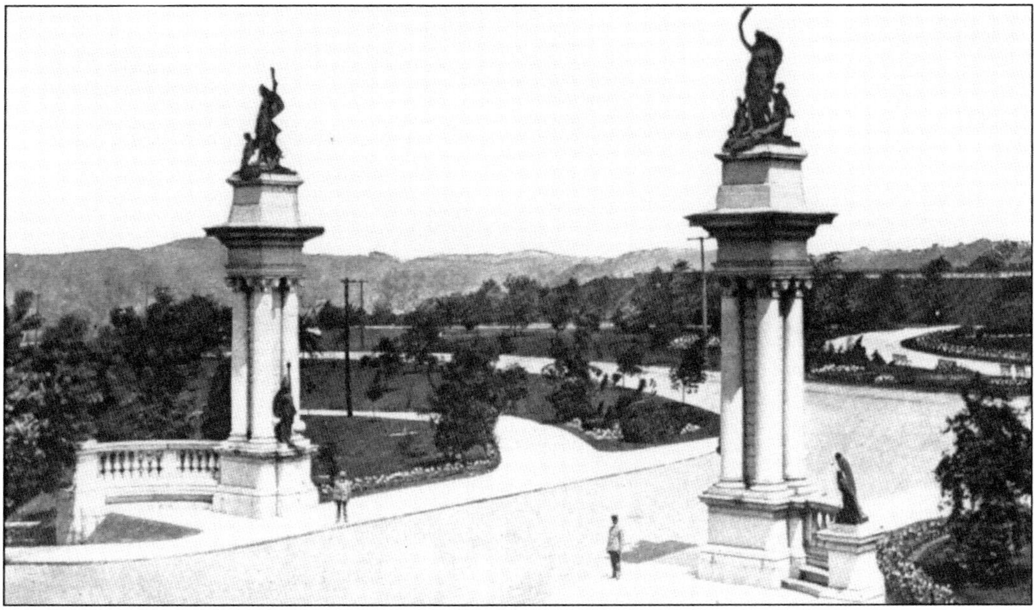

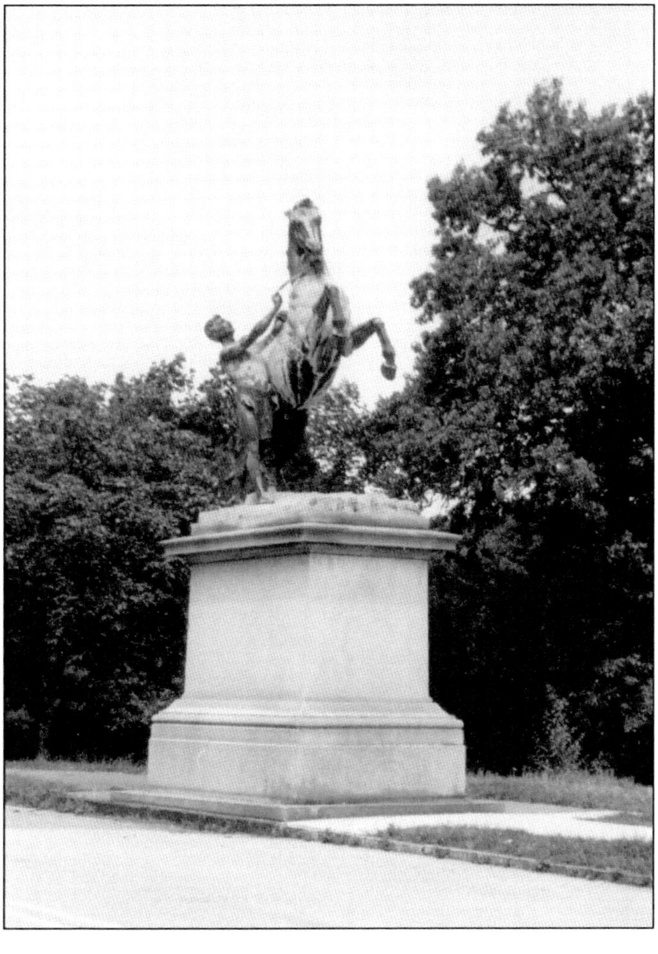

ENTRANCES AT HIGHLAND AND STANTON AVENUES. Bigelow's desire for public improvement and a "city beautiful" that would inspire its inhabitants to moral and civic virtue prompted him to bring New York City sculptor Moretti to Pittsburgh to beautify its public parks. Both the Highland and Stanton Avenue entrances were completed by Moretti, who was trained in Siena and Florence. The neoclassical gates at the Highland Avenue entrance were completed in 1896. The heroic art nouveau bronzes hold lights and gesture welcome. They have been described as copies of "the gates at Munich" and verify America's tendency to turn to Europe for cultural respectability. The Stanton Avenue sculptures, pictured at the right, were completed four years after the main gates (1900) and are modeled after the famous *Horses of Marly* by French sculptor Guillaume Coustou (1677–1746).

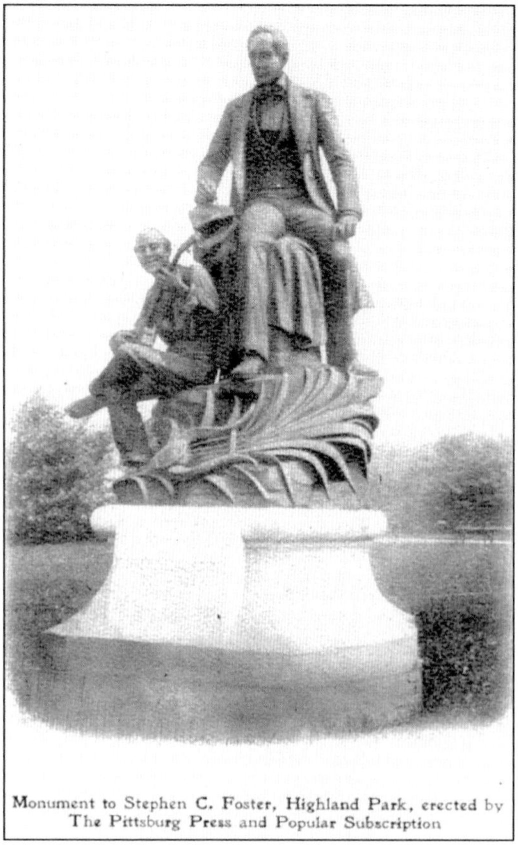

STEPHEN FOSTER MEMORIAL, 1900. When dedicated in Highland Park, 3,000 children from Allegheny City and McKeesport sang Stephen Foster melodies under the direction of Victor Herbert. Nearly 50,000 people lined the Highland Avenue parade route. Marion Foster Welsh of Chicago, Foster's only daughter, unveiled the statue, and Pres. James Buchanan's nieces placed a wreath. After persistent vandalism, this work by Giuseppe Moretti was removed to Oakland in 1944.

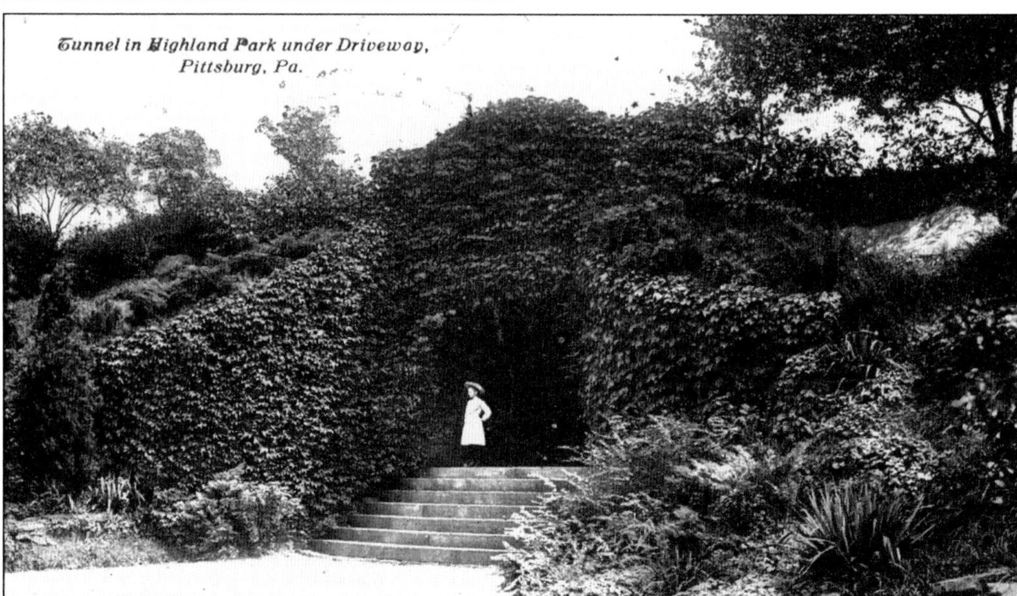

TUNNEL, C. 1910. As signified by the spelling of "Pittsburg," this scene was taken before 1911, when the "h" was restored to the city's name. It shows an ivy-covered stone access under a road in Highland Park.

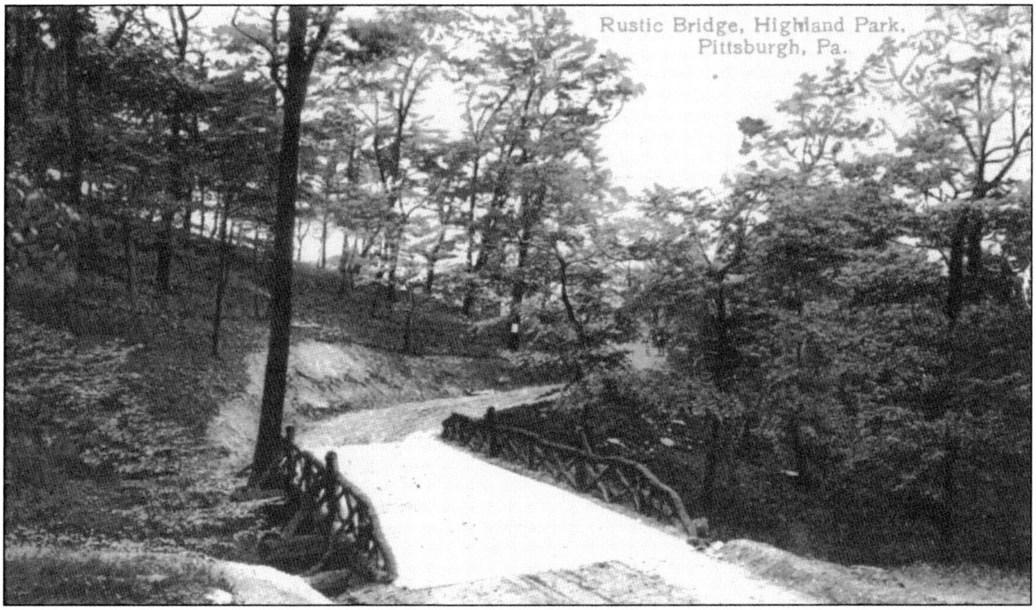

RUSTIC BRIDGE AND RUSTIC SPRING, C. 1910. The "rustic style" advocated by Andrew Jackson Downing (1815–1852) was firmly ensconced in America by the mid-19th century. His publications were filled with designs for rustic work for gardens and porches. Calvert Vaux, along with Frederick Law Olmsted, lavishly incorporated rustic structures and foot bridges in their design of New York's Central Park in 1857. Pittsburgh's parks, established decades later, followed suit with rustic adornments as shown in these pictures. A simple bridge carried a road in the park, and the spring provided a refreshing stopping place for park visitors.

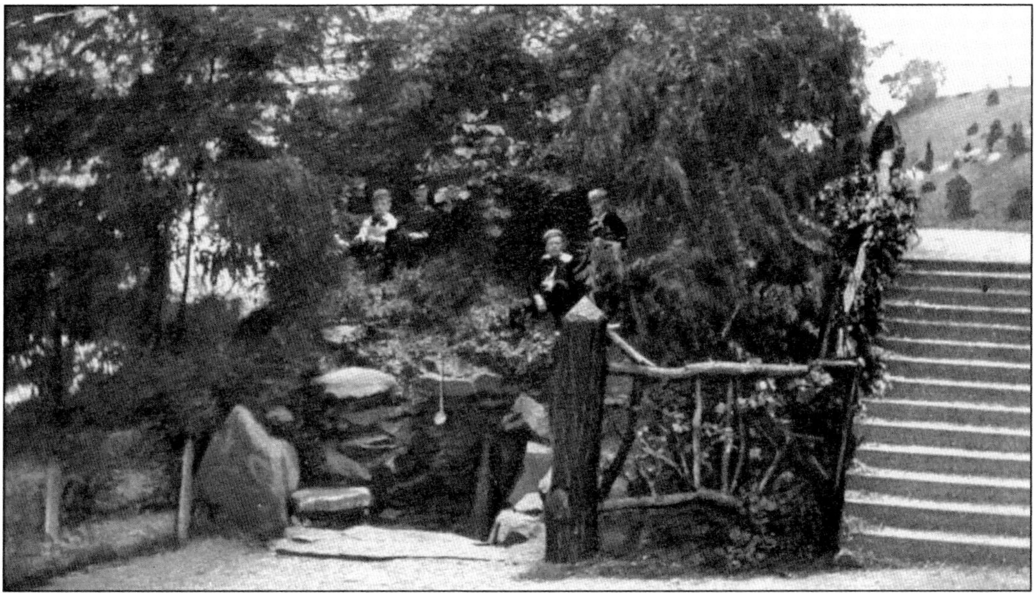

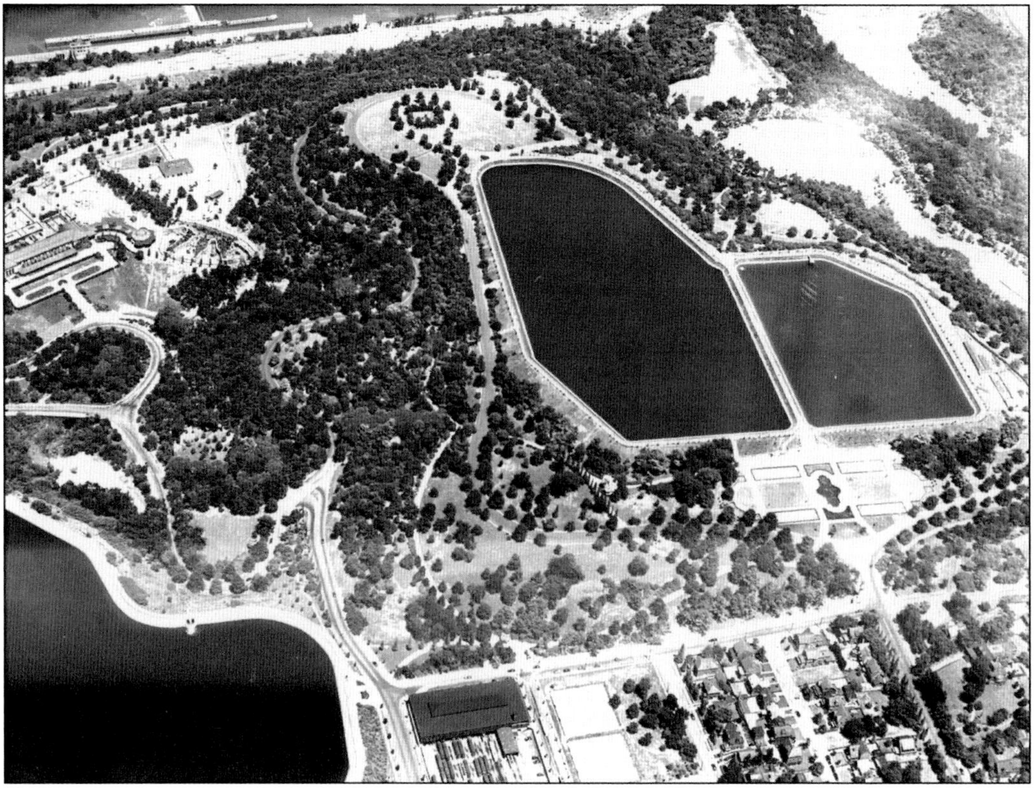

AERIAL VIEW OF HIGHLAND PARK, 1941. This picture, looking north, shows Reservoir No.1 to the right, with Reservoir No. 2 at the lower left. Above it, to the upper left, is the Pittsburgh Zoo. In the distance, at the top, are Allegheny River Boulevard, the Allegheny River, and Lock and Dam No. 5. At the top center is Mount Bigelow at 1,068 feet elevation, and at the bottom center is the trolley car barn, since demolished and replaced in 1962 by the Park Lane high-rise apartment building.

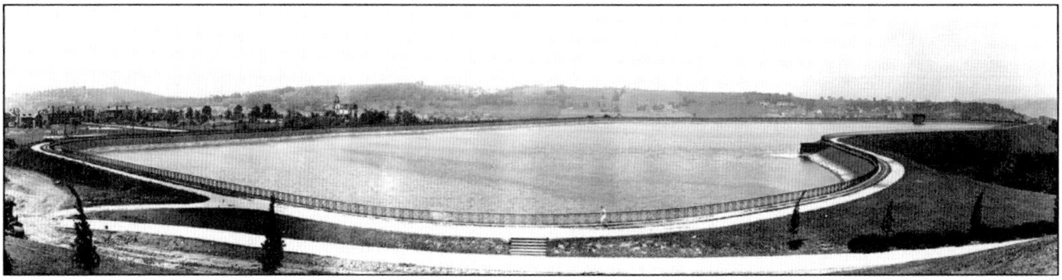

RESERVOIRS. Reservoir No. 1 was built in 1879, and Reservoir No. 2 in 1903. Each has a capacity of 120 million gallons. In this 1927 photograph of Reservoir No. 2, the King mansion can be seen near the center beyond the far shore, as well as other residences along North Negley Avenue. The mile-long walkway around Reservoir No. 1 serves as a favorite recreation spot for runners, joggers, and walkers.

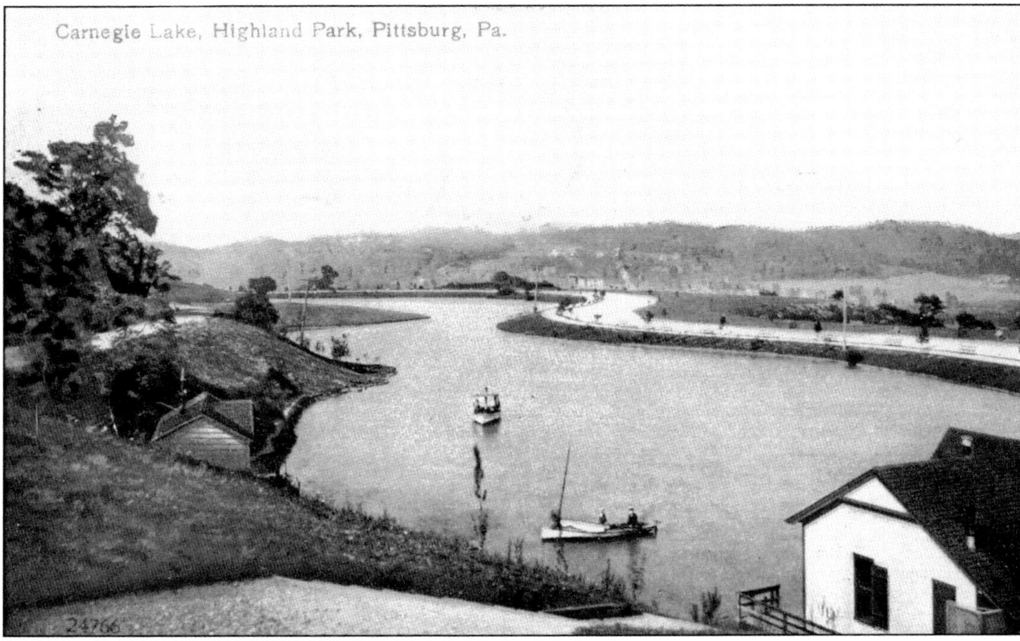

CARNEGIE LAKE, 1909. This lake was originally the Brilliant Reservoir, built to serve as a halfway station for water pumped from the Allegheny River to the upper basin. No longer needed because of improved pumping capability, it was converted to a pleasure lake and named in honor of Andrew Carnegie (1835–1919). In 1932, a portion was taken to make room for the present swimming pool.

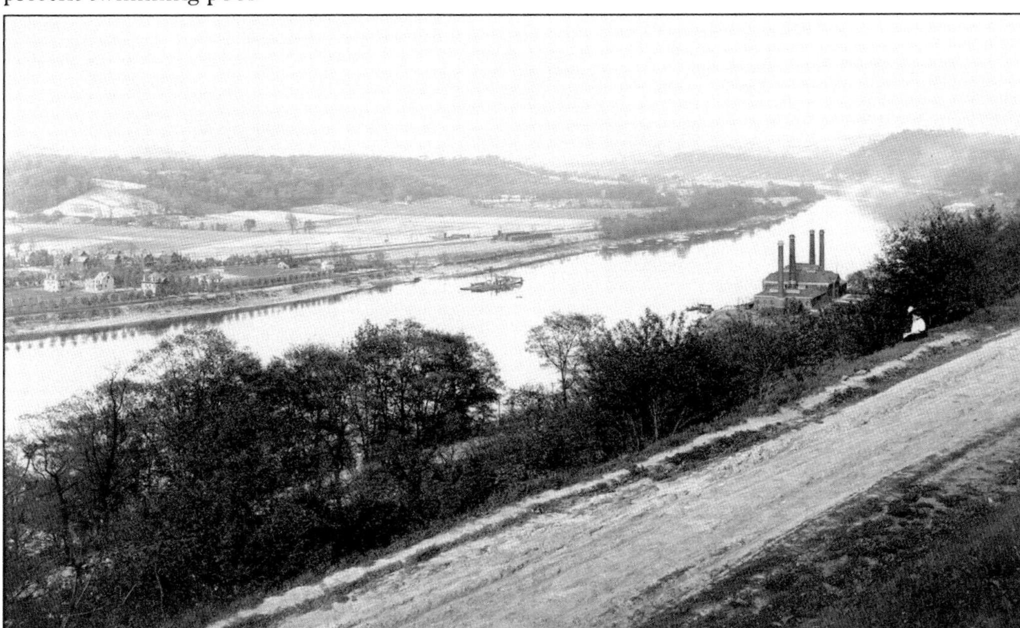

BRILLIANT PUMPING STATION, C. 1900. This station, built in 1879 and located on the south bank of the Allegheny River, pumps municipal water from the city water treatment plant on the opposite side of the river to the Highland Park reservoirs. Across the river is the town of Aspinwall, which was incorporated in 1892

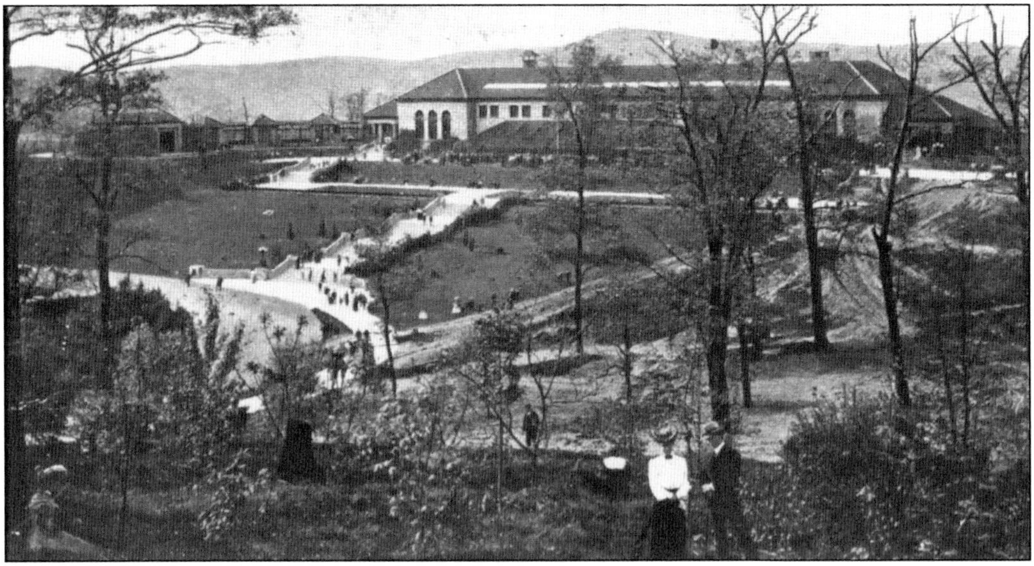

Zoological Garden, 1898. On Christmas Eve 1895, Christopher Magee, political boss and Magee-Women's Hospital founder, gave the city a "zoological garden." Built on 20 acres in Highland Park, it opened on June 14, 1898, with 200 animals that were kept in a large Victorian-style menagerie building. In 1899, Schenley Park's "live animal collection" closed and its 350 animals were sent to the new Highland Park zoo. It was demolished in 1985.

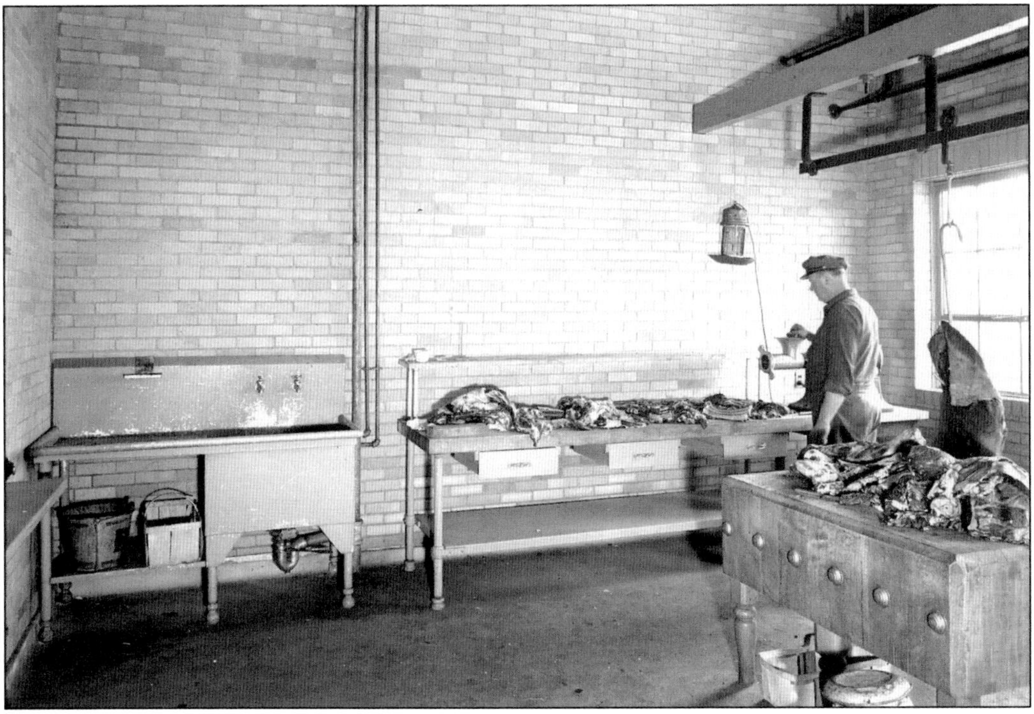

Zoo Butcher Shop, 1941. Changes in the zoo in the 1930s stopped the practice of feeding the large carnivores horse meat from the city's stock of deceased workhorses when a policy of feeding the animals government-inspected beef was instituted. Changes were again made in the 1970s when the zoo reverted to using horse meat because it was more cost effective.

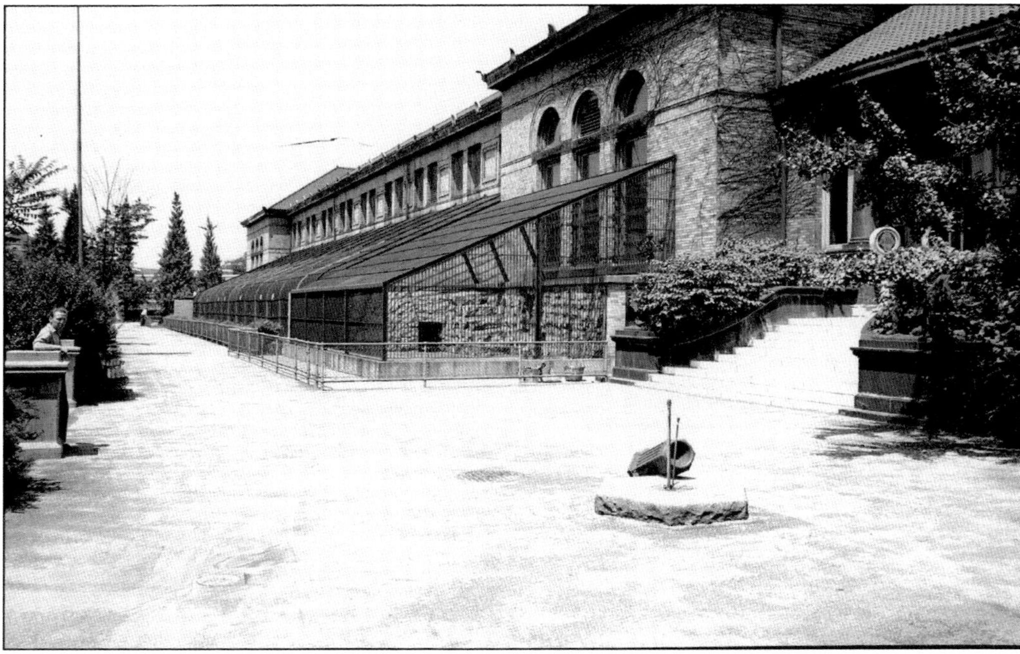

CAT CAGES, 1940. These cages were original to the zoo when it was first opened. Designed by J. L. Silsbee of Chicago, the zoo was first opened in 1898. The cages were in use until the main zoo building was taken down in 1985. Once described as a "Poster Stamp Collection," it had pairs of several different types of cats.

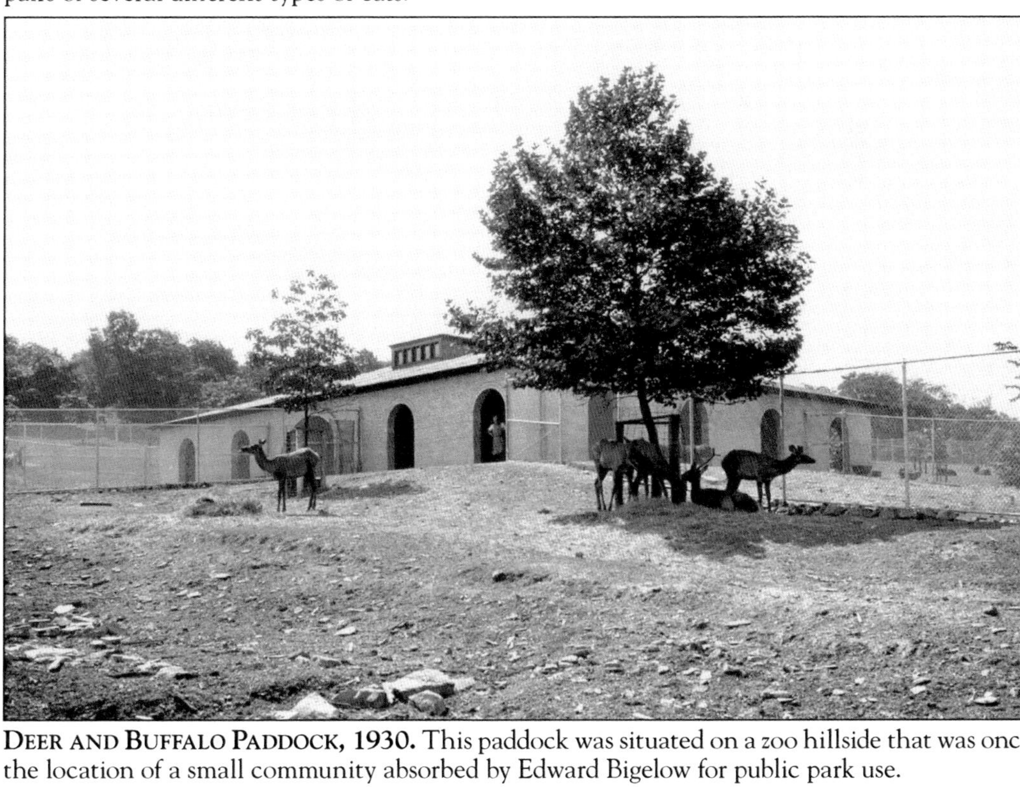

DEER AND BUFFALO PADDOCK, 1930. This paddock was situated on a zoo hillside that was once the location of a small community absorbed by Edward Bigelow for public park use.

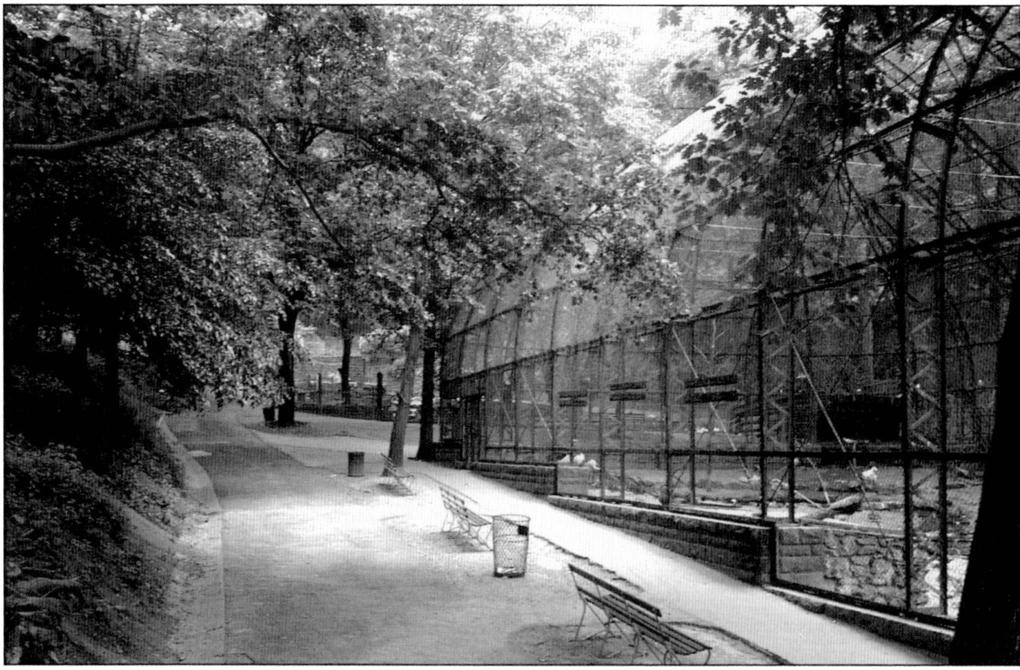

BIRD CAGE, 1961. This former birdcage was part of the early Zoological Garden in Highland Park, as the zoo was first known. It followed the pattern of early ideas of housing animals for public view, now changed to more habitat-friendly presentations throughout the present zoo.

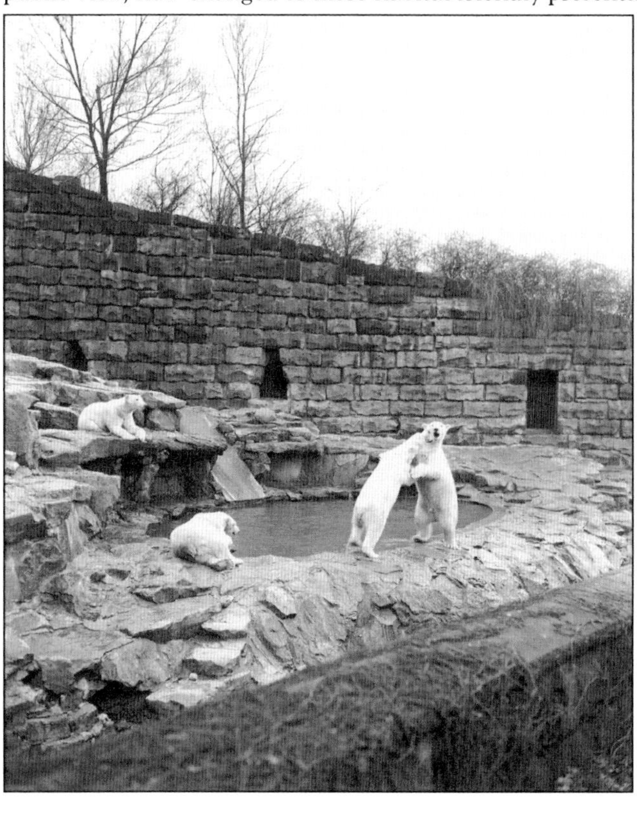

POLAR BEARS, C. 1948–1955. The addition of the outdoor bear exhibits in 1937 began an evolution from the caging of animals to placing them in a more natural environment. A WPA project enabled the construction of a "barless" habitat. Today the transformation continues with more than 4,000 wild animals in areas such as the African Savanna, Asian Forest and indoor Tropical Forest, and a newly opened Polar Bear exhibit.

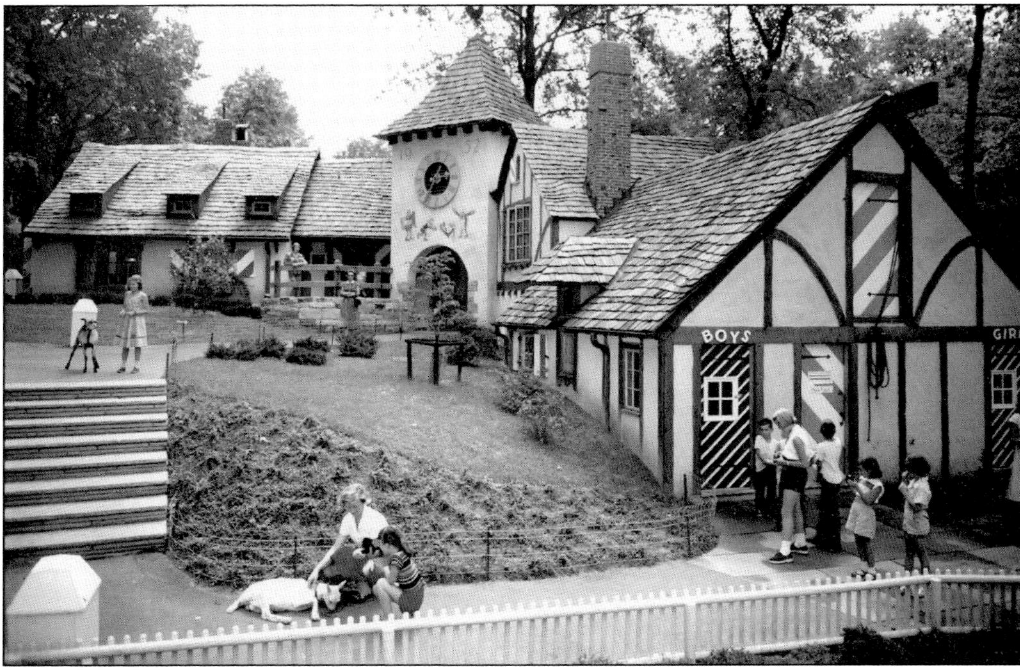

CHILDREN'S ZOO, 1953. Opened in 1949 with a grant from the Sarah Mellon Scaife Foundation, children walked on the spongy tongue of a whale and visited a giant piece of cheese, home to mice. This Mother Goose theme was thought inappropriate for animal exhibition and was abandoned in 1986. A new Kid's Kingdom opened in 1995 and is regarded one of the three top children's zoos in the country.

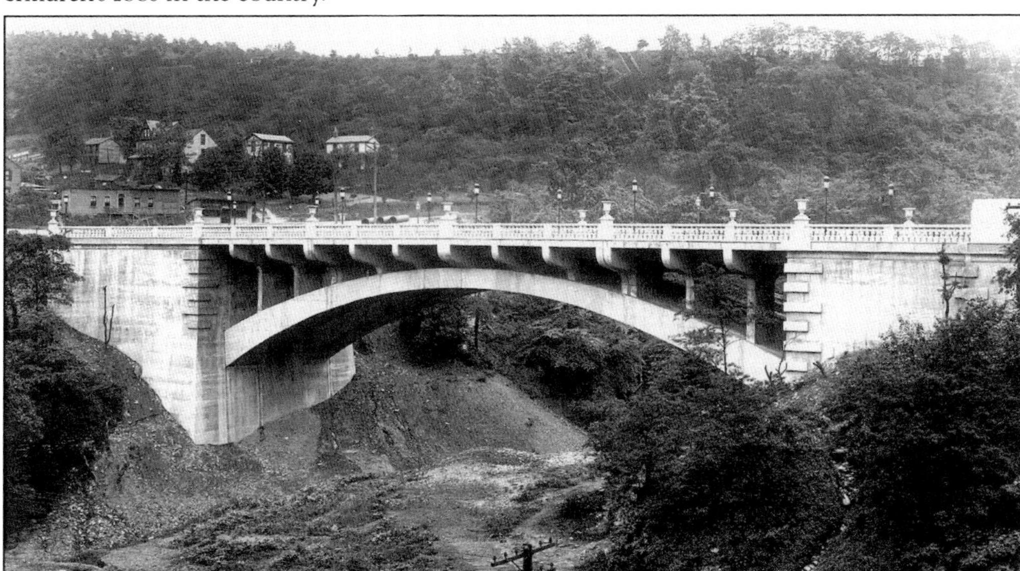

HETH'S RUN BRIDGE, 1914. Marking the northern entrance to Highland Park and the Pittsburgh Zoo, this once picturesque bridge has been ravaged. Heth's Run, which was crossed by a 90-foot high arch, has been filled with rubble. The bridge's most impressive features have been removed, including the carved pieces along the southern side; most of the 14 urns; and all of the handsome ornamental lampposts.

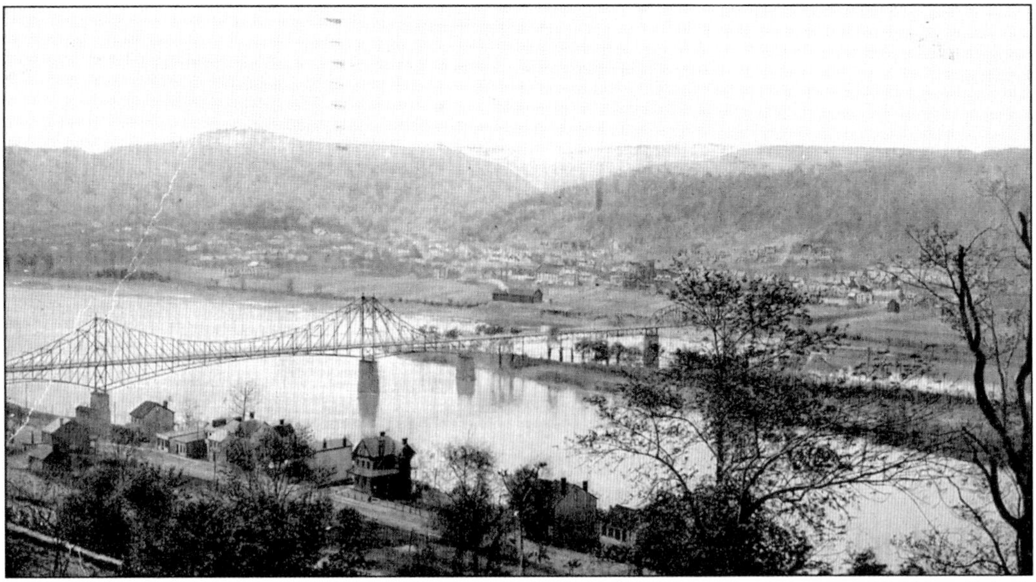

SHARPSBURG BRIDGE, EARLY 1900S. This bridge, built in 1902, connected Highland Park with the community of Sharpsburg on the north shore of the Allegheny River. The bridge was replaced in 1938 with the present Highland Park bridge, 400 feet upstream.

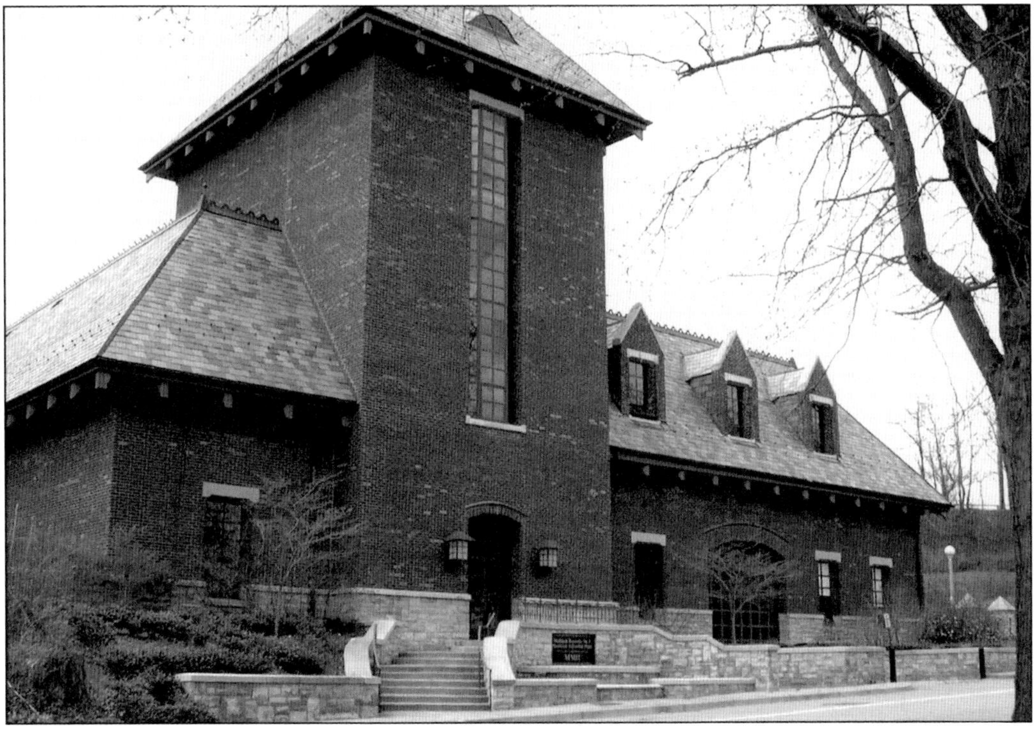

WATER FILTRATION SYSTEM, 2002. This building houses a highly efficient microfiltration plant that purifies 20 million gallons per day of water pumped from Reservoir No. 1 into Pittsburgh's mains. Installing this innovative technology avoided the need to cover the scenic, 18-acre reservoir with a protective rubber membrane to comply with environmental regulations. It is the first major installation of its kind in the United States.

Eight

NOTABLES

Alexander Negley, his son Jacob, and Jacob's son-in-law Thomas Mellon are perhaps the first names to come forth in a roster of notables in the valley. Followed by Andrew W. Mellon and William Larimer Mellon, they helped to build the cornerstones of development in the East Liberty Valley through real estate, road building, transportation ventures, banking, and community enterprises.

In 1861, Charles Lockhart started the commercial oil refinery business in America with his Brilliant Oil Works near the Allegheny River, in what is now Highland Park. This operation was the forerunner of the international Standard Oil Company. George Westinghouse produced a myriad of inventions and developed numerous processes that were the impetus for great industrial progress. Westinghouse also drilled the city's first gas well on his property on Thomas Boulevard, leading to the formation of the Equitable Gas Company. Alfred Hunt started what was to become ALCOA in his Shady Avenue home.

Peabody High School, opened in 1911, has proudly graduated an exceptional list of notables, many of whom are featured in the pages that follow. Among some not pictured here from Peabody are philosopher and writer Kenneth Burke; professional athletes Kevan Barlow, Mike Barnes, and Mel Bennett; and billionaire hedge fund manager and philanthropist David Tepper.

For this publication, the challenge was to choose candidates for presentation from a tremendous output of famous talent spawned in the neighborhoods of the valley. What is evident is that the pioneering, innovative, and creative spirit of the valley's population continues to bring scientific and artistic enrichment to the neighborhood and the nation.

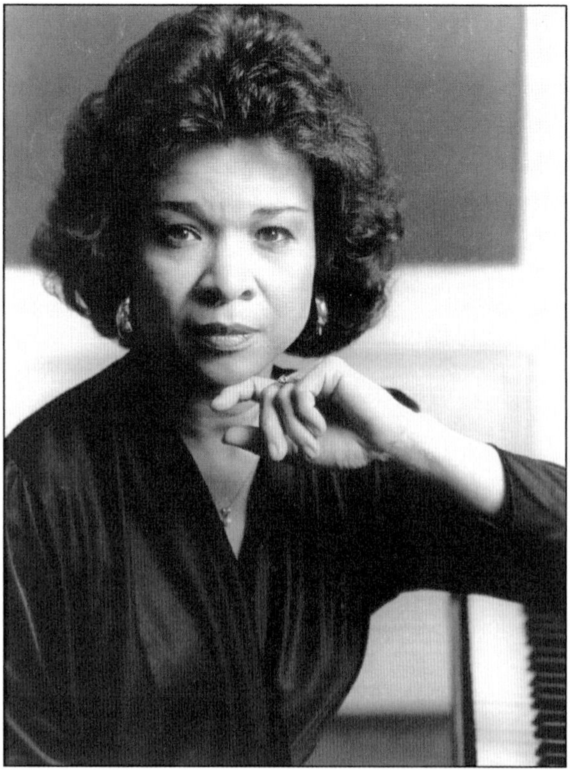

PATRICIA PRATTIS JENNINGS. An East End native, Patricia Jennings recently retired as principal keyboard of the Pittsburgh Symphony Orchestra, where she served for over 40 years. She graduated from Westinghouse High School in 1958 and earned her Master of Fine Arts from Carnegie Mellon University. Between 1988 and 1994, she published a series of newsletters titled *Symphonium*, which successfully encouraged symphony managers to hire talented African American instrumentalists from all over the country.

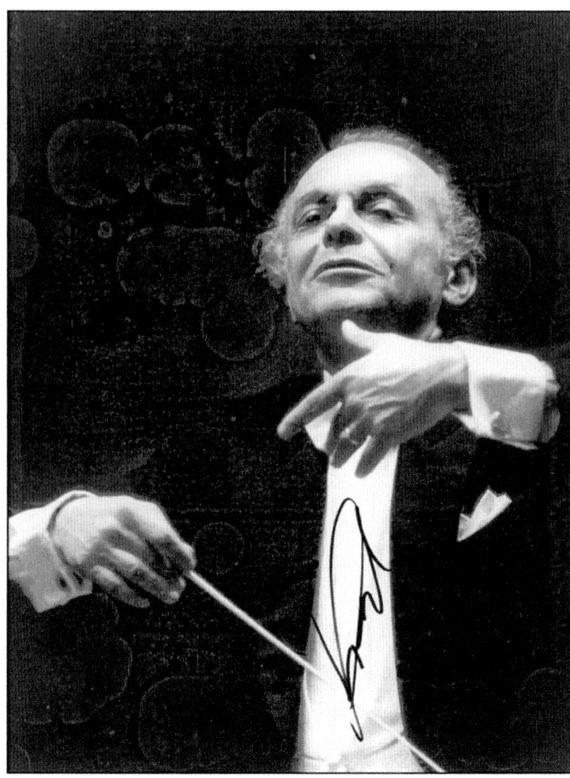

LORIN MAAZEL. A world-renowned symphony conductor and composer, Lorin Maazel conducted the Pittsburgh Symphony Orchestra from 1984 to 1996. A child prodigy, he graduated from Peabody High School in 1946.

MARY LOU WILLIAMS (1927–2002). This popular jazz composer and pianist grew up in the East End and graduated from Westinghouse High School. She arranged music for Duke Ellington and performed with him. Her works include "Mary Lou's Mass," commissioned by the Vatican. At the time of her death, she was artist in residence at Duke University. A Pennsylvania Historical Marker is in front of Lincoln School, which she attended.

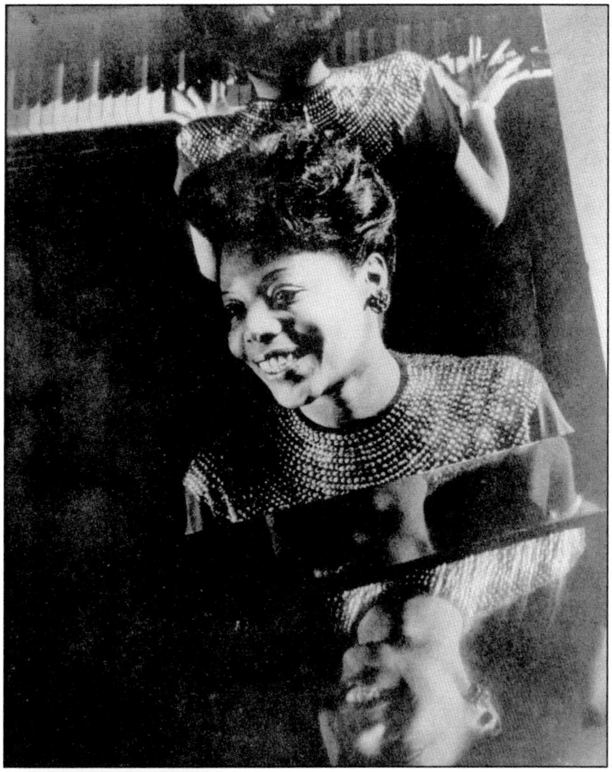

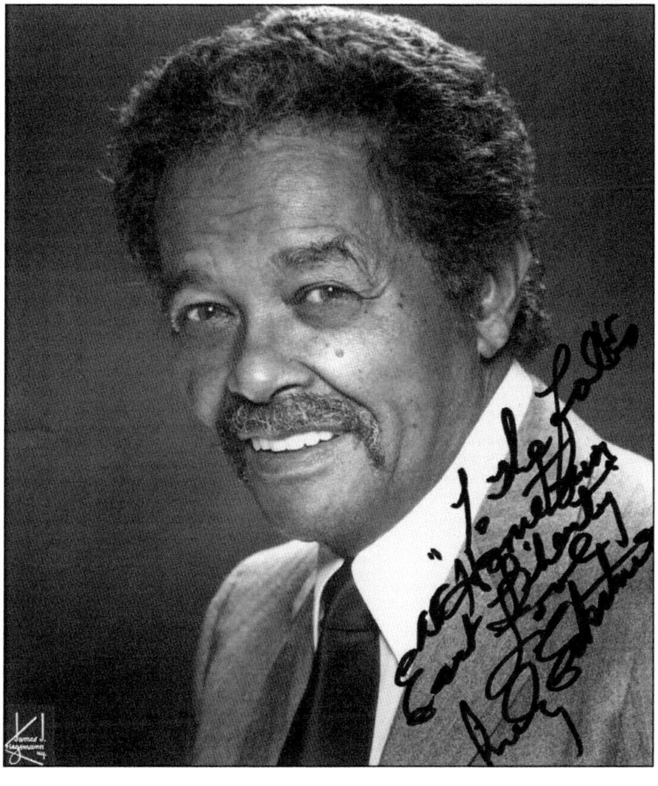

BILLY ECKSTINE (1914–1993). This famous African American jazz balladeer and bandleader was an East Liberty native. His innovative style and sponsorship of new talent helped revolutionize jazz in the 1940s. One of the nation's most popular vocalists, he had 11 gold records. He attended Peabody High School and grew up at 5913 Bryant Street where a Pennsylvania Historical Marker has been placed. He died in Pittsburgh.

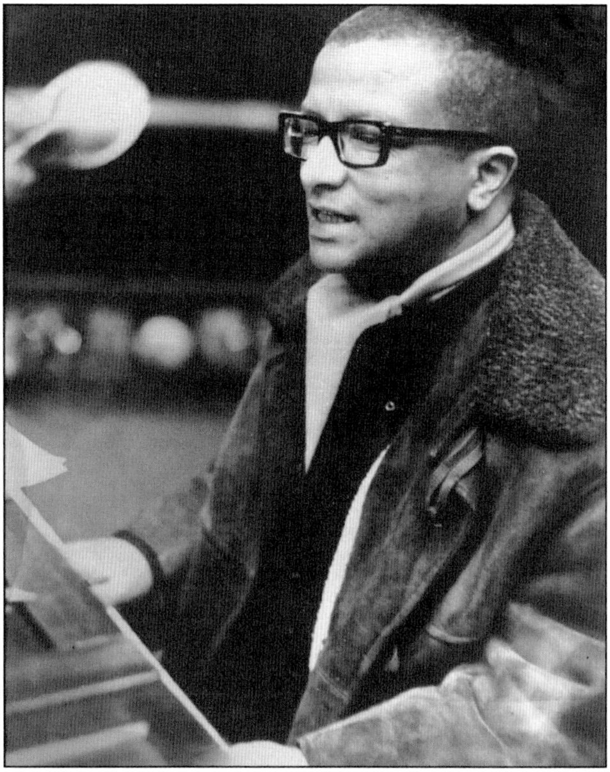

BILLY STRAYHORN (1915–1967). This 1934 graduate of Westinghouse High School was a jazz musician and lyricist. He joined the Duke Ellington Orchestra in 1939 as a composer and arranger. His most famous arrangement was "Take the 'A' Train," which became Ellington's theme song. His work is celebrated with a historical marker in front of his high school and by the Kelly-Strayhorn Theatre on Penn Avenue.

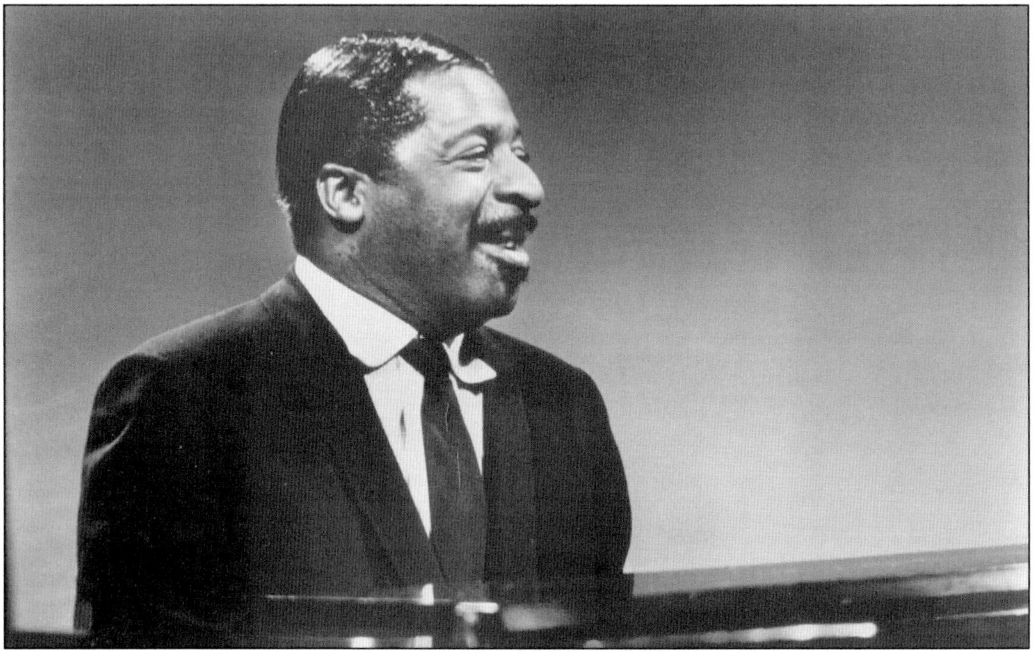

ERROLL GARNER (1921–1977). A well-known American jazz pianist, Erroll Garner's distinctive and melodic style brought him both popular acclaim and the admiration of peers. He is generally credited with having bridged the gap for jazz musicians between nightclubs and the concert hall. Garner is buried in the Homewood Cemetery.

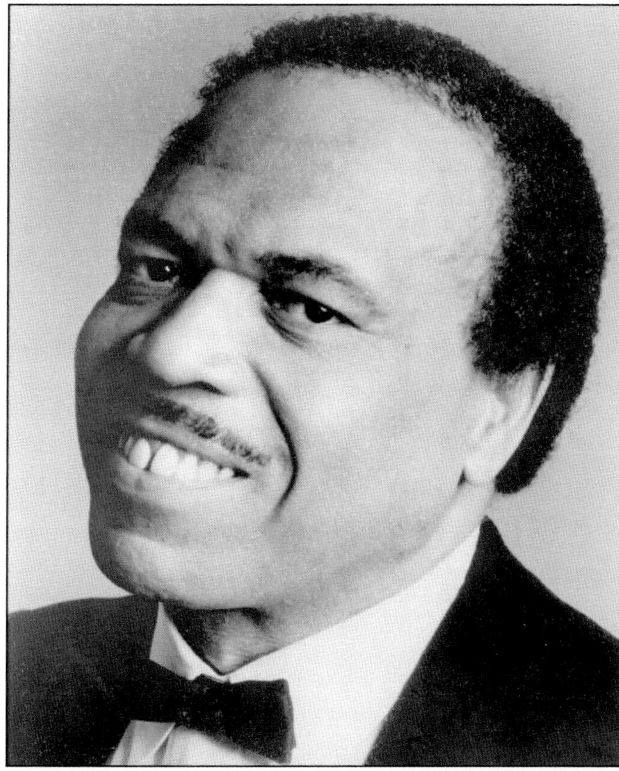

Robert Mosley (1927–2002). A 1946 graduate of Schenley High School, Robert Mosley was a renowned opera singer. A celebrated bass-baritone, he played the lead role in the Metropolitan Opera production of *Porgy and Bess*.

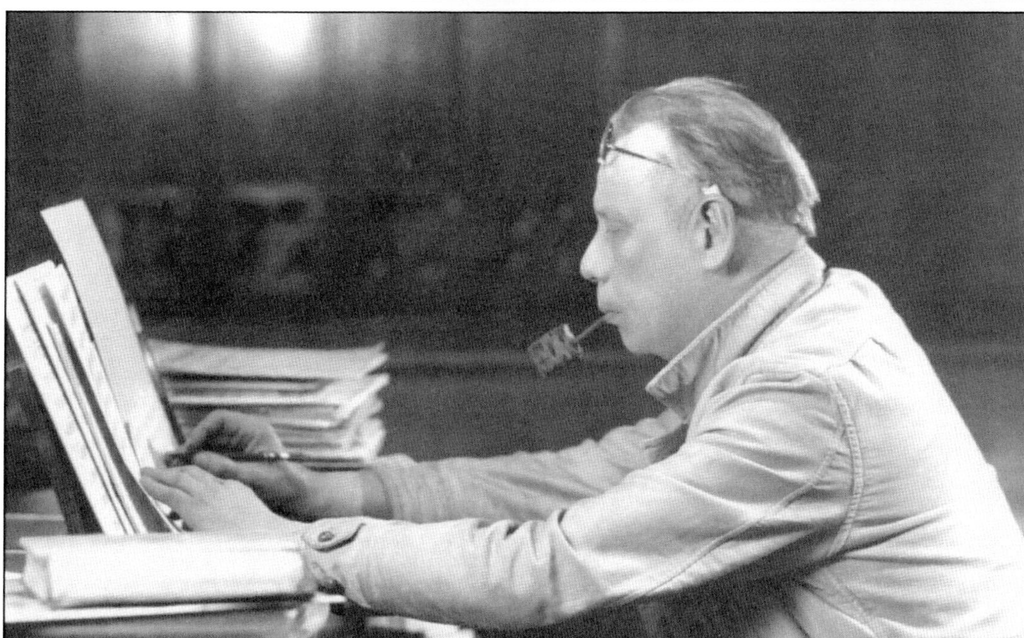

Harvey Gaul (1881–1945). A prominent American organist, conductor, and composer, Harvey Gaul spent 35 years at Calvary Episcopal Church. Besides composing prolifically for the organ, he was music critic for the *Pittsburgh Post-Gazette* and the first music director of radio station KDKA.

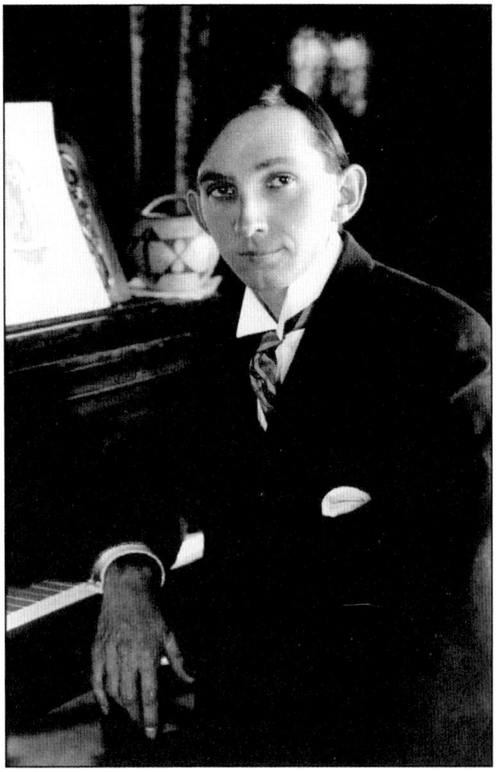

CHARLES WAKEFIELD CADMAN (1881–1946). Charles Cadman was a leading composer of the early 20th century, among the first incorporating Native American themes. Although a serious composer of operas, he also gained fame with such pseudo–Native American songs as "From the Land of the Sky-Blue Waters." He was musically educated in Pittsburgh, an organist at East Liberty Presbyterian Church from 1907 to 1910, and in 1908 became music critic for the *Pittsburgh Dispatch*.

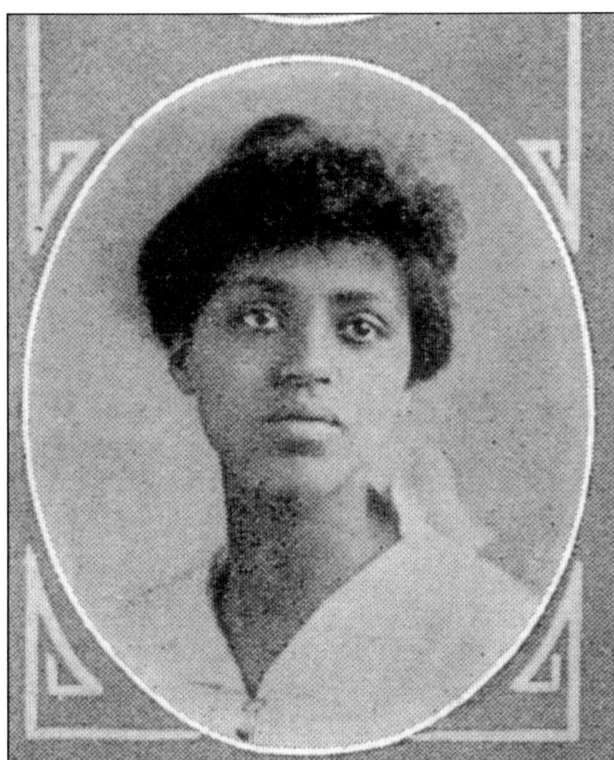

EDITH SPURLOCK SAMPSON (1901–1979). Edith Spurlock graduated from Peabody High School at the age of 14. She served Associated Charities of Pittsburgh as its first African American social worker. Holder of a law degree, she was appointed by Pres. Harry Truman in 1950 as an alternate delegate to the United Nations, and later served on the United States Commission on the NATO.

SELMA BURKE (1900–1995). This noted African American sculptor lived in Pittsburgh from 1968 to 1981. She directed the Selma Burke Art Center in East Liberty and spent much time working with black youth, introducing them to the world of art. She studied sculpture with Maillol in Paris and drawing with Matisse. One of her most famous works, a bust of Pres. Franklin D. Roosevelt, can be seen on the U.S. dime.

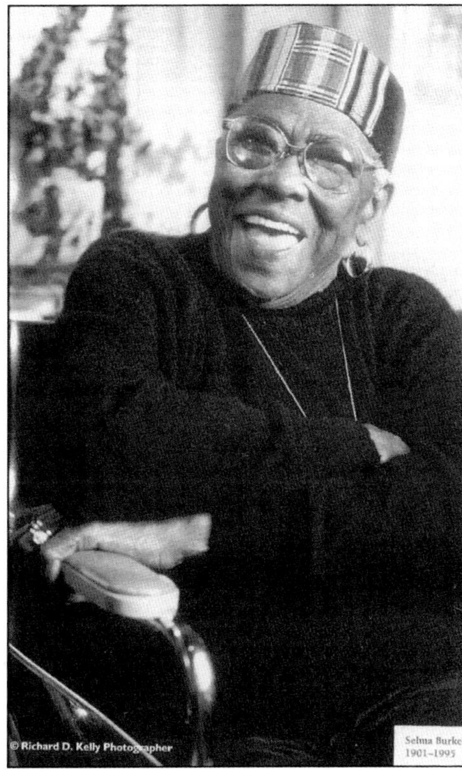

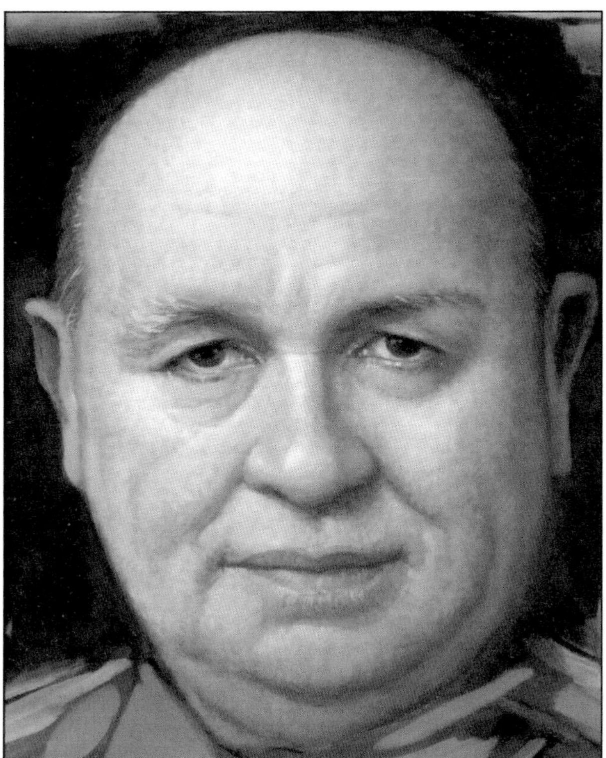

ROMARE BEARDEN (1911–1988). This widely acclaimed African American artist graduated from Peabody High School in 1929 and from New York University in 1935. His aim in art was "to redefine the image of man." He was elected to the National Institute of Arts and Letters in 1972 and received the National Medal of Arts in 1987.

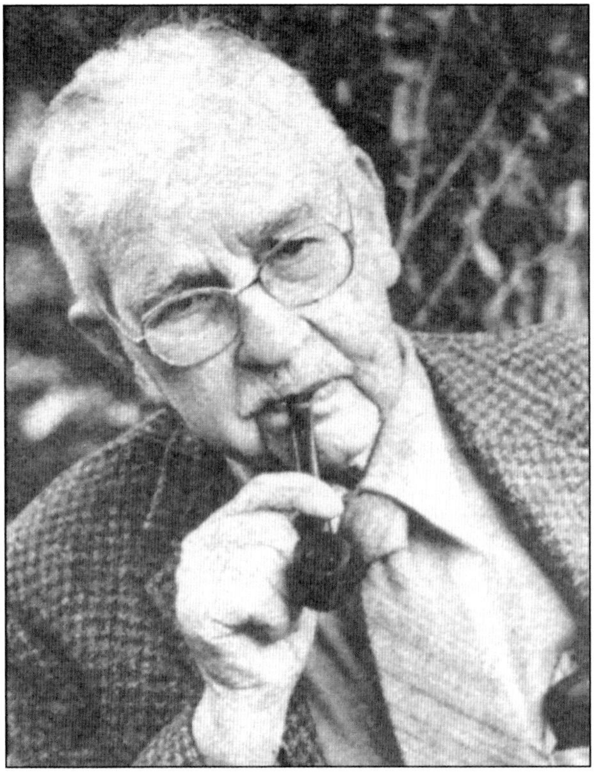

MALCOLM COWLEY (1898–1989). Malcolm Cowley, a 1915 graduate of Peabody High School, was a prominent critic, author, and poet. A 1920 Harvard alumnus, Cowley is best known for his books *Lost Generation*, *Exiles Return*, and *Blue Juniata*. He helped institute the Viking Portable Library series in the 1940s with the *Portable Hawthorne* and the *Portable Hemingway*. Viking published the *Portable Malcolm Cowley* by Donald Faulkner in 1990.

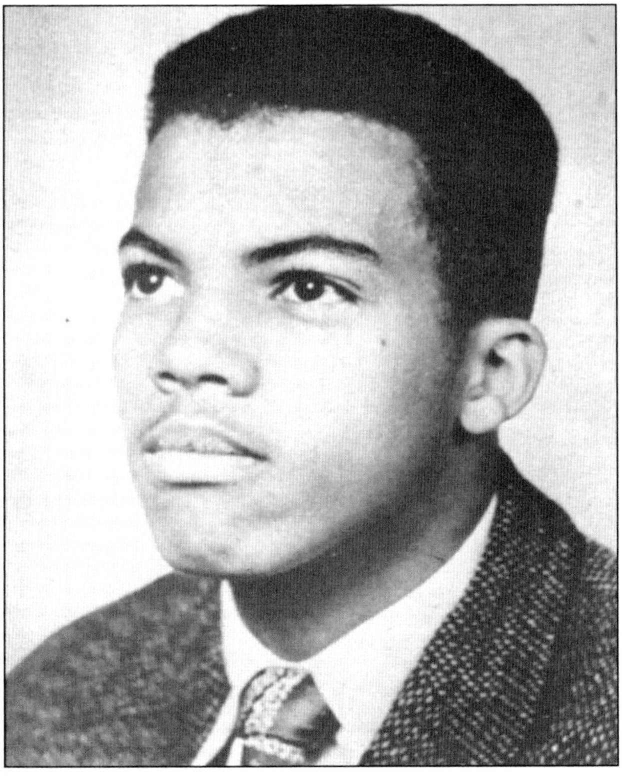

JOHN EDGAR WIDEMAN. A star athlete, valedictorian, and senior class president in 1959 at Peabody High School, John Wideman attended the University of Pennsylvania where he was Phi Beta Kappa in 1963. He was awarded a Rhodes scholarship at Oxford. He has written many short stories and several novels, the best known being his trilogy based upon his Homewood experiences. He currently teaches at the University of Massachusetts.

GEORGE S. KAUFMAN (1889–1961). George Kaufman was one of the most successful Broadway playwrights, twice winning a Pulitzer Prize. Born in East Liberty and a 1921 Peabody graduate, he moved to New York City and was the editor of the influential drama page of the *New York Times* from 1917 to 1930. He produced some 40 plays and musical comedies in his career beginning in the 1920s, working with Moss Hart and others.

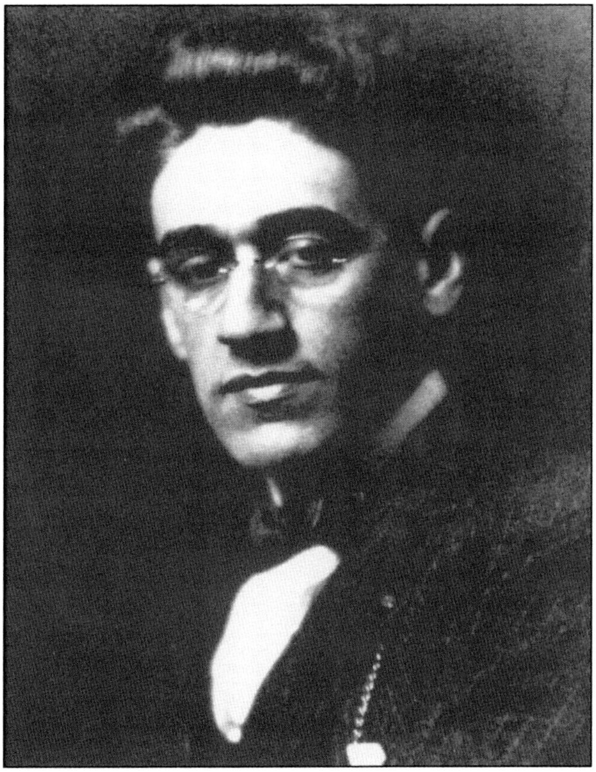

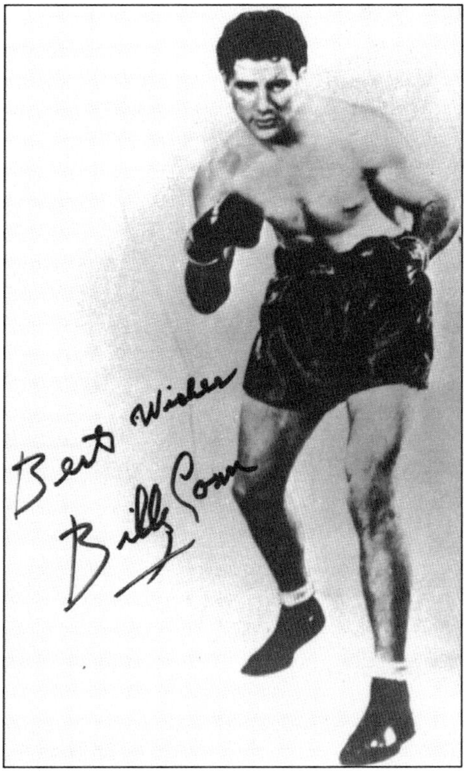

BILLY CONN (1917–1993). An East End native, Billy Conn was the light heavyweight champion from 1939 to 1941. His fight with Joe Louis in 1941 at the New York City Polo Grounds was one of the greatest fights of the century. Conn, outweighed by more than 25 pounds, came within two rounds of dethroning Louis. His career record was 63 wins, 12 losses, and 1 draw, with 14 wins by knockout.

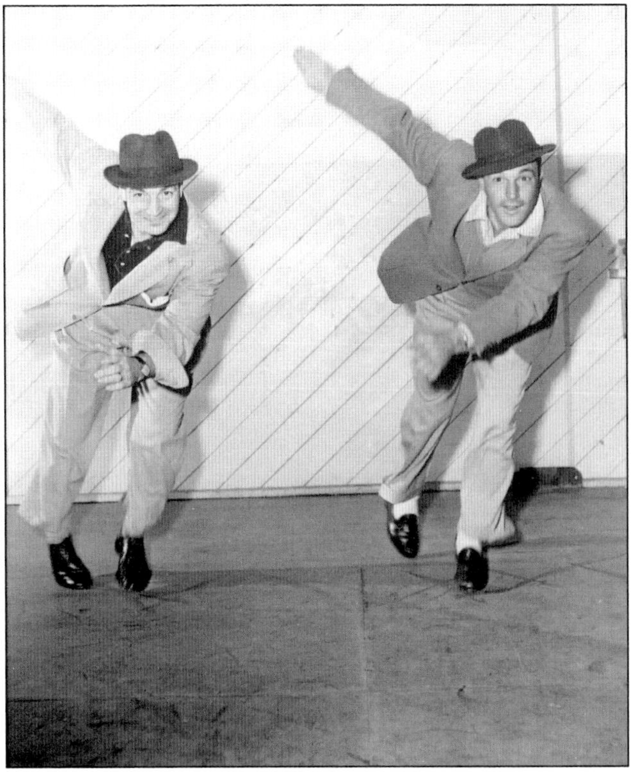

KELLY BROTHERS. These men, alumni of Peabody High School, were acclaimed for their dance performances. This photograph shows a rehearsal at MGM Studios in 1954 for *Deep in My Heart,* the one movie that Gene Kelly (1912–1996), seen on the right, did together with his brother Fred (1915–2000). Gene's most famous movie was *Singing in the Rain*. In 1987, a one-block section of South Whitfield Street was designated as Gene Kelly Square.

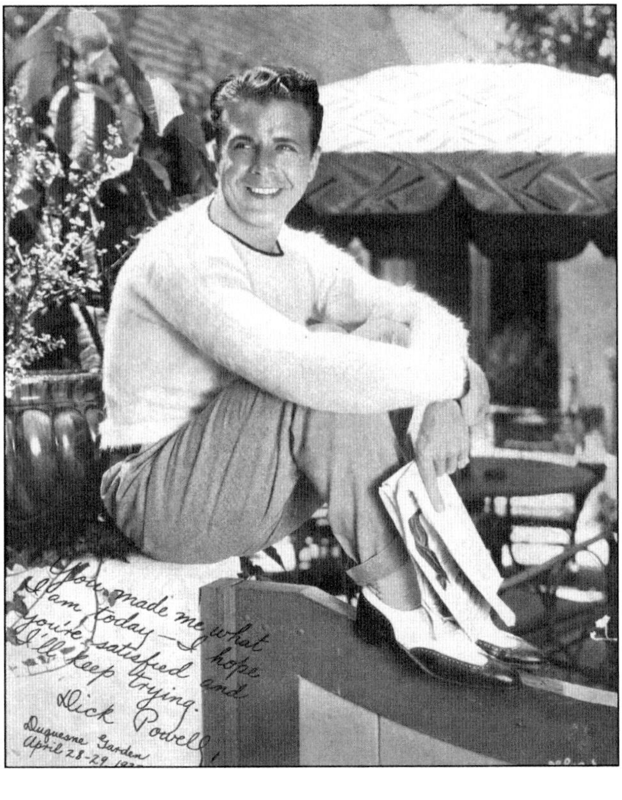

DICK POWELL (1903–1963). Dick Powell was the master of ceremonies at the Enright Theatre. In 1929, he was reported in the *Pittsburgh Post-Gazette* to have a "knack for crooning soft ballads through a megaphone." By 1932, he was bound for Hollywood and stardom.

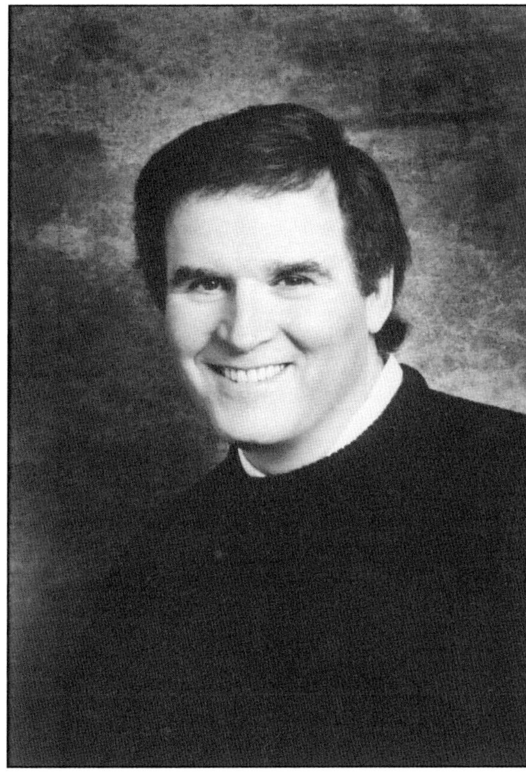

Charles Grodin. This well-known Broadway and Hollywood actor, author, and talk show host attended Fulton Elementary School and Peabody High School. Graduating from Peabody High School in the early 1950s, Charles Grodin was class president for four years. Grodin has served as a commentator on *60 Minutes*.

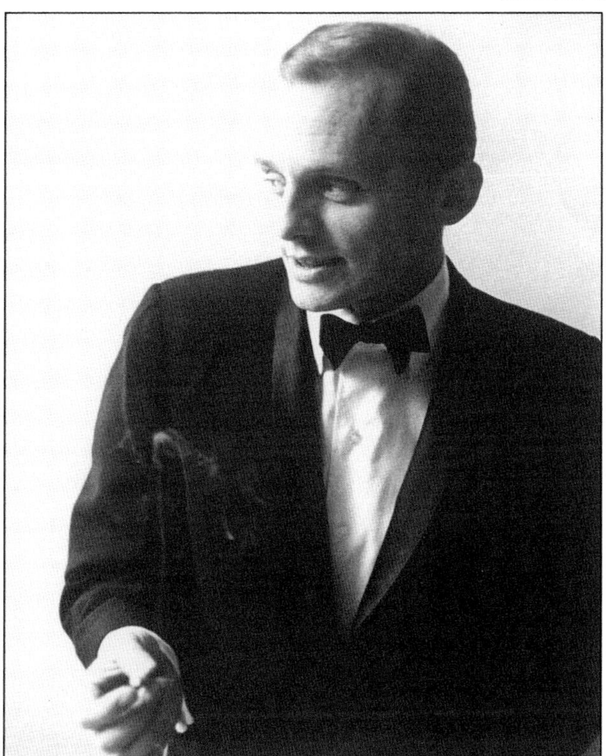

Frank Gorshin (1933–2005). A 1951 Peabody High School graduate, Frank Gorshin was a popular movie actor and impressionist. While in high school, he worked as an usher at the Sheridan Square Theatre, where he learned to impersonate famous screen personalities such as Al Jolson, James Cagney, and Edward G. Robinson. He played the Riddler in the television series *Batman*. He was nominated for an Emmy award.

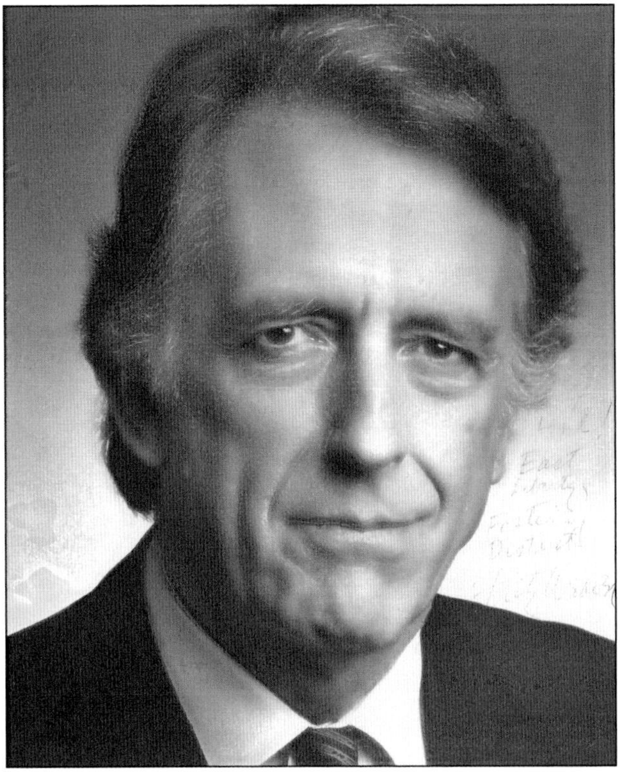

FRITZ WEAVER. Fritz Weaver, a noted Broadway and Hollywood character actor, attended Peabody High School.

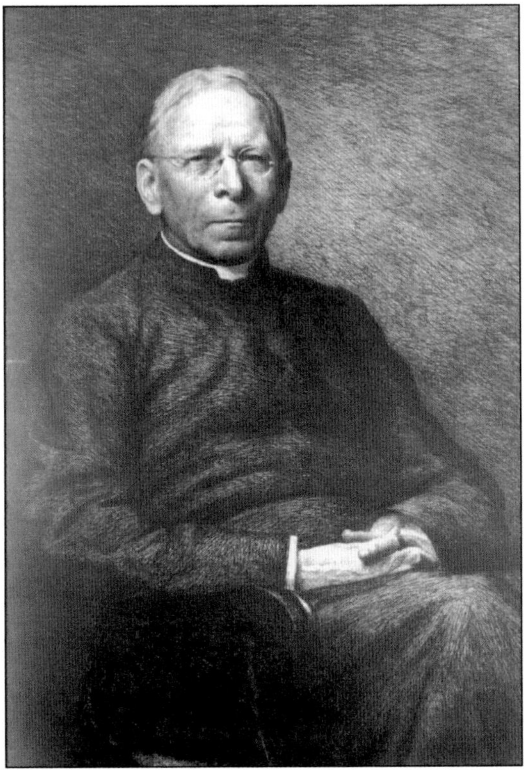

GEORGE HODGES (1856–1919). George Hodges was an influential Episcopal theologian who served as rector of Calvary Episcopal Church from 1881 to 1894. An early leader in promoting the social gospel, he was involved in several important ecumenical and philanthropic activities. In the forefront of the settlement house movement, he established Kingsley House (now Kingsley Association) in 1893.

Nine

From Redevelopment to Rebirth

For almost a century, East Liberty was a bustling center of commerce and a good place to live. After World War II, it began showing signs of decline as a retail center and losing residents, who were moving to the suburbs. By 1953, several long-standing East Liberty businesses had failed and merchants turned to the Urban Redevelopment Authority (URA) of Pittsburgh to create a plan that would curtail this loss of business and people.

A plan was launched by the URA in 1960 to create a mall similar to those that were growing and expanding in the suburbs. Penn and Highland Avenues and Broad Street were turned into pedestrian malls closed to automobile traffic in the most bustling parts of the area. The road configuration was changed to a series of new one-way streets that formed a ring around the main business district (Penn Circle). The 500-acre, $68 million project required the obliteration of several roads and the demolition of blocks of neighborhoods and institutions. Pittsburgh's housing authority constructed three large, 20-story apartment buildings to help alleviate the overcrowding in neighboring Homewood, partially caused by the earlier demolition of the lower Hill District to create the Pittsburgh Civic Arena.

These well-intentioned redevelopment efforts failed to preserve East Liberty as a market center, and in a matter of a few years, it became a blighted neighborhood. Population fell drastically and of the 575 or so businesses in the late 1950s, fewer than 100 remained in 1979.

Community groups then rallied to bring new life to East Liberty. In 1986, some roads were returned to their pre-1960 traffic pattern; several more are planned to follow. Deteriorated housing projects were demolished in 2005. The success of new stores such as Home Depot and Whole Foods sparked further investment in East Liberty, attracting national and local retailers. The Regent Theatre is now a performing arts center renamed the Kelly-Strayhorn Theatre. New restaurants, boutiques, clothing and grocery stores, and residential projects bring promise to the transformation of East Liberty into a modern version of the thriving neighborhood it had once been.

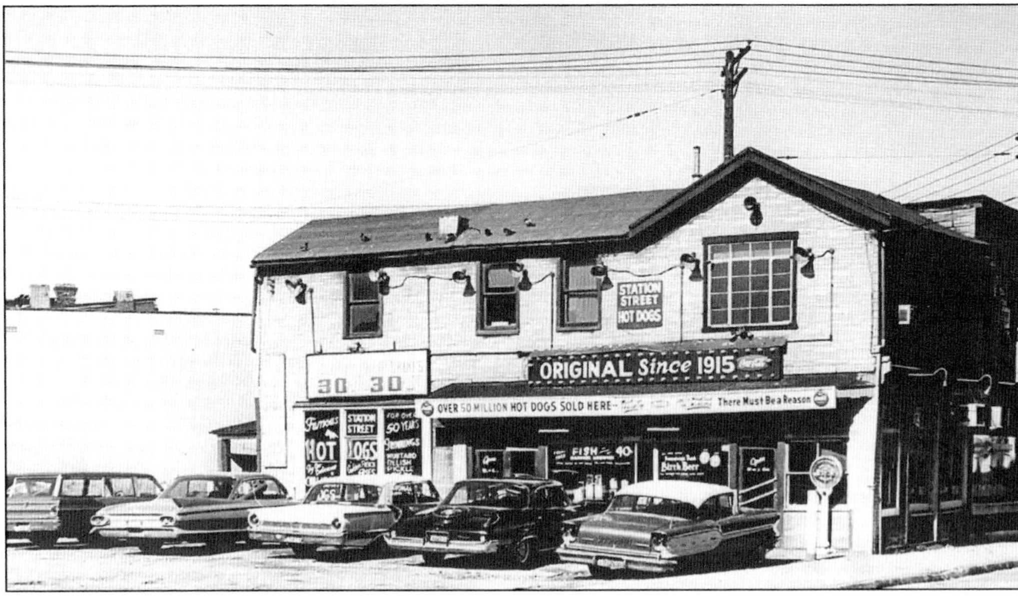

ORIGINAL STATION STREET HOT DOG SHOP, 1950S. This family store at Larimer Avenue and Station Street was in business from 1915 to 1969, when it relocated to a new building on Broad Street near Larimer Avenue, with carhop service from 10:00 a.m. to midnight. It closed in 1980 and remained vacant for many years. After complete remodeling by owner Robert Tortorete, it reopened in 2007.

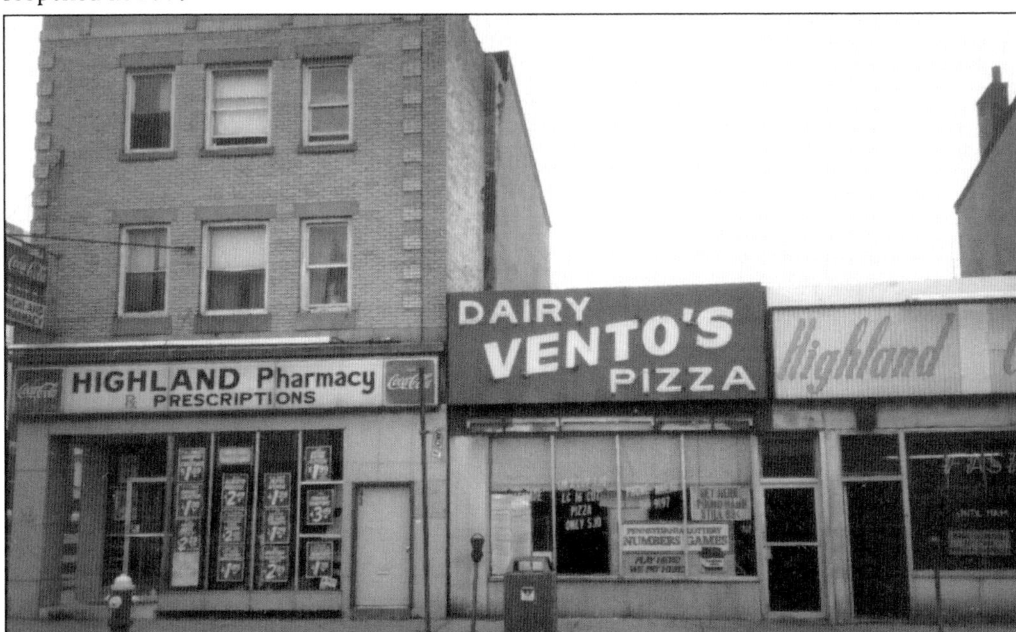

VENTO'S PIZZA, 1960S. Born and raised in East Liberty, Al Vento started a delicatessen on North St. Clair Street in 1951. When his rental place was demolished for a playground, he relocated in 1956 to Margaretta Street, where he started selling his popular pizza. When Margaretta Street became East Liberty Boulevard, he moved to North Highland Avenue, pictured here. He moved again in 2000 into his new store on Highland Avenue beside Home Depot.

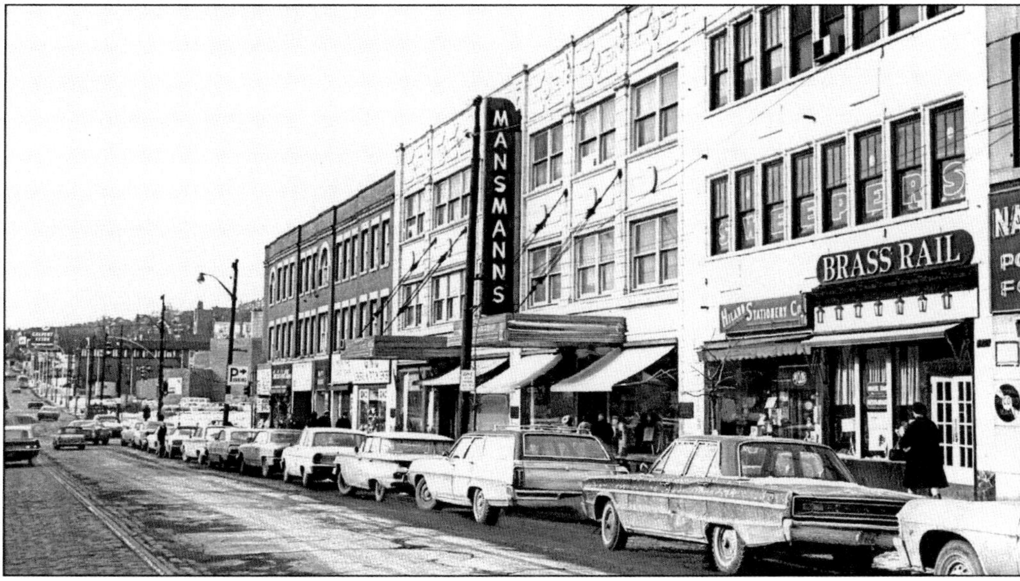

Penn Avenue, 1960s. Before the redevelopment, the 5900 block of Penn Avenue was one of the busiest shopping areas in East Liberty. The venerable Mansmann's Department Store is featured prominently in this photograph.

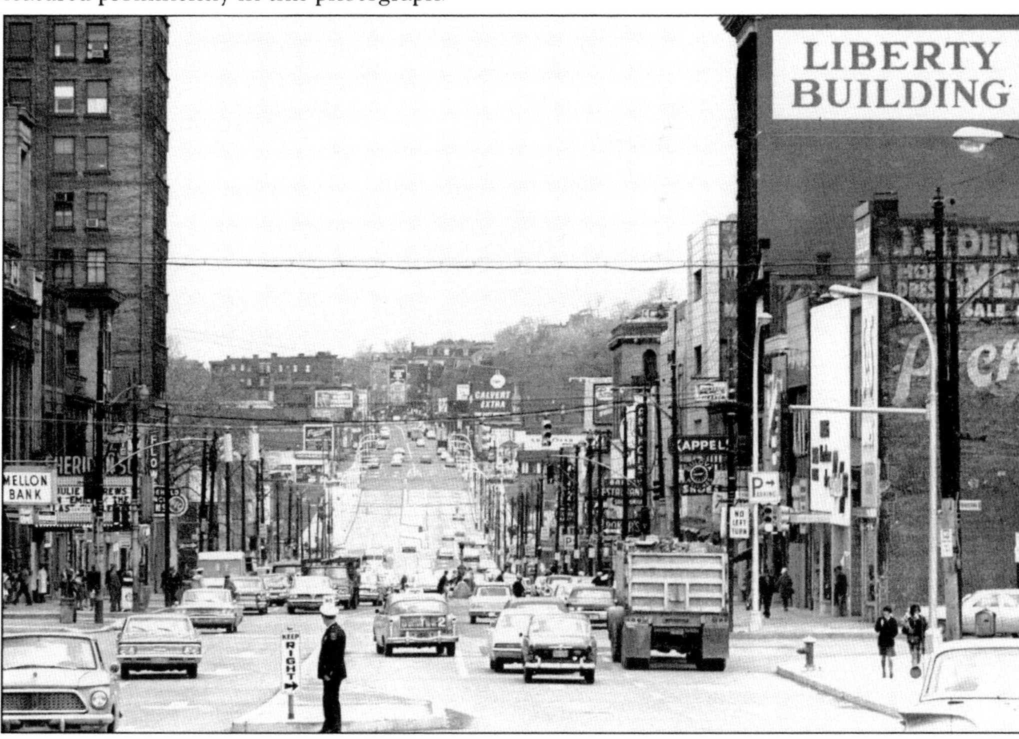

Penn Avenue, 1965. Looking west, this view shows traffic on one of the main business thoroughfares before redevelopment. On the south side of the street are the Sheridan Square Theatre and Peoples East End Bank, both since demolished, as well as a Mellon Bank and a flower shop. The Liberty Building on the north side now houses East Liberty Development and a number of professional offices.

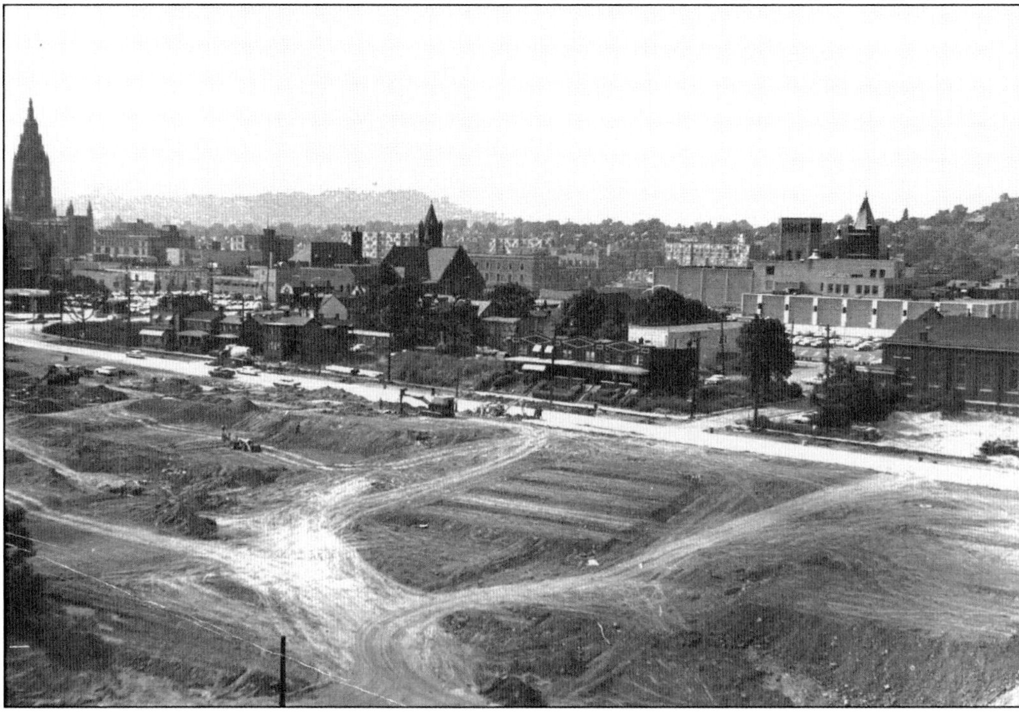

DEMOLITION, 1960S. This photograph dramatically shows the demolition of entire blocks as part of the redevelopment of East Liberty.

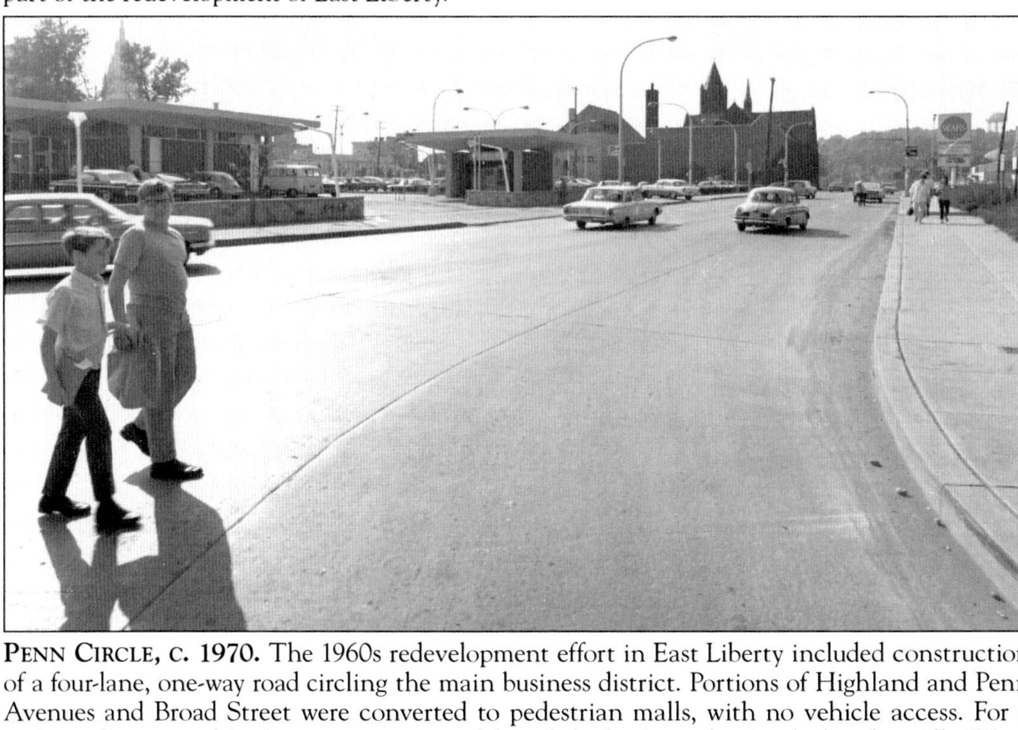

PENN CIRCLE, C. 1970. The 1960s redevelopment effort in East Liberty included construction of a four-lane, one-way road circling the main business district. Portions of Highland and Penn Avenues and Broad Street were converted to pedestrian malls, with no vehicle access. For a variety of reasons, this plan was not successful, and the business district declined rapidly. Work now underway to restore the vitality of the area is beginning to bear fruit.

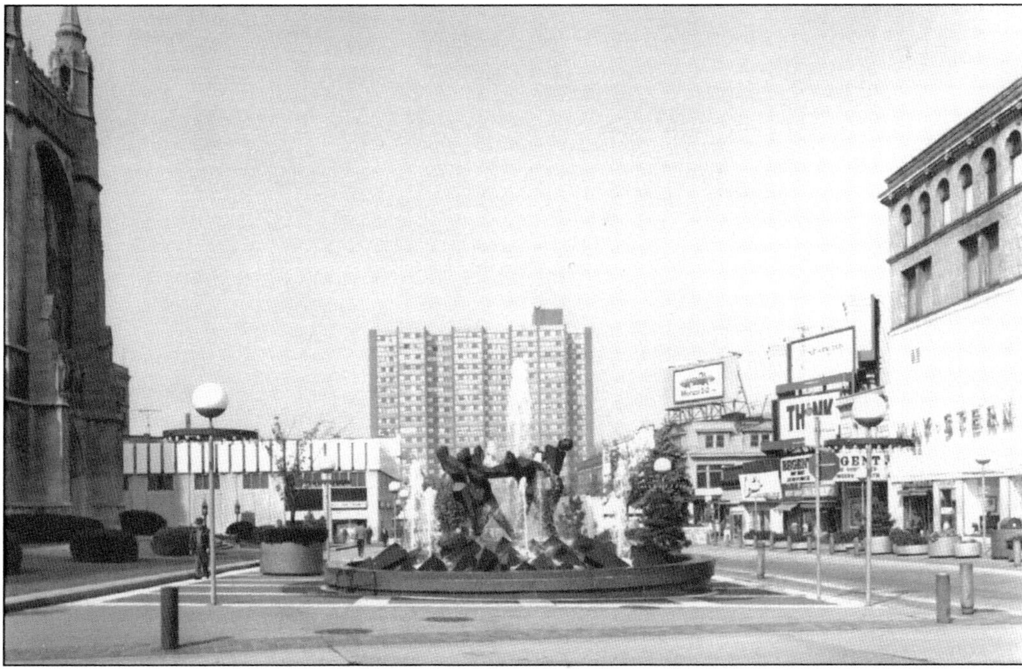

Joy of Life, 1969. Commissioned by the Urban Redevelopment Authority, Virgil Cantini's fountain sculpture was the focal point of the new East Liberty Mall. The unrest and violence of the 1960s moved Cantini to express an idea of unity through figures with locked arms. To correct the unsuccessful mall model, Penn Avenue was reopened to through traffic in 1986, necessitating relocation of the fountain to Baum Boulevard at South Whitfield Street.

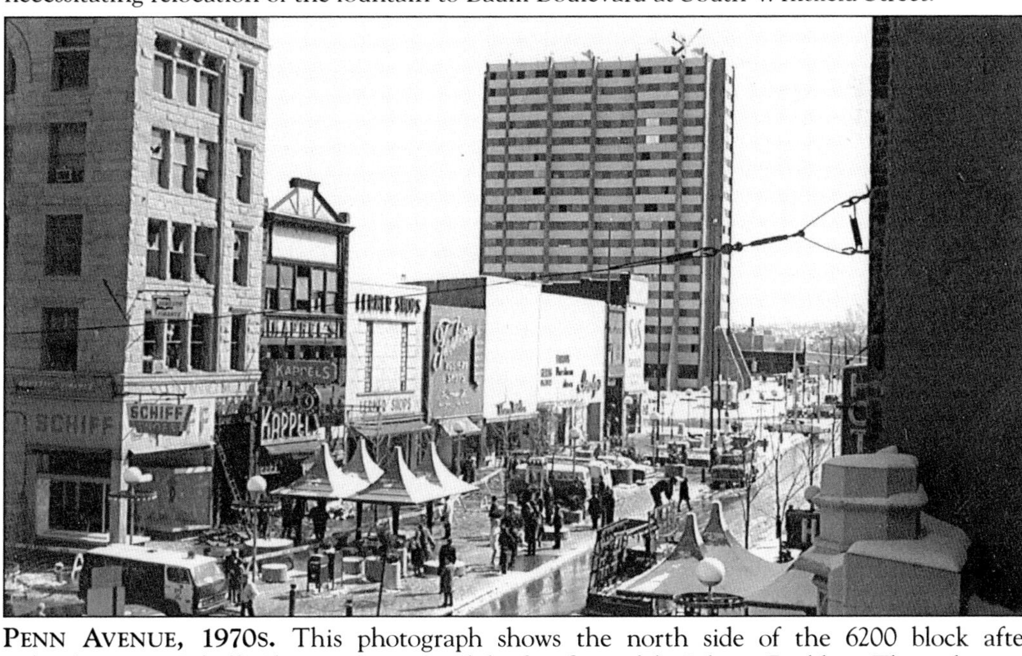

Penn Avenue, 1970s. This photograph shows the north side of the 6200 block after redevelopment. Schiff's Shoe store occupied the first floor of the Liberty Building. The pedestrian mall filled the middle of the street. The 20-story Liberty Park high-rise apartment building dominates the eastern end of the block, at Broad Street and Penn Circle East.

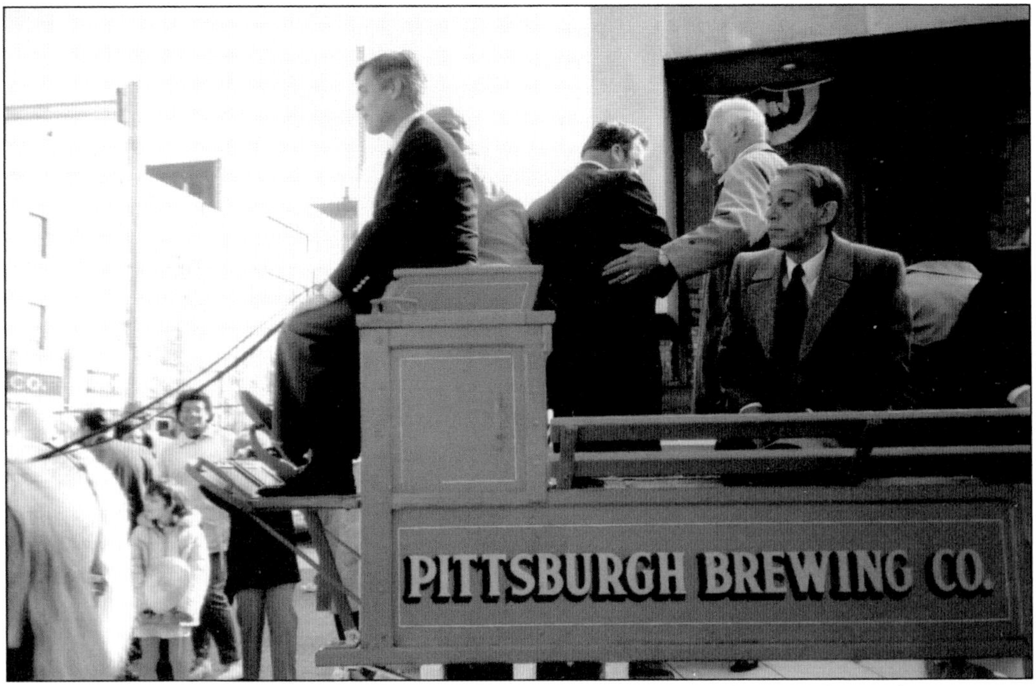

OPENING PENN AVENUE, 1986. Mayor Richard Caligiuri is shown driving a horse-drawn wagon at the celebration of the reopening of Penn Avenue to vehicular traffic. After 25 years, the main streets in East Liberty once again are accessible by automobile.

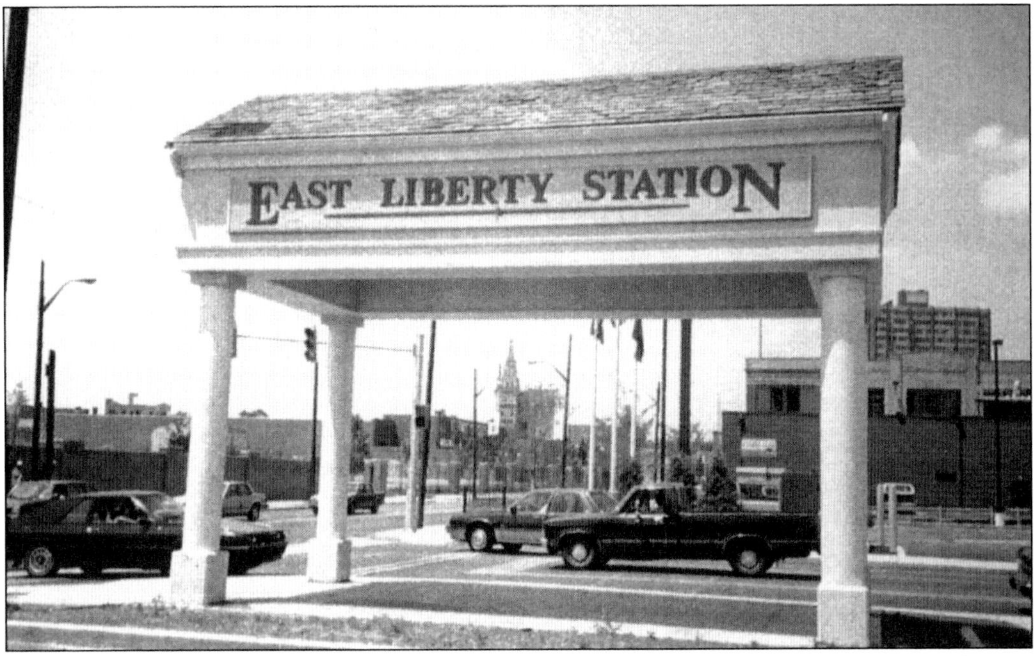

SHOPPING CENTER, 1987. This modern shopping center was built on Penn Avenue on the site of the original East Liberty station of the Pennsylvania Railroad, and named, appropriately, East Liberty Station. It has continued to grow, and change, under its current name of Village of Eastside.

BIBLIOGRAPHY

A Legacy in Bricks and Mortar: African-American Landmarks in Allegheny County. Pittsburgh: Pittsburgh History and Landmarks Foundation, 1995.

Cleland, Hugh. *George Washington in the Ohio Valley*. Pittsburgh: University of Pittsburgh Press, 1955.

Collins, Jr, John, *Stringtown on the Pike*, East Liberty Chamber of Commerce, 1966.

Downes, Randolph C. *Council Fires on the Upper Ohio*. Pittsburgh: University of Pittsburgh Press, 1977.

Evert, Marilyn and Vernon Gay. *Discovering Pittsburgh's Sculpture*. Pittsburgh: University of Pittsburgh Press, 1983.

Gangewere, R. Jay, Marilyn Evert, and James D. Van Trump. "Highland Park." *Carnegie Magazine* 54:6 (June 1980): 7–17.

Johnston, William G. *Life and Reminiscences from Birth to Manhood of Wm. G. Johnston*. New York: Knickerbocker Press, 1901.

Kelly, John M. *J. M. Kelly's Handbook of Greater Pittsburg*. Pittsburgh: the J. M. Kelly Company, 1895.

Kidney, Walter C. *Landmark Architecture, Pittsburgh and Allegheny County*. Pittsburgh: Pittsburgh History and Landmarks Foundation, 1997.

———. *Pittsburgh Bridges: Architecture and Engineering*. Pittsburgh: Pittsburgh History and Landmarks Foundation, 1999.

———. *Henry Hornbostel*. Pittsburgh: Pittsburgh History and Landmarks Foundation, 2002.

Mellon, Thomas. *Thomas Mellon and His Times*. Pittsburgh: University of Pittsburgh Press, 1994.

Miller, Annie Clark. *Early Land Marks and Old Names in Pittsburgh*. Pittsburgh: Pittsburgh Chapter Daughters of the American Revolution, 1924

Mulkearn, Lois and Edwin V. Pugh. *A Traveler's Guide to Historic Western Pennsylvania*. Pittsburgh: University of Pittsburgh Press, 1954.

Municipal Year Book, 1913, City of Pittsburgh. Digital Research Library of the University Library System, University of Pittsburgh, Pittsburgh.

Negley, Georgina G. *East Liberty Presbyterian Church Centennial Celebration*. Pittsburgh: Murdoch, Kerr and Company Press, 1919.

Rasmussen, William M. S. and Robert S. Tilton. *George Washington – the Man Behind the Myths*. Charlottesville: University Press of Virginia Press, 1999.

Stewart, Howard. *Historical Data, Pittsburgh Public Parks*. Pittsburgh: Greater Pittsburgh Parks Association. 1943.

Stotz, Charles Morse. *Point of Empire; Conflict at the Forks of the Ohio*. Pittsburgh: Historical Society of Western Pennsylvania, 1970.

Toker, Franklin. *Pittsburgh: An Urban Portrait*. University Park, Pennsylvania: the Pennsylvania State University Press, 1986; reprinted Pittsburgh: University of Pittsburgh Press, 1994.

Van Trump, James D. and Arthur P. Ziegler Jr. *Landmark Architecture of Allegheny County Pennsylvania*. Pittsburgh: Pittsburgh History and Landmarks Foundation, 1967.